THE NORTHWEST
PASSAGE OVERLAND

The two English travellers flanked by those who almost certainly saved their lives. From left to right: 'Mrs Assiniboine', Louis Patenaude ('The Assiniboine'), Dr W. B. Cheadle, Viscount Milton, and 'The Boy'.

THE NORTHWEST PASSAGE OVERLAND

The Epic Journey that Helped
Create Canada

E. C. Coleman

AMBERLEY

About the Author

E. C. Coleman served in the Royal Navy for thirty-six years, which included time on an aircraft carrier, a submarine, and Nelson's flagship, HMS *Victory*. During that time he mounted four Arctic expeditions in search of evidence from the 1845 Sir John Franklin Expedition. He has written many books on naval, polar, medieval and Victorian subjects and contributed the foreword to two volumes of Captain Scott's diaries. His interest in the Grail legend is longstanding and he is currently researching a new (and linked) work on the Knights Templar.

First published 2017

Amberley Publishing
The Hill, Stroud
Gloucestershire, GL5 4EP

www.amberley-books.com

British Library Cataloguing in Publication Data.
A catalogue record for this book is available from the British Library.

ISBN 978 1 4456 7007 2 (paperback)
ISBN 978 1 4456 7008 9 (ebook)

Typesetting and Origination by Amberley Publishing.
Printed in the UK.

Contents

Acknowledgements   7

Introduction   8

1   From the Atlantic to the Assiniboine – Sunburn and
Indigestion   14

2   Rum and Red River Carts on the Fort Ellice Trail   29

3   Sioux, Cree, Buffaloes and the Saskatchewan   40

4   Goodbye to Messiter, Hello to Fort Milton   55

5   A Wolverine Winter, Starvation and Incontinence   71

6   Joined by the 'Assiniboine' Family,
Burdened by Mr O'B   92

7   Bears, Mosquitoes, a Forest Fire and the Athabasca   112

8   The Yellowhead Pass and the Naming of Mountains   127

9   Disaster on Canoe River – a Headless
Indian and Hell's Gate   143

10   Farewell to Mr O'B – Royal Engineers
on the Cariboo Road   164

11   Lake Steamers, the Goldfields, and Whist
with the Royal Marines   190

12   An American Lady, San Francisco,
the American Widow – and Home   222

Epilogue   236

Index   252

Acknowledgements

I am enormously grateful to Margaret Bertulli of Winnipeg for her help, encouragement, accommodation, and guidance. I am deeply obliged to Sarah Allan and her family who welcomed me to their delightful God's Mountain – a place well named. To Sue Breeson, upon whom I inflicted the onerous task of reading the first drafts. Her tolerance, insights, and stoicism were received with much gratitude. To my wife, Joy, for her patience, support, and permission to proceed. To my two sons, Edmund and Rupert and their families for putting up with the same tale frequently told; Edmund specifically in his role as 'Ed Coleman – Photographer' for his professional help with the images. To Graeme Paterson, for providing a technophobe with a communications link, and to all the motels, hotels, and lodges who gave me a generous 'Forces Discount'. To the kind people at 'Herbaria', St. Louis, Missouri, for their help with 'Brown Windsor Soap', which I thought was a spelling mistake. To the owners of Milton Hall, Covington, Virginia, for their kind help with the close of Milton's life. To Ivor Hallam, for his great generosity, to the owners of Camp Lake for their tolerance of my footprints across their snow, and their permission to take photographs. Also to the many Canadians who helped with directions, advice, and assistance. In particular, I would like to thank the traffic policeman who cut my speeding fine in half as I 'got the message', and the young lady in the government office who, amazed at my payment within half an hour, cut the fine in half again. Thank you all.

Introduction

Anyone seeking a pair of archetypal Englishmen from the middle of Queen Victoria's reign would be hard pressed to find better examples than Lord William Wentworth Fitzwilliam, Viscount Milton, and Walter Butler Cheadle. Milton, the eldest son of Earl Fitzwilliam, was aged 23 and of slight build. Educated at Eton and Cambridge University, he was egocentric, delicate in health, temperamental, petulant, indolent, and easily offended. At the same time, however, had circumstances so provided, Milton was the type of young aristocrat who would have been in the forefront of the Charge of the Light Brigade, or leading his men over the top from the trenches on the Somme or at Passchendaele. Cheadle, on the other hand, was no aristocrat, coming instead from the gentle confines of the rectory. The son of The Reverend James Cheadle, the Vicar of All Saint's Church, Bingley, Yorkshire, the 26-year-old Cheadle was heavily built, strong, bearded, humorous, determined, and unimpressed by social rank or petulant behaviour. Also Cambridge-educated, Cheadle had already achieved a Bachelor of Arts degree in addition to his Bachelor's degree in medicine, and was intent upon continuing his studies until qualifying as a Doctor of Medicine. He was also among the top ranks of Cambridge oarsmen, and only missed rowing in the Oxford-Cambridge boat race through the untimely death of a relative.

Neither man had experienced the rigours of a long overland journey. Milton had paid a short visit to the Canadian Red River settlement (now Winnipeg, Manitoba), but the trials of an extended – and possibly hazardous – passage through barely explored territory lay beyond both men's experiences. Undeterred by this, and adopting the English practice of doing as little preparation as possible (a method that prevailed until after Captain Scott's assault on the South Pole), they set off to find an overland route to the Cariboo goldfields of British Columbia. As it was, they were pre-empted by a few others – a small party led by Norfolk-born teacher John Jessop, taking a more southerly route; Captain Palliser's expeditions across the southern prairies and the through southern passes of the Rocky Mountains; Dr Henry Youle Hind's mapping of much of the Assiniboine and the Saskatchewan rivers; and a large group of men (and a pregnant woman) – known appropriately as 'The Overlanders' – who encountered varying fortunes along a similar route to that taken by Milton and Cheadle. Milton always referred to them as 'the Canadians' or 'the emigrants' while, to Cheadle, they were 'the Americans', or 'the Yankees'.

After wintering in a self-built log cabin and suffering appalling difficulties as they made their way down the Thompson River, Cheadle's announcement at Fort Kamloops – while on the edge of starvation and clothed in rags – that they were 'a mere party of pleasure' has given rise to the idea that they were the first tourists to visit that part of the world. Others, however, including Jane, Lady Franklin (the widow of the explorer, Sir John) accompanied by her niece, Sophie Cracroft; and Lord Dunmore and his soldier friends (encountered en route by Milton and Cheadle), had already visited different parts of British North America for no better reason than their personal enjoyment. In the end, the outcome of their journey was far more important than a route to the goldfields or laying a path for subsequent tourists.

Neither Milton nor Cheadle were imperialists. Like most other Britons, from politicians and civil servants to the women in the weaving mills, they had no interest in obtaining yet more territory that would be a drain on the national coffers. British Columbia, however, was already British territory – a beautiful and promising land that was clearly under the covetous gaze of the United States of America. With its vast natural resources of coal, gold, timber, and furs and with its harbours and ports perfectly situated to provide for the Pacific Fleet and for Pacific markets, British Columbia was worth holding on to. On their return, Milton and Cheadle – especially the former as a Member of Parliament – provided staunch support for the confederation of British Columbia with the Dominion of Canada. Furthermore, if it took a railway to seal the arrangement, then they knew the route the railway should take – a route they had traced across wide prairies, through spectacular mountains, and along mighty rivers.

It is sometimes suggested that Cheadle was selected by Milton as his personal physician to accompany him on an arduous journey. Doctors, however, even in mid-nineteenth century British North America, were not exactly rare and it is far more likely that the partly qualified Cheadle was chosen for his other, more practical, qualities. Milton himself later wrote that he had been 'fortunate enough to obtain the assistance of my friend, Dr Cheadle, of Caius College, Cambridge; to whose energy and perseverance the success of the enterprise is mainly to be attributed'. Nevertheless, Milton was suffering from a condition which, while not immediately life threatening, would have benefited from the support of someone with both sympathy and medical knowledge. This condition has often been described as epilepsy despite there being little, if any, supporting evidence for this claim. Although numerous medical documents from Milton's early life still exist, they never mention epilepsy. Cheadle, called to treat epilepsy in others on his journey, never mentions epilepsy with regard to Milton. The condition was still shrouded in mystery and its treatment had hardly changed since the Middle Ages. Less than five years had passed since the first effective treatment for epilepsy – the prescribing of potassium bromide – had been discovered. Even if Cheadle took bromide on the journey with him, it could not be seen as proof of epilepsy in Milton as the drug was commonly found in medicine chests of the day. In addition, the prescribing of bromide brought about its own dangers. Once prescribed, the patient could be expected to suffer from the symptoms of 'bromism' – vomiting, sleeplessness, confusion of the mind, memory lapses, palpitations, and an unsteady gait. Just as epilepsy itself would have prevented anyone taking part in such an arduous journey, so would the effects of the only known treatment. Furthermore, it is highly unlikely that anyone suffering from epilepsy would have embarked – or been allowed to embark – upon a journey of any serious proportion. Such was the view at the time, that sufferers of the condition were frequently incarcerated in mental homes, although kept separate from the mental patients – on the grounds that the mentally ill had to be protected. The degree to which Milton's affliction was used against him, even by his closest family, is astonishing. In 1861, he announced to his father that he was engaged to Dorcas, the daughter of Lord Chichester, and niece of the Marquess of Donegal. Earl Fitzwilliam was horrified, and retaliated by writing to the fiancée's family telling them that his son suffered from fits and consequential mood swings. The engagement was immediately ended.

It is more likely that Milton was suffering from psychologically induced hyperpnea, a condition brought about through anxiety or stress especially in ultra-sensitive sufferers who feel that they are being ignored, under-valued, or otherwise personally offended – a classic Milton reaction. The sufferer hyperventilates until a carbon dioxide-oxygen imbalance occurs, which causes the blood vessels in the brain to constrict. This, in turn, can lead to dizziness, chest pains, fainting, and convulsions in which the hands and wrists contort and the feet become straight and rigid. For many years the answer to an attack was to make the sufferer breathe into a paper bag, but modern thinking stresses the need to find the cause of the basic anxiety or stress. It is unlikely that Cheadle – who was frequently referred to as Doctor in the various accounts of their journey – would have understood the underlying cause of the condition, but his presence would have acted as a reassurance to Milton.

According to his own account, Milton's reasons for attempting to cross much of British North America was that he had 'resolved to investigate for myself the nature of the country between the Red River and the Rocky Mountains; and to penetrate, if possible, by the shortest route to the gold region of Cariboo – an enterprise hitherto unattempted'. There was good reason to attempt such a route. With the exception of the scarcely surveyed fur traders' or native Indian routes, no communication existed eastwards from British Columbia. The much hoped-for Northwest Passage across the top of North America had failed to materialise at the cost of many lives. Consequently, all goods had to be sent by sea, usually via San Francisco, to the Pacific coast of Panama. In practical terms, gold had to be sent to the San Francisco mint, assayed and converted into currency – all to the advantage of the Americans. The Panama isthmus then had to be crossed by wagon or mule train before a vessel could be found, usually from New York, to cross the Atlantic to Britain. Should United States' aggression over, for example, territorial ambition, lead to diplomatic rupture, the Pacific route could be easily blockaded. On the other hand, if communication by road or rail could be established between British Columbia and the eastern colonies of Nova Scotia, New Brunswick, Prince Edward Island, Newfoundland, and the Province of Canada (modern-day Ontario and Quebec), the dependence upon American goodwill and territorial restraint would be avoided. Between the eastern colonies and the Rocky Mountain border of British Columbia lay the vast area of river-laced and lake-studded prairies owned by the Hudson's Bay Company and known as Rupert's Land. An attempt at colonisation had been made in this area around the junction of the Red and Assiniboine rivers. Known as the Red River Colony and started by displaced Scots, the colony had seen little success and had frequently been under attack by the mixed-blood Métis who saw the colony as an attempt to dispossess them of their land. Elsewhere in Rupert's Land, communication was by trails connecting Hudson's Bay Company's forts or posts. Beyond these outposts, most of the country lay in the hands of the native Indians, many of whom worked for the company in the roles of guides, hunters, and trappers.

The Indians of British North America had fared well enough under the control of the Hudson's Bay Company. Treated fairly and assisted where possible, the Indians soon discovered that it was not generally in their interest to attack the white settlers and travellers. Overall, a degree of trust had grown up between the natives and the newcomers that was almost totally unknown in the United States. There, 'the only good Indian is a dead Indian' policy ensured a continuing conflict between the two races that blighted any chance of co-operation. Sophia Cracroft, accompanying her aunt Jane, Lady Franklin, on a journey to British Columbia in 1861, noted the 'merciless policy of the Americans who avow without the least hesitation that they would just as soon shoot an Indian as a dog. We have had this said to us repeatedly.'

As far as Milton and Cheadle were concerned, it soon became clear that without the aid of their crippled Assiniboine Métis guide, with his wife, son, and dog named Papillon, it is unlikely that they would have survived their journey. It is equally probable that many modern readers will note with disquiet the readiness with which the two travellers, in common with all white men passing through or living in that part of the world, resorted to their guns to kill any bird or animal within range. In part, it may be excused where it was done in the cause of enquiry. Strange and exotic creatures are unlikely to remain on hand tamely allowing close examination. Mr J. Edward Gray, the British Museum's 'Keeper of the Zoological Collection', requested that the Hudson's Bay Company should obtain specimens of a wide range of animals ('fit for stuffing'), including cariboo and deer ('It is very desirable that the horns are preserved with the skins'), bears ('black', 'white', 'cinnamon' and 'grisly'), badgers, hares, and 'the American Bison'. Mr Grey further requested: 'It is desirable that specimens of the young and old animals should be procured of each of the kind and if there is a difference in their colour or appearance during the summer and winter a specimen exhibiting these particulars.' Equally, on the prairie or in the pine forests, it would be expected that animals and birds would be shot or trapped for food. The wholesale slaughter of buffaloes, however, merely for their tongues, not only seems excessive, but proved to be so, to the loss of later generations. An example of hunting for sport in North America was recorded by Colonel Richard Dodge, an experienced US Army officer. In company with another US officer and three English gentlemen, the hunting party returned after three weeks with '127 buffalo, 2 red deer, 11 antelope, 154 turkeys, 5 geese, 223 teal, 45 mallard, 49 shovel bills, 57 widgeon, 38 butter-ducks, 3 shell-ducks, 17 heron, 6 cranes, 187 quail, 32 grouse, 84 field-plover, 33 yellow legs, 12 jack snipes, 1 pigeon, 9 hawks, 3 owls, and 2 badgers'.

When Milton and Cheadle published their account of the expedition, *The Northwest Passage by Land*, they were accused of exaggerating some aspects of their story in the name of novelty and sensationalism. But there was no need for exaggeration or embellishment. The journey undertaken by Viscount Milton and Doctor Cheadle in 1862 and 1863 stands alone in its courage, fear, squabbles, humour, and dangers; uniquely so, perhaps, for 'a mere party of pleasure'.

1

From the Atlantic to the Assiniboine – Sunburn and Indigestion

On Thursday 19 June 1862, the Allan Line vessel *Anglo-Saxon* sailed from Liverpool, bound for Quebec in the Province of Canada. On board were two young Englishmen eager to search for an overland route to the Cariboo goldfields of British Columbia. They were not interested in the gold itself, just in a means of crossing the vast prairies and passing through the mountains that barred the path for all but the Indians and the most intrepid fur trappers. A route which, if successful, would greatly reduce the dependence upon the United States for the facilities to transport goods – including gold – from British Columbia to Great Britain.

The youngest of the pair was the 22-year-old Lord William Wentworth Fitzwilliam, Viscount Milton, the eldest son of the 6th Earl Fitzwilliam – the sixth-richest man in the country. Some idea of his wealth may be gauged from the splendour of his family seat. Wentworth Woodhouse, near Rotherham in Yorkshire, built between 1724 and 1750, was twice the width of Buckingham Palace, and had approximately 350 rooms connected by 5 miles of corridors. The house had more than 1,000 windows, a stable for 100 horses, and it required more than 1,000 people to run the house and gardens. The saloon with its pillared gallery had a marble floor, and the Whistlejacket Room was built to accommodate a 1762 George Stubbs painting of one of the eighteenth-century family's favourite racehorses. The house was believed to have inspired Jane Austen as a model for 'Pemberley' – Mr Darcy's ancestral home – in her novel *Pride and Prejudice*. Furthermore, Darcy's name is 'Fitzwilliam' in the book. In Austen's *Persuasion* there is a Captain Wentworth, while in her *Emma*, the heroine's family name is 'Woodhouse'.

The slightly built and emotionally sensitive Milton had previously visited the Red River Colony established around Fort Garry at the junction of the Assiniboine and Red rivers (now Winnipeg, Manitoba). The visit had awakened his interest in a westward expansion from the colony, across the plains of Rupert's Land, and through the mountains to British Columbia – a land on which the United States gazed with unabashed envy. Not only would successful expansion need an east-west route, it would also provide a brake on American territorial ambition. Milton not only had the private funds for such an enterprise as he was about to embark upon, but also the political ambition to urge the case for the east-west linking of British North America in the face of possible United States aggression. A firm alliance of colonies stretching from the Atlantic to the Pacific north of the 49th Parallel would certainly counter any threats from the south.

Milton's friend and companion was Walter Butler Cheadle, a medical student at Cambridge University who came from Bingley in Yorkshire, where his father was the local church incumbent. A heavily built and bearded man with a commendable record for competitive rowing, the 26-year-old Cheadle had a high level of humour matched only by his outrage at other people's discourtesies – including Milton's. A practical man, Cheadle never retreated from difficulties, preferring to tackle any problem head on.

At Londonderry, 200 emigrants bound for the colonies and the United States embarked on the *Anglo-Saxon*. Although there was a marked difference between the 'steerage' and the 'saloon' classes, there was enough tolerance on both sides for them to mix, especially at times of entertainment. Not that there was a lot of mixing or entertainment in the first few days as stormy weather laid many passengers low. Eventually, once the rolling and pitching had been mastered, and the weather abated somewhat, Milton and Cheadle were able to meet their fellow saloon passengers. These proved to be as varied in character as they were in appearance. Two were Roman Catholic bishops returning from Rome. One, a 'round fat oily man', smoked a meerschaum pipe and enjoyed all the delights of earthly comforts; the other, speaking French and of a 'puritanical' demeanour, enjoyed snuff and abstinence. A jolly Irishman enlivened the evenings with his singing while another man, who claimed to have been an army officer, an assertion doubted by everyone, boasted that he could out-drink any other passenger. His noisy bragging was handled by supplying him with enough drink until he collapsed and could be bundled out of the way into his cabin. A Mr Gray (a 'complete Yankee in appearance'), was loud in his talk of the Civil War – then being fought between the Union and the Confederate States. Although born in a slave state, Gray was in the peculiar position of both despising slavery and hating the slaves ('not human beings'). He was, however, pleased to hear from Milton that 'American women are the most beautiful in the world'. Bartholomew Gugy was a Quebec lawyer, politician, and colonel in the militia who added to the saloon amusement by suffering grievously from seasickness and constantly wailing that 'it was most demoralising thing a man can go through, it is degrading to lie on one's belly on the floor, with one's head over a basin; to be a slave of one's squeamish stomach, & a disgusting beast in the face of the company. No Sir, I shall never hold up my head again among my fellow men.' His 'fellow men' reacted by bursting into laughter. All this was watched at a distance by an enigmatic young woman of 'solitary habits and pensive taciturnity'.

Of most interest among the passengers, however, was a former Etonian named Charles Alston Messiter of Barwick House, near Yeovil, Somerset, a young man of independent means on the lookout for adventure. He had joined the ship as it was the only one that permitted him to bring his bloodhound Druid ('a son of Grantley Berkeley's celebrated dog') which he hoped to try out against wolves. He recorded that he had 'met two English gentlemen, also on their way to the West, and intending, like myself, to fit out at Fort Garry, on Lake Winnipeg, so we agreed to join company for so long as it suited us'.

In an effort to relieve the boredom of the voyage, the saloon passengers played shovelboard, bridge, backgammon and chess, or talked about food, the weather, or each other. Bets were laid on the distance covered each day, and on which foot the pilot would first place on the deck when he boarded to take them into Quebec. Milton stayed in his bunk for most of each day, and even the active Cheadle was forced to speak sharply to the cabin steward about the man's objectionable habit of waking him up for an unwanted breakfast. But, as the *Anglo-Saxon* approached the Newfoundland banks, a new subject for conversation arrived in the shape of the battered, mastless hulk of a ship that drifted silently past. The following day, fog and icebergs brought home the probable reason for the abandoned vessel. Now, with their own ship's siren blaring out across the murky waters, all eyes peered into the thickening mist at towering icebergs in the hope that their ship would not endure the same fate. Terrible stories about ships lost with all hands became the chief topic of conversation as the *Anglo-Saxon*'s bows crashed through vast fields of broken ice.

On the morning of 30 June, the passengers awoke to a beautiful, blue-sky day with Cape Race in view and the entrance to the Gulf of St Lawrence ahead. Milton and Cheadle, with a few others, engaged Mr Gray in a debate over the United States. The American claimed that the Southern States had no right to secede from the Union as, in the case of Louisiana, the state had been purchased from the French, others partially, so they therefore 'belonged' to the Union. When he asked, 'Would Scotland be allowed to separate?' it was pointed out that Scotland did not 'belong' to England and there was no parallel case in the Union of the United Kingdom. Gray then declared that, if it came to a war between the United States and Great Britain, every Irishman, and every English immigrant to the United States, would side against the British. However, he continued, the United States did not want British North America – the obvious bone of contention between the USA and Great Britain. The USA planned instead to invade Mexico.

The following day, after a course of instruction on navigational instruments given by the captain, Cheadle joined Milton, Messiter, and Gray in an inquiry into an alleged theft of 15 gold sovereigns from one of the steerage passengers. The man, a Staffordshire miner, had met a stranger the night before the ship sailed from Liverpool. After a drink, during which time the miner revealed he had the sovereigns in his purse, the stranger suggested they had a meal. On this being arranged by the miner, he returned to find the stranger gone. Much later, when the ship had left Ireland, he had checked his purse only to find that his sovereigns had been replaced by counterfeits. Upon examination, Cheadle and the others felt that the man was telling the truth and proposed a collection to replace some of the lost money. At this, Colonel Gugy – now recovered from seasickness, and who had not attended the inquiry – roundly denounced the miner as an impostor. In consequence, another inquiry was held, also concluding that the miner was telling the truth. Eventually, £7 was collected and presented to the man who wept with gratitude – the only non-contributors among the saloon passengers being the colonel and the two bishops.

After a passage of eleven days, and on arrival at Quebec, the young woman, who had remained aloof from the general company, was seen to be rushing up and down the landing stage in a state of great agitation. Clearly, she had expected to have been greeted by her lover but, with no one there to meet her, she was finally seen rushing to the telegraph office in a state of 'frantic excitement'. Later the same day, however, she was seen in the company of a young man and as 'placid as ever'. She had married within 'an hour' of arrival. The end was not so happy for the *Anglo-Saxon*. A year after she had disembarked the Milton party at Quebec, she ran aground off Cape Race and became a total wreck, with 238 lives lost.

In company with Messiter, Milton and Cheadle booked into the Russell Hotel where they discovered the advantage of having a senior aristocrat as part of the team. As he was unpacking, Milton was disturbed by a man walking into the room, picking up a small leather bag, and demanding that Milton 'trade' it. When the viscount refused, the man stated that it was Milton's fault for not coming to an agreement, turned on his heel, and disappeared with the bag. Milton, dumbfounded, let the matter go. Shortly afterwards, the stranger reappeared, returned the bag with abject apologies saying that he had not realised that Milton was an English lord. He then offered five pounds of tobacco in compensation – which Milton accepted. That evening, some of the tobacco was enjoyed along with tall glasses of mint julep and a game of billiards before the English trio retired to their beds.

Following a visit to the Plains of Abraham – the site of Wolfe's victory over Montcalm in September 1759 – a sextant was purchased for £6, before returning to the ship to continue the voyage up the St Lawrence. At Montreal, gunpowder and percussion caps were obtained and Cheadle complained at beer being priced at 1s a bottle. In the evening they joined the captain of the *Anglo-Saxon* as he dined with a friend ('thoroughly Scottish'). Throughout the meal, the Scotsman insisted on explaining in great detail the Indian game of La Crosse, to the immense boredom of his listeners. Breakfast the following morning found the Scotsman again present. To their intense irritation, he opened the conversation by saying 'Bye the bye, Sir, have you heard of the game of La Crosse? Played by the Indians...' He then repeated the previous night's entire monologue. The event was missed by Messiter who was busy spending £4 on a Newfoundland pup, to be named Sailor.

Toronto was reached on 7 July, when they booked in to the Rossin House Hotel. Having time to spend in the area, they decided to visit the Niagara Falls. At first they found the spectacle 'disappointing', a response, they decided, from relying too much on overblown illustrations and written accounts. However, after time spent watching the falls on a moonlit summer evening, they reassessed their opinion and found the scene to be 'very fine'. The night was spent at a local hotel, where the party was constantly pestered by a 'Captain Hutchinson' who insisted on introducing his friend 'Major Kane' with exaggerated elegance. Once it was discovered that there was an English lord present, the pair resorted to an over-familiar fawning and loud offers of drinks and accommodation in Toronto. This was followed by tall stories of how Hutchinson had covered himself with glory in the Queen's service during fighting in southern Africa. Major Kane, on the other hand, hinted that he had been sent to the area in case of any American aggression. On their return to Toronto, Milton, Messiter and Cheadle found themselves besieged by the two 'military' men who, once again, bought round after round of drinks in a desire to impress. Their undoing, however, came when Milton walked into the hotel bar to hear Hutchinson boasting to a group of listeners about his new-found friends, 'Capital fellows, got devilish intimate with them.' At this, he realised that Milton was in the room and was then heard to ask in a whisper if he had been overheard. But it was too late, the damage had been done and the pair were never seen again, leaving Cheadle to ponder whether either of them was 'a sharper, or merely an impertinent fool'.

From Toronto, the next destination was intended to be the Wisconsin city of La Crosse, via Detroit and Chicago. Having booked berths in a 'sleeping car' they found that there were only two vacant bunks in the gentlemen's compartment. As a result, although only married men were allowed into the ladies' compartment, Messiter was offered a berth with the ladies – a berth made vacant by a lady passenger offering to 'squeeze into' a bunk already occupied by a married couple.

Detroit proved to be a disaster. Faced with American customs officials demanding thirty per cent duties on their guns, and with delays in inspecting Messiter's large travelling case, the train left without them. Messiter, furious at having lost his place in the ladies' compartment, demanded to see the senior customs officer. The official, possibly intimidated by the enraged Messiter, but more likely impressed by Milton's social rank, proved to be an accommodating man and supplied them with a pass excluding them from import duties until they reached Fort Garry. The delay meant that they had a few hours to spend in Detroit. Cheadle considered the city to be 'a large straggling place' full of Americans with 'sallow faces, large straw hats, clean shaven cheeks & moustaches, or beards'. He was not impressed with the language spoken by the inhabitants with its repeated use of 'I guess' in the place of 'I suppose'. Nor was he impressed by the train that took them to Chicago. His fellow passengers were 'very promiscuous' with the ladies failing to draw the dividing curtain of their compartment and watching 'with great satisfaction' as the gentlemen dressed. Just four years earlier, one passenger on the line was George M. Pullman, who was so unimpressed with the conditions of the sleeping car in which he was travelling that he determined to produce something better. Unfortunately for Milton, Cheadle and Messiter, the new, comparatively luxurious 'Pullman Sleepers' did not appear until two years after they had passed through.

Matters did not improve on arrival at Chicago. Having booked into Briggs House Hotel they found themselves in a place where the waiter talked to Milton 'as if he had been his own brother'. A stage magician known as 'Herr Hamburger' tried (unsuccessfully) to obtain

Milton's sponsorship by removing a handkerchief and other items from Cheadle's pockets. The people exhibited a 'general rudeness' by 'pushing past without begging pardon' and the shopkeepers served them 'as if they were doing a favour'. To top it all, Cheadle later found that his best pipe and six ounces of tobacco was missing and suspected 'Herr Hamburger' may have had something to do with it.

La Crosse was reached, at last, on 11 July. There they boarded a stern-wheeled Mississippi paddle steamer where, much to his shock, the appalled Cheadle found that breakfast was at 6.30am. Grotesquely early breakfast or not, the journey along the river to St Paul proved to be through attractive, even beautiful, country. The voyage was marred, however – at least for Cheadle – by the amount of swearing among the other passengers. The use of oaths such as 'by Jesus Christ' and 'God Almighty' was especially prevalent, leading – presumably by divine influence – to a number of groundings. As a result, their destination was not achieved until several hours after dark.

St Paul, the capital city of the State of Minnesota, and consisting mainly of log cabins, had little to offer the party except for a last chance to stock up with powder, ammunition, and tobacco. Milton had $30 stolen from his belt (left unguarded on his bed), and Cheadle found he could get a better rate of exchange for his sovereigns from a tobacconist than from the official Exchange Bureau. They were also depressed to find about thirty of their fellow countrymen were living in impoverished conditions in the town. They had been gripped by tales of fortunes to be made in the gold fields of British Columbia, but had fallen victim to fraudsters who had charged them £40 to conduct them northwards but had abandoned them in northern Minnesota. Messiter noted that although 'none of them ever having done any manual labour before' and included several 'broken-down gentlemen', they were forced to chop wood, sweep the streets, and undertake other lowly jobs in order to survive.

Even worse was the news that the river boat they intended to use to take them up the Red River to Fort Garry was delayed. At this, they decided to travel 320 miles by stagecoach to join the Red River at Georgetown, north-west Minnesota. Once there, they intended to buy canoes, and paddle their way north. Consequently, at the first opportunity, they caught the train to St Anthony, 6 miles from St Paul and the start of the Great Pacific Railroad to the Pacific coast – still under construction, but already reaching far across the plains. St Anthony was also the starting point for the four-horse 'express wagon' which would transport them to Georgetown. More of a stage-wagon than a stage-coach, the conveyance was uncomfortable, hot, and overcrowded. Beneath a canvas cover stretched over metal hoops, three padded benches were suspended by leather straps. Luggage was placed in the rear along with a seat for the conductor. Both the conductor and the driver were armed with a rifle and a pistol in case of unwanted attention from the local Indians. Milton and Messiter – with his two dogs – managed to secure seats on the outside, one alongside the driver, the other joining the conductor. Cheadle, however, was forced to endure the journey on the inside, keeping company with 'Yankee women chattering like magpies' and two German women with four fractious babies between them. So cramped was the inside of the stage that Cheadle, trapped on one of the swaying benches, could only with the greatest of efforts extract an arm to wipe the sweat from his brow or brush away the multitudes of mosquitoes that had descended to torment the passengers. After a journey of 70 miles some relief came on arrival at the overnight stop at St Cloud ('pronounced as spelt'), although Cheadle had to sleep on the floor of the wayside house ('as objecting to bed fellows').

The following day's journey of a similar distance was made considerably better by the absence of the Americans, but Cheadle still had to put up with the German women with their bawling babies – and the clouds of humming mosquitoes. With some daylight still remaining on their arrival at the next overnight stop, Sauk Centre, the party went in search of ducks to provide something more interesting to eat than the usual fare of salt pork. Although they managed to bring down several of the birds, they could not be reached as they had fallen into the water, and nobody wanted to strip off to retrieve them due to the ubiquitous mosquitoes. When the landlord of the wayside house learned of this he informed them that they should have taken his dog, Rover, as he was a trained gundog. The next morning, the party offered the landlord $20 for Rover, a terrier-like animal about the size of a beagle. This offer resulted in the man's wife and sister rushing into the room and smothering the dog with loud affection while breaking into tears. Retreating in the face of this onslaught, the party repaired to the stage empty-handed. However, just as they were about to set off, the landlord arrived with Rover tied to a length of string. He had, it transpired, managed to persuade the women that the money would be of greater use than the dog. Consequently, Rover brought the number of expedition dogs up to three. More ducks were shot before their arrival at the oddly named overnight stop of Pomme de Terre. Again the birds fell into the water. This time, however, despite the much promised skills of Rover, Messiter stripped off to collect them. His reward was not only to lose his powder flask, but also to be so badly bitten by mosquitoes that he was unable to sleep that night.

They reached the Red River the next day, at Fort Abercrombie. Manned by 'slovenly' soldiers, the fort was surrounded by dozens of Indian lodges. The Sioux had gathered at the fort to receive an annual subsidy owed to them by the US authorities in payment for lands surrendered to the Government. In the main, the subsidy consisted of blankets and ammunition, the latter needed for the coming buffalo hunt. Only a portion of the supplies had arrived and the Indian Agent had refused to hand any out until the full stock had been delivered. Under their chiefs, the tribe had sat patiently waiting for their supplies for four weeks, but nothing had been handed over, and their condition had been ignored. Unable to leave to go hunting in case the goods arrived in their absence, the chiefs were coming under pressure to act on behalf of their people as the families starved around them. Overall, an atmosphere of menace began, and bands of young braves were beginning to gather in the woods. Now, as the stagecoach arrived, the only thing stopping a full-scale attack was the Chippewa chief 'Hole-in-the-day' having been locked up in the local jail – his tribe would not join the Sioux without him. Two days later, on their arrival at Georgetown, rumours abounded of Sioux war bands being spotted in the area singing their war song –

Iaxica-canze-maye-ca-e,
Niyakee-bawahunhen-we.

(The white people have made me angry,
I will butcher them alive.)

The small settlement on the Buffalo River was the most southerly trading post of the Hudson's Bay Company. A contemporary account describes the place as 'composed of one Store, at which you can buy nothing; one Hotel at which we could buy neither grog nor victuals; one Barricks & some three or four Indian wigwams & one dwelling House'. The 'Barricks' provided accommodation for a company of the Minnesota militia made up mainly of Irishmen and Germans who strutted around with great swagger and heroic posturing. Not surprisingly, many of the inhabitants had left in search of safety at St Paul.

Rather than wait around for an expected Indian attack, or for the delayed steamboat, Milton and Cheadle purchased one birch bark canoe for $6 and hired another for $2.50. One of the canoes was still full of bullet holes after being grabbed during an ambush by Sioux against the Assiniboine Indians, the other was in an almost as bad condition. Nevertheless, on the water, Cheadle found them to be 'cranky' but acceptable. In a race against Lyman Bullock Goff and his new bride, Almira – two Americans they had met who were paddling a dugout canoe – he was soundly 'licked'. Revenge, however, was gained when Goff revealed that they intend to use their canoe to reach Fort Garry. Messiter and Cheadle then amused themselves by embarking upon a catalogue of entirely fictional tales revealing the terrifying hazards of the river from barbaric Indians, which 'evidently produces an effect'. Astonishingly, sixty-four years later, Goff wrote an account of the meeting. According to his version, he met 'Milton, and his Squire, Doctor Cheadle'. Apparently, the 'Squire' 'was a gentleman, but the viscount was 'a snob of the first water'. After having purchased their dugout canoe, the American couple intended to join the party of Englishmen on their way to Fort Garry but, 'rumours of Indians, however, changed our minds'. The day after Milton and Cheadle arrived at the post, they learned that they need not have invented lurid tales to alarm a couple of American newlyweds. Just before Milton's party was due to leave on their journey along the Red River, they heard that the stagecoach following the one on which they had travelled northwards had been attacked and the conductor killed. Yet more reports of painted Sioux war bands arrived. It was clearly time to move on.

On the morning of Monday 21 July 1862, having (probably more in hope more than expectation) arranged for their baggage and the two large dogs to be forwarded to Fort Garry, one canoe bearing

Cheadle and Messiter, and another carrying Milton and Rover, entered the muddy waters of the Red River. On board they had flour, fat, salt and pemmican (pounded dried meat embedded in its own solidified fat), a frying pan, a soup kettle, a basin, an axe, and a coffeepot. For hunting and for defence, each canoe carried a shotgun, powder and shot, a revolver loaded with six bullets, and a rifle with ten bullets. The country through which they would be travelling was the ancestral land and hunting grounds of the Sioux, Assiniboine, and the Chippewa – none of whom would be in the mood for gentle negotiations. They had intended to hire a guide, but the collection of drunkards and misfits remaining at the post provided no one of merit, and so they set off, trusting to their own skills and the whims of Providence with a 'jolly feeling of independence'.

The first part of the journey bode well as the canoes were gently paddled in a generally northwards direction as the river snaked through the flat country in a succession of numberless bends. Despite a burning sun, both Milton and Cheadle had rolled up their sleeves. The doctor soon came to the view that they were in danger of being badly burned and rolled his sleeves down again. Milton refused to do so. A couple of ducks were shot and they landed to try and cook them skewered on a stick – 'failure'. After an extended rest, they returned to the river and paddled until it was almost dark before landing again to set up camp and prepare a meal. Only then did they realise that they carried no dry wood for a fire and the wood close at hand was already wet with early dew. Trying to prepare a meal in the dark proved to be a 'great bother'. With little but barely edible duck to eat, no tent, swarms of mosquitoes, and the constant awaking at every sound for fear of Indians, the night turned out to be 'exceedingly disagreeable'.

Having achieved about 25 miles on the first day, it was hoped that such progress could be maintained. The poor condition of the canoes, however, soon ended such ambitions, and much of the day was spent sealing and resealing leaks. In all, no more than 7 or 8 miles were achieved on the second day. Rover's fortunes, on the other hand, improved when it was found that the pemmican was inedible – at least for humans. Learning from their experience the previous night, camp was established while light still remained and they soon had a recently shot goose sizzling in the frying pan. Unfortunately, the axe handle broke while wood was being chopped for the fire.

By now, Milton's arms, long exposed to the sun, had badly blistered and he found it impossible to paddle. As a result, Cheadle and Messiter had no option but to tow him and Rover. Messiter, not a natural river traveller, later complained that the paddling was 'very monotonous, especially as we often paddled for an hour and more, only to find ourselves within a few hundred yards of where we started from, the river having wound in almost a complete circle'. They nevertheless again managed to achieve a distance of about 25 miles. This gave Milton the chance to note the wildlife that flourished by the river. He recorded squirrels, woodpeckers, and hawks. 'Swarms' of black and golden orioles competed in display with 'gaily plumed' kingfishers. At night 'a hundred owls hooted round us' while, from nearby lakes, the sad calls of loons rolled with a dismal drone across the prairie grass. The initial enthusiasm was, however, beginning to wear thin as they paddled along the 'monotonous', meandering river channel with flat, featureless prairie extending to the horizon beyond the high banks.

After wasting an almost entire day repairing the canoes which leaked 'abominably', the party decided to try to make up the time by paddling through the night while towing Milton, who promptly went to sleep. With the sun's first rays, a camp was made ashore beneath a tall bank. Three hours later they woke 'half baked'. Their campsite was not only protected from the wind, it also faced directly south. Wearily, and with the two old Etonians squabbling over Milton's self-inflicted sunburn, the camp was abandoned and the canoes put back on the water.

On the sixth day after leaving Georgetown, both canoes were almost lost when they shot a series of rapids. Milton was cast adrift and almost collided with a mid-stream rock as Cheadle and Messiter struggled to avoid other hazards. The excitement resulted in a lot of bad language and, after the canoes went aground and had to be dragged clear, they clambered back on board 'each abusing the other'. All animosity was, however, quickly forgotten when they came face to face with the white-hulled sternwheeler *International* hauling up against the rapids. Following a struggle against the fast-flowing stream, both canoes were hoisted on board the steamer and the party invited to stay for dinner. Learning that the vessel would not be back for at least a week they decided that they would continue in the canoes and took to the river once again, amply supplied with cheroots, salt pork and flour, and glowing from the effect of several brandies. They had also learned that they had managed to cover 113 miles in the six days.

Most of the following ten days were spent in search of food. They found success with the occasional fish or duck, but their search for an elk proved wholly unsuccessful. In addition to breaking their only axe, and snapping the handle off their frying pan, they squabbled ceaselessly over the best method of producing bread in the remnant of the pan, and suffered such rains and storms that their canoes were almost swamped. The continuous deluge prevented any attempt at lighting a fire at their muddy campsites. Consequently, it was with great joy that, at five o' clock on the morning of the eleventh day, they awoke to the sound of the steamboat whistle. The *International* was on her way north and Captain Butler had spotted their camp. With no need for encouragement, the party jumped on board, Milton getting a splinter in his foot and Messiter being reunited with Druid and Sailor. Little, however, was allowed to obstruct the route to the dining saloon where great justice was done to the ample fare provided – the breakfast was 'wonderful! ditto dinner, ditto tea'.

Starvation having been avoided, merely being on board the vessel did not necessarily mean the removal of other dangers. Constructed at Georgetown and launched just over two months earlier, she proved to be too long for the sinuous river and, during the first 48 hours of her maiden voyage, collided with the bank on three occasions, lost her funnels, wrecked the pilothouse, and damaged the stern wheel.

Writing a few years later, a passenger in the *International*, Colonel W. F. Butler, noted:

The *International* was a curious craft; she measured about 130 feet in length, drew only two feet of water, and was propelled by an enormous wheel placed over her stern ... Her engines were a perfect marvel of patchwork ... pieces of rope seemed twisted around crank and shaft, mud was laid thickly on boiler and pipes, little jets and spurts of steam had a disagreeable way of coming out from places not supposed to be capable of such outpourings. Her capacity for going on fire seemed to be very great; each gust of wind sent showers of sparks from the furnaces flying along the lower deck, the charred beams of which attested the frequency of the occurrence.

Something of the domestic conditions on board may be understood from an account by another passenger, B. Peyton Ward, who wrote:

> The crew were a set of scoundrelly looking half-breeds; the passengers all of the rough, dirty-handed, try-to-make-their-fortune species, and the solitary woman looked crushed under the responsibility of representing the show of her sex ... We were not provided with washing materials in our cabins, but there was a general washroom where the basins were covered with a thick coating of filth, and there was an equally offensive common towel.

The second day onboard saw the steamboat calling at the frontier post of Pembina, a place, according to Colonel Butler, which was pervaded with 'a sense of dirt and debauchery'. For Cheadle, it was little more than 'huts and half-breeds'. The customs house agent, having sent his family away, had fortified the upper storey of his house, destroyed the stairs, and entered his building by a rope ladder to a window – a ladder which he drew up each night. On his bed he had gathered a formidable collection of firearms with suitable ammunition placed by each weapon. Messiter, in particular, was impressed by the agent's intention to sell his life dearly.

With such preparations in hand to face the approaching threat, Milton and his party were glad to leave. Once across the border, they were back in British North America, and Fort Garry was only a day away. Not that Cheadle could sit back and enjoy the view. As the vessel repeatedly ran aground, he tended to Messiter who had been violently ill from over-eating, and dealt with Milton's sunburn. Both the viscount and Cheadle suffered from severe indigestion, arising from the same source as Messiter's discomfort.

At two o'clock on the afternoon of 7 August, the *International* left the Red River and steamed the few hundred yards up the Assiniboine River to a landing stage on the south bank. On the north bank, immediately opposite, lay Fort Garry with its stone walls and round towers. Milton and Cheadle had, at last, reached the start of their overland journey.

2

Rum and Red River Carts on the Fort Ellice Trail

As the *International* came alongside the landing stage, she was immediately boarded by a number of men, mainly Métis, whose job was to unload the ship's cargo of supplies for the fort. Among them was the tall, strong figure of Louis La Ronde, a French 'breed' who had accompanied Milton on his previous visit to the colony. In the mid-nineteenth century, mixed-race people of French descent were known as 'Métis'. Those with British – usually Scottish – ancestry preferred 'half-breed', while the white colonists usually referred to most of the mixed-race people as 'breeds'. Mixed race people with a Cree or Ojibway Indian background were known as 'Bungays'. The Métis, in particular, were devout Roman Catholics. Even in the great June and September buffalo hunts, the first rule was: 'No buffalo shall be run on the Sabbath.' La Ronde had been awarded the Arctic Medal for the time he had spent in accompanying the naval surgeon Sir John Richardson in an overland search for the missing explorer, Sir John Franklin. La Ronde had later joined the search party led by Dr John Rae, a Hudson's Bay factor who earned infamy by rushing home to gain the reward for 'discovering' Franklin's fate when only two days march from possible survivors. Even worse, with personal malice towards the Royal Navy, Rae had invented tales of cannibalism among Franklin's men.

Eager to be of service to Milton one more, La Ronde invited the party to put up their tent close by his house. A single tent was used as it allowed all of them to shelter beneath Messiter's mosquito net. As it was early evening before the party had completed ferrying their baggage and dogs across the river, it was decided that a visit to the fort could wait until the morning. Before turning in, Cheadle attended to Milton's sunburn, a condition exacerbated by an outbreak of boils on one of his legs. The doctor prescribed 'perfect rest & cold water bandage; quinine & port wine'.

The following morning, having had breakfast and a pipe of tobacco, and with Milton's ailments attended to, Cheadle set off for the nearby fort – named after Nicholas Garry, the Deputy Governor of the Hudson's Bay Company between 1822 and 1835. The 12-foot high, 4-foot thick stone walls of the fort were finished at each corner with a round tower, each tower holding four small artillery pieces and provided with a musket gallery and loopholes. The walls enclosed an area of about 4 acres on which were built the governor's residence, the chief factor's house, the clerk's house, the men's quarters ('bachelor's hall'), the office, the canoe house, the fur house, and the Hudson's Bay Company's stores ('the Indian shop') – the latter stuffed with clothes, blankets, fire steels, scalp-knives, files, awls, scissors, twine, beads, thimbles, needles, pins, guns, gun parts, flints, powder, shot, and copper or tin kitchen ware. An Indian hunter bringing in a pack of furs would have his catch valued by the trader. With this done, he would be presented with a number of small wooden tokens. These, in turn, were returned to the trader in exchange for goods from the store.

The community attaching itself to the fort extended about 10 miles along the Red River, and about the same distance up the Assiniboine. In all, about 3,000 people had settled around the junction of the two rivers, the majority being Métis families.

Cheadle's first port of call was to the house of William McTavish – the Governor of Assiniboia (as the Red River settlement was known). McTavish was a tall, gaunt Scotsman with red hair and a matching bushy beard. He had been in command at the fort since 1857, and had been appointed governor the following year. Cheadle found McTavish to be 'very civil' and prescribed medicine for the governor's servant who was suffering from 'English cholera' – a virulent form of diarrhoea. The fort's executive officer, accompanied by his daughter, took Cheadle to see another patient outside the fort, calling at the post office en route to see if there were any letters for the party. On the way, the carriage hit a post and the man and his daughter were thrown out, the latter falling under the carriage wheels, fortunately with little injury. After attending to the new patient, Cheadle was invited by the girl's father to stay for lunch and was served not only cold beef, but also with tales of the country through which he intended to travel. His host was well known as a killer of grizzly bears and told of a time when a bear attacked his camp and dragged off one of his companions 'like a baby in arms'. Several men received serious wounds before the animal was brought down by gunfire. Suitably fortified after such stories with a pipe and a glass of port, the doctor walked back to the fort only to be caught in a thunderstorm and thoroughly soaked.

At La Ronde's house, Cheadle found Messiter busily pressing on with his preparations but not too busily to prevent him from accepting an invitation to that night's 'half-breed ball'. Such dances were a regular event during their stay at the fort, and were noted for their wild, abandoned dancing to the fiddle, the Métis men dressed in their finery of company regulation light-blue coats, red or blue flannel shirts, and corduroy trousers gathered at the knee with beadwork. To this they added a distinctive, decorated sash; long woollen stockings with red or blue fringed leggings; and moccasins decorated with beadwork. On their heads they wore hats decorated with feathers, or caps garlanded with tinsel bands. From their necks a powder horn was suspended, while from their belt hung a tomahawk – which also doubled as a tobacco pipe. Messiter found the Métis women 'very handsome ... anywhere else you would have taken them for Spaniards; the only thing which spoiled them was their hair, which was always very straight and coarse.'

While Milton remained laid low by his sunstroke and boils, Cheadle and Messiter fell to arguing whenever the opportunity rose. A trip downriver in a dugout ended with them swearing at each other and, in the early hours of the following morning, unable to sleep due to a violent thunder storm, they long and loudly debated the use of the phrase 'damn it'. On the fifth day at the fort, the pair had another 'fierce argument' over the 'salvation of savages'. At this, Messiter set up his own tent and moved out of the shared accommodation taking his mosquito net with him – much to Milton and Cheadle's subsequent discomfort.

When not arguing, socialising or assembling their supplies, it was important to obtain suitable horses for the forthcoming journey. Whenever one of them heard of a promising animal, they tried to keep it from the others, for one reason – that it would avoid price increases through competition. Messiter proved himself to be the best at the game. Knowing that Cheadle had heard of a first-rate horse some distance from the fort and intended to go after it the next day, Messiter acted promptly. As Cheadle strolled into the fort after breakfast, he was not amused to find Messiter had ridden out overnight and was now smugly parading the animal in front of admiring Métis. La Ronde recommended that Cheadle buy a strange looking horse that suffered from an enlarged head, a crooked foreleg, and an extra-long tail. Despite finding the animal 'sluggish', Cheadle took the Métis' advice and, demonstrating humour over practicality, named the horse Bucephalus after the legendary steed of Alexander the Great. With their horses secured, the party gave Cheadle the responsibility of purchasing or hiring a means of transporting their supplies overland. This took the shape of the ubiquitous two-wheeled Red River cart, a construction that was almost entirely made of wood, and capable of carrying a load weighing up to 900lb. The wheel rims normally remained unshod but, in some case, a 'tyre' made of buffalo hide was shrunk onto the rim, and leather strips were used as bindings. At least two spare axles had to be carried as they very quickly wore out. Requiring no metal, the carts could be quickly and easily repaired anywhere that wood could be found, the repairs completed with buffalo rawhide lacing known as 'shaganappi'. Crossing rivers provided little inconvenience as the body of the cart could be floated across with the wheels carried on board. They were, however, noted for the extraordinary noise of their passing.

Three carts were obtained, with three oxen to haul them. The necessity for each member of the party to have his own cart was indicated by Cheadle's own list of purchases from the fort's store – 3 hundredweight of flour, 1 hundredweight of pemmican, 8 gallons of rum, 20 pounds of tobacco, 22 pounds of gunpowder, 56 pounds of lead shot, 32 pounds of ball cartridge, 1 blanket, 1 buffalo robe, 20 pounds of tea, 10 pounds of coffee, 14 pounds of salt, 3 pounds of pepper, 2 yards of duffle and 1 pair of beaverteen (coarse cotton) trousers. He also purchased from Madame La Ronde 12 pairs of moccasins, 1 caribou-skin hunting shirt, 1 pair of moose-skin breaches, and 1 pair of moose-skin leggings. There was also the need to carry the supplies of any guides or hunters who may be required en route. To ensure the weights balanced out equally between each cart, La Ronde would go on his hands and knees under each cart's axle and lift it clear of the ground adjusting the loads as necessary. Cheadle took his responsibility very seriously and could have been annoyed when a drunken ('very silly and laughing at nothing') La Ronde conspiratorially informed him that Milton had said: 'Damn the doctor's carts'.

In addition to La Ronde, the party hired three other Métis: Jean Baptiste Vital, Tousaint Voudrie and Athanhaus Bruneau. The latter, the son of a magistrate, was talkative and agreeable, but with little experience. Vital was a 'sinister-looking dog' of great pretensions, and Voudrie was considered 'simple'.

As the final preparations were being made, the fort was honoured by a visit from Colonel Charles Alphonsus Murray who, at the age of four, had received the titles 3rd Baron Dunmore; 7th Lord Murray of Firth, Moulin and Tillemot; 7th Viscount of Fincastle; and 7th Earl of Dunmore. The twenty-one-year-old aristocrat was on a hunting expedition with Captains Cowper and Thynne from the Guards regiment stationed at Montreal. They were on their way to Fort Ellice, on the Assiniboine River, to hunt buffalo and grizzly bears. It was a brief visit but, being only a last breath away from becoming an earl himself, Milton had a brief, yet unexpected, moment in the company of someone near his social equal. On the final evening at the fort, the party were joined by Dunmore and his fellow officers at dinner at the home of the bishop of Rupert's Land. The bishop lived with his sister and proved a hospitable host providing their guests with turkey, veal, and beef, all washed down with two bottles of port. On their return Milton stayed up late in the company of La Ronde's daughter 'fixing hunting shirt'.

The following day, both Cheadle and Messiter were ready to leave, but Milton was some way behind in his preparations. The doctor tried to urge the viscount to speed things up, but received only a fractious response. Milton then decided that he needed another cart. As they waited for this to be arranged, Messiter gave

Cheadle the surprising information that capital punishment had been abolished in the settlement. The last murderer had been given ten months in prison, but the community thought that was too severe, so it was reduced to three. While inside, the prisoner made a lot of money by making harnesses.

On the morning of 23 August, Cheadle called on the governor to raise funds from a bill of exchange. The governor agreed to do so, but only as a personal favour to the doctor. Apparently, Milton had caused annoyance by his 'abuse' of the Hudson's Bay Company hospitality. Unfortunately, Cheadle told Milton of this at lunch, just before they were about to depart. Instead of leaving, the insulted viscount stormed over to the governor's house to tell McTavish that he has got everything wrong. One way or another, the matter was smoothed over and, at last, Cheadle noted in his journal, '& *start!* at 4.'

As they left Fort Garry, word began to trickle in of a wave of Indian attacks in Minnesota. Under the leadership of the Sioux Chief Little Crow, and goaded into action by starvation and lack of Governmental concern over their plight, the Winnebago Indians advanced on St Paul from Mankato in the south-west, the Chippewa poured down from the north-west, while the Sioux attacked from the south-east. The Indians mercilessly attacked the white population wherever they could be found. With increasing savagery and brutality that shocked the nation; men, women and children were slaughtered in their hundreds. Among the dead were the previous owners of Messiter's dog Rover – early victims of the first Indian War.

The trail the travellers had chosen was known as the White Mud River – or Fort Ellice Trail, which meant following the bank of the Assiniboine River. After just one night out of Fort Garry, one of the oxen vanished. The animals had proved to be aggravatingly slow, so it was decided to exchange them for horses. La Ronde asked permission to attend a wedding close by and was allowed to do so. He returned in a hopelessly drunken state and collapsed snoring into the mud.

The following day, Voudrie suggested that they all attend the wedding reception of one of his cousins. Messiter, anxious about more delays, did not approve, but it was eventually decided that they should attend in order to avoid any offence. The event was held in a two-roomed house packed with Métis, one room being used to contain the food and copious drinks, the other served as the 'ballroom'. It did not take Milton long to start dancing with the bride – a young woman of about sixteen or seventeen. Although he performed in a somewhat more stately manner than the other dancers, his version of the fiddle-led 'double shuffle and stamp' received wide and enthusiastic approval. Cheadle and Messiter, however, looked on with mild disapproval and refused to join in. Eventually, with no one knowing the whereabouts of La Ronde, a very reluctant Milton was dragged away. An attempt by drunken partygoers to stop them leaving on the grounds that there was no water for at least 15 miles was ignored, and they headed for a small settlement 1½ miles away under the command of a Mr Lane. There they ran into another large group of drunken Métis who insisted on treating them to corn whisky. Lane assured them that they could continue with safety. This they did, with Milton sulking and Messiter fuming at the delay. Matters were not improved when Messiter discovered that Rover was missing. He turned his horse and, cursing loudly, went off in search of his dog. Just at that moment, La Ronde turned up full of apologies for his drunken antics. Shortly after his return, however, after a muttered conversation, both he and Milton decided that they would join in the search for the missing dog and went back the way they had come. Unfortunately for their true intent, they ran into Messiter who was accompanied by Rover. Nevertheless, instead of returning to the carts, they returned to the celebrations and did not get back for several hours. The following morning, so bad was the atmosphere between the two old Etonians that Cheadle had to force his horse between them to prevent a fight breaking out.

Near Portage La Prairie, a farming-based community of about sixty homes, they called at a house in the hope of obtaining some milk to discover that the owner was a Scotswoman who was delighted to see them. She had recently come up the Red River on board the *International* and had asked the captain to fly the British flag when in British territory. The captain had refused, so when he next looked up he saw a dishcloth flying instead. Another Stars and Stripes was run up, only, much to the woman's delight, to be promptly hauled down and replaced by the British flag as a salute of musket fire from other British passengers rattled out. While enjoying the woman's hospitality, Cheadle looked at himself in one of her mirrors and saw that, after a week on the trail, his appearance was 'not prepossessing'.

Two days later another argument broke out, this time over whether it was a Saturday or a Sunday. La Ronde was asked to adjudicate and came down on it being a Saturday. Consequently, a ham was cooked for the following day's dinner. In the early hours of Monday morning, after a supper of mushrooms, Messiter leapt from his camp bed shouting that they were being attacked by Indians. He rushed from his tent and grappled with Voudrie who was at a marked disadvantage through wearing nothing but his shirt. The commotion woke up La Ronde, who was sleeping under a cart. Forgetting where he was, the half-breed jumped up – severely cracking his head. Within moments the camp was in uproar with everyone rushing round trying to find the cause of the commotion. Eventually, Messiter returned to his bed beneath a shower of verbal abuse from his travelling companions. But not everyone returned to their beds; in the morning it was discovered that Vital had disappeared. There had been some friction over the last few days between Vital and Cheadle over the former's tendency to avoid work and to ride all day in one of the carts. The Métis' increasingly sulky manner had made Cheadle think that he might 'bolt' as he 'don't like pedestrian exercise'. La Ronde, however, was of the opinion that, as Vital had served with Captain John Palliser during his 1857 expedition into the region, his experiences of the Blackfeet Indian tribe had 'funked him'.

That noon, the party encountered a cart train on its way from Fort Carlton, and letters were handed over for delivery at Fort Garry. La Ronde also arranged for a 'loutish lad' named Zear to join them in the place of the absconded Vital. After dark that night, another cart train was met. The leader handed Cheadle a letter from Lord Dunmore stating that the earl was at Fort Ellice suffering from jaundice and would welcome a visit from the doctor. Cheadle and Messiter immediately set off for Fort Ellice to attend to Dunmore's needs. Carrying the coffee pot and with two biscuit-like cakes known as 'galettes' each, they left Milton – as usual, slow to respond to anything requiring his departure from his bed – to catch them up later with a vital supply of rum. They intended to survive through the three or four days' journey on a readily available supply of ducks, snipe, prairie chickens, and geese. Several had been shot when Milton turned up with the rum, but without his ration of galettes, causing Cheadle to mutter about the 'rather short commons' – Messiter, however, was not too concerned; he described galettes as 'not bad when hot, but only fit for making bullets when cold'. The rest of the evening, before they retired to their tent, was enlivened by the horses' attempts to escape. After several long-distance chases, and despite being 'enfarged' (hobbled by the forelegs), the horses charged past the tent yet again. This time the travellers, too tired for further exertion, gave up and went to bed. The following morning the horses were found nearby and, having caused enough excitement, were easily recaptured.

A breakfast of watered rum, ham and galette helped to fend off the chill of an early September morning. After a day of steady progress across the prairie, they reached the gentle, wooded hills at the northern tip of Shoal Lake. That night it rained and the thermometer fell. By the following morning Cheadle was wet and the air was 'very cold and raw'. That evening, after overtaking another cart train, they were standing on the eastern bank of a loop in the Assiniboine River looking across at a high plateau on which could be seen the wooden buildings of Fort Ellice. A large flat-bottomed boat was tied alongside the opposite bank and, following the instructions they had been given by one of the cart trains they had met, they fired two shots into the air to attract the attention of the ferryman who would take them across. No one, however, came in response to the firing. After some time, two Métis were seen walking along their side of the river. After explaining their situation, one of the Métis volunteered to wade across and collect the boat, which proved to be half-full of water and floating debris. With the obliging Métis continuing on their way, Messiter decided to load two horses on to the boat. He had barely pushed off from the bank when the boat sank, leaving two horses and one former Etonian floundering in the river. With Messiter and the animals back on dry land, they agreed to try to wade or swim across. This method proved successful and, having climbed the steep bank on the far side, they discovered that the buildings they had seen had been abandoned – a new fort had been built about a mile-and-a-half further north.

At last arriving at their wooden-walled destination, they found the fort gates firmly closed, causing them to create a 'great hullabaloo'. Eventually, the gates were opened by a drunken Indian wearing just a breechcloth who shook Cheadle's hand with enormous enthusiasm before running off to inform the fort's chief trader. This proved to be Mr William McKay, a bearded giant of a man with blue eyes set in a bronzed, weatherbeaten face. He greeted his unexpected visitors warmly in his bare feet, before providing them with food and a place to sleep. They were less impressed, however, with his news that Lord Dunmore had already left the fort, and was now on a buffalo hunt – news that Cheadle felt was 'rather provoking'.

The following day, while waiting for the carts to arrive, Milton and Cheadle strolled around a collection of Métis and Indian lodges clustered close by the fort. The conical tepees, made of buffalo skin supported on pine poles, were the portable homes of Indians of the Assiniboine, Chippewa, and Cree tribes. They had been on a hunting expedition with the Métis (many of whom were closely related to the Indians) when four of their party – two women, a man, and a boy – were killed by a Sioux raiding party. The enemy were eventually driven off, with the loss of one of their braves, but the hunting party decided to seek the protection of the fort. One of the lodges had symbols pointed on the outside indicating the number of enemies the owner had personally killed.

For much of the day, the Indian men found little else to do but get drunk and start fighting with each other. During his visit to the lodges, Cheadle attended to a man lying in his shelter groaning from injuries received during such a fracas. The women turned their skills to the making of pemmican, pounding dried buffalo meat into a powder before soaking it in the animal's fat. When everything had hardened into a lump, the end product was highly valued as a means of long-lasting and portable nourishment – although a later traveller through the region, the Reverend G. M. Grant, suggested that pemmican 'needs all the sauce that hunger supplies to make it palatable'. During mealtimes, the Indians gathered in the fort where they were given food and tobacco by the chief trader, while the other traders supplied them with alcohol.

The following day was spent 'idling' until La Ronde rode in with the sunset. From the Métis, Milton and Cheadle learned that two of the cart axles had broken, and two replacements had been purchased with rum. Another of the carts had defective wheels, which also needed to be replaced. The carts themselves had been taken across the Assiniboine and were now just beyond the junction of that river and the Qu'Appelle – a smaller river joining from the south.

In the morning, the party rode to inspect the carts. Cheadle returned to the fort with money to pay for the new wheels. Milton also returned with a gaudy 'calumet' smoking pipe and a gun, which he hoped to exchange for one of the Indian lodges. On his first inspection of the Indian's tepees, he had been impressed with the protection provided by the portable shelters, and he was determined to try and barter for one. Eventually, he found one of the Indians prepared to trade his home by settling for the pipe and a cart cover – the latter in order to provide shelter for his family until he had built a new lodge.

The next day, 8 September, Cheadle suddenly remembered that it was his father's birthday. The realisation brought on a wave of homesickness and thoughts of his 'poor Father'. His mood was lifted slightly when Mr McKay refused any payment for his hospitality, but was dashed again when, riding from the fort, he got into an argument with Messiter who, with flaring temper, called Cheadle 'a fool'. The clergyman's son merely turned and pointed out that his companion was behaving in an ungentlemanly manner. After a while, Messiter apologised and the incident was forgotten.

While at the fort, La Ronde had lost his horse, Old Rouge. Milton and the Métis decided to return for a final search, the viscount taking with him a silver cup he had brought from home – it was now to be a gift given to McKay in gratitude for his generosity. A search for the horse failed until Milton announced that he would give a £2 reward for the animal's return. Within minutes it materialised from 'the back of the fort'.

3

Sioux, Cree, Buffaloes and the Saskatchewan

Setting off from their camp between the Assiniboine and the Qu'Appelle rivers on Tuesday 9 September, the party were just over 300 miles from Fort Garry and about the same distance from their immediate destination, Fort Carlton. They passed through gently rolling prairie, speckled with thickets of pines and aspens, and skirted by swamps. By now their mornings were greeted by ice on the water, cold rain, and hail. Any living creature that walked or flew was brought down by 'pot shots' to provide their food. A wide variety of ducks, prairie hens, badgers, and even a skunk found their way into their cooking pot – the latter accompanied by a smell that 'pervaded everything'. With the increasing cold, Messiter's dogs soon lost their enthusiasm for hunting and, when they failed with their guns, the party were forced to resort to their limited supply of galettes and 'richaud' (pemmican cooked in a little water, flour, and onions).

Milton's Indian lodge proved to be a popular addition to their equipment, and nights would be spent around a fire beneath its shelter as the Englishmen regaled their astonished Métis companions with tales about the speed of steam trains, and the short time it took to cross the immensity of the Atlantic Ocean. The vast size of London and its population vied with the modern marvel of Brunel's ship *Great Eastern* in astounding La Ronde and the other local men. The Métis also found it difficult to understand the outsiders' view of animals. The party had not long been on the trail when Cheadle's horse, Bucephalus, began to misbehave. On inspection, Cheadle discovered that the horse was suffering from girth galls and saddle sores. Rather than causing the animal to continue suffering, he simply took the reins and walked alongside. The Métis were 'much astonished' at this behaviour and loudly protested that it was, 'All right, monsieur. Indian horses always so – not hurt him'. Cheadle ignored the protests and walked the entire day, covering 20 miles. For the next few days, he travelled and hunted on foot, until a boil on his leg forced him to resort to the cart. When the ailment subsided, he rode Bucephalus in the morning, but walked in the afternoon.

Milton was rapidly gaining a reputation as someone extremely reluctant to leave his bed. On one occasion, early in the trek, he used an overnight bleeding nose as his excuse to remain beneath the sheets, causing a long delayed departure. Messiter, his fellow Etonian, fumed with impatience and threatened to take some of the carts and Voudrie, and press forward alone. Although sympathising, Cheadle was not alarmed, believing that Messiter's threat 'won't come off'. After a week of delayed starts, Cheadle and Messiter resorted to 'great yells' to get Milton's early morning attention.

On Thursday 18 September, on a cold, cloudy day sprinkled with hail, and with Messiter nursing the bruises he had received when thrown from his horse the previous day while in pursuit of a wolf ('at least three summersaults'), the party arrived at Touchwood Hills – a pleasant district consisting of low, rounded hills, fringed by 'bluffs' (thickets of pine and other prairie trees). The place had been home to a Hudson's Bay Company fort that served to supply travellers on the trail to, and from, Fort Carlton. Only a year or so earlier, the fort had been abandoned and the site was completely deserted. Camp was set up a couple of miles further west alongside a lake with a 'round wooded island in centre, very like a miniature Derwentwater'. While there, the conversation turned to the possibility of a distraction by journeying down the Mackenzie River. The river was a gateway to the Arctic with its water feeding into the south-eastern corner of the Beaufort Sea. Much used by fur traders and attempts to find the fabled Northwest Passage, the river was an exciting prospect. All depended, however, on their progress towards the great barrier of the Rocky Mountains. As they discussed the possibility of new destinations, but were joined by a new companion. A scrawny, clearly starving, 'Indian dog' suddenly appeared and made short work of scraps of pemmican thrown in his direction. It was agreed by all that the animal should be allowed to join them as a 'train dog' – useful for alerting the humans to hiding birds and animals that might be added to the evening's meal.

As they continued westwards from Touchwood Hills, both the surroundings and the relative harmony of the journey began to change. The great prairie continued, but the trees began to become more and more scarce. Of greater concern, however, was the fact that much of the available water proved to be brackish, with a high saline content. Some of the shallower lakes had dried out leaving a crust of salt, others turned out to consist of nothing more than light-coloured mud surrounded by rushes. On one occasion, their saviour turned out to be Milton's horse who, of his own accord, raced into one of the few remaining thickets and discovered a 'fine sheet of water'.

Cheadle had a bad day when he woke to find the boots and socks he had left by the fire to dry out had been badly burned. He lost part of a shot bag he had borrowed from Milton and, shooting at a succession of ducks and snipes, he missed them all. He then chased a badger, who escaped just before it began to pour down with rain. To complete his catalogue of misfortune, both he and Messiter broke out with 'the itch' – believed to have been caught from Zear, the Métis boy who had joined them as they approached Fort Ellice. Then Messiter fell out with Milton and the pair spent an entire day squabbling. Cheadle, refusing to get involved, went shooting and found his old skill had returned, adding ducks to the night's meal.

An entire week was spent crossing the prairie before they arrived on the bank of the southern branch of the Saskatchewan River, only to find the Hudson's Bay Company barge – used by travellers to cross the river – was 80 yards away on the far bank. The Métis were immediately set to work collecting timber for a raft. When the work was completed, the raft was used to collect the barge, which was then used to ferry the baggage and men across, leaving the horses and the carts to be brought over the following day.

The next morning, the carts were taken apart and reassembled on the other side as the horses were made to swim across. During all this activity, Messiter managed to offend Cheadle who (no doubt still suffering from 'the itch') replied with uncharacteristic venom. Messiter immediately lost his temper and began to roundly and offensively abuse the doctor. Cheadle left the carts and walked a dozen miles ahead to avoid any further conflict. When the carts caught up with him, he found that Messiter and Milton were engaged in a violent quarrel that was on the verge of coming to blows. The prospect of spending the coming winter in Messiter's company was beginning to look increasingly unattractive.

If, however, nothing more than a change of company was needed, the wait was over. After a chase in pursuit of Milton's horse, he and Cheadle rode westwards, past Duck Lake, for about 6 miles. Suddenly, in a wide, shallow valley below them, they could plainly see Fort Carlton with the North Saskatchewan River curving beyond. They were 550 miles from Fort Garry, and a third of the way along their planned route.

On entering the fort, Milton, Cheadle, and Messiter were invited to join the fort's factor, Alexander Lillie, for a substantial tea. As the Métis erected the lodge between the fort and the river, they dined off buffalo steaks in a wooden building that was heavy with the aroma always associated with trading posts – pine resin, tobacco, buffalo hides, drying meat, and people. The fort had originally been built in 1810, and had been rebuilt twice since in response to the increased trading activity. Solidly constructed with a high wooden palisade and with square towers at each corner, the fort was intended to provide security for the fur trade and defence for the people involved. Buffalo meat was brought in by the Indians (mainly of the Blackfeet tribe) to be made into pemmican. The high-calorie preparation was supplied to the many fur trappers who frequented the fort when not away trapping. The furs were brought up the Northern Saskatchewan to be taken on to Fort Garry or Cumberland House by 'brigades' of carts along the Carlton Trail or by canoes and more substantial 'York boats' along the Saskatchewan. From both posts, the furs were taken to ports on Hudson's Bay or, from Fort Garry, down the Red River to join the Mississippi where the cargoes could reach as far south as the Mexican Gulf.

All the commercial enterprise required a sound administrative base. This was provided for by the fort's clerk, a Scotsman named Alexander. Having tried and failed to achieve success in a variety of other fields, he had ended up as a Hudson's Bay Company clerk at a salary of £24 a year, with his food and lodgings. He wore a threadbare purple dressing jacket edged with gold cord and a battered cap to match. This mode of dress apparently attracted much admiring attention from the Indian women. Alexander's tendency towards eccentricity, however, almost proved to be his undoing when a Sioux Indian Chief named White Cloud arrived at the fort to negotiate a peace treaty with the Cree. The Sioux Chief was a noted warrior who was well-built and more than 6 foot tall. One day, while being entertained by the clerk in his cabin, White Cloud noticed a couple of pairs of boxing gloves and asked what they were for. Alexander replied that they were used by white men when learning to fight. The puzzled chief, like most Indians, knowing nothing about fighting with fists, asked for an explanation. Taking away the chief's pistol and knife and locking them away, the clerk put a pair of gloves on the chief, and a pair on himself. Then, telling the White Cloud to 'stand on his guard', Alexander knocked him to the floor. Whether or not the clerk was aware that such an action constituted one of the most grievous insults to an Indian, is not clear, but the shocked chief rose to his feet, only to be knocked down a second time. Exploding with rage, White Cloud pulled off his gloves and demanded the return of his weapons. Alexander refused and much to his surprise, the chief rapidly calmed down and asked to be allowed to leave the cabin. When asked what he would do if allowed outside, the chief replied that he would gather up his warriors – camped just outside the fort – and return and kill everyone in it. At this, the clerk took up a pistol and aimed it at White Cloud's head while telling him that, unless he withdrew his threat within five minutes, he would be shot dead. The minutes passed with neither man making a move. Just as the five minutes were about to expire, Alexander placed a bottle of whisky on the cabin table. White Cloud remained totally impassive, and the clerk's finger tightened around the trigger. With the tension in the cabin at breaking point, Alexander placed a second bottle of whisky on the table. Suddenly, White Cloud relaxed, smiled, shook Alexander's hand, and left the cabin gleefully clutching his two bottles of whisky.

Shortly afterwards, the Sioux chief demonstrated his reliability once he had given his word. A group of his tribesmen were behaving badly inside the fort and the factor, Lillie, asked White Cloud's help in removing them. The chief simply strode into the fort and blew on his war whistle. Instantly, his warriors tumbled out of the store and other places they had been congregating and mustered around their chief. He then ordered them to leave the fort immediately. Invited by Lillie to visit the fort's kitchen for a reward, White Cloud was shocked and embarrassed to find one of his braves inside finishing off a meal that had been provided by the cook. Without a second's hesitation, the chief picked up a log from the fireplace and sent the man senseless to the floor while expressing the hope that the malingerer was dead. Such an incident was not unusual when Indian honour was at stake. At the peace treaty negotiations, a Cree Indian looked into the lodge where the talks were being held and recognised an old enemy among the Sioux. The man was sat with his back against the skin of the lodge. Seeing this, the Cree crept around the outside of the tepee to the position where his enemy was sat and, thrusting through the tent skin, stabbed the Sioux in the back. There was an immediate uproar, especially among the Sioux who were heavily outnumbered by the Cree. The chief of the Cree, however, placed himself at the entrance to the lodge and demanded that the assailant be brought to him. When the man was hauled to the doorway, the chief took a tomahawk from his belt and killed him on the spot. The negotiations restarted within minutes – honour restored for all parties.

Following a 'famous sleep', during which time 4 inches of snow fell, Cheadle (now reconciled to an 'agreeable' Messiter) breakfasted on fried potatoes and tea with milk before making preparations to move on to winter quarters. La Ronde suggested that they should find a site in the territory belonging to the Wood Cree, a tribe currently at peace with all their neighbours and, unless provoked, unlikely to prove a threat. This meant a journey of about 80 miles north-north-west of Fort Carlton towards White Fish Lake. This would find them on the edge of the vast pine forest that continued far to the north. Not only would they find fuel and building material, but they would also be close to the great herds of buffalo that roamed the area. That evening, the doctor went to the fort to obtain a supply of sulphur, which he made into an ointment to be applied to 'the itch' that was continuing to affect both him and Messiter. He also bought three pairs of Indian buffalo hide moccasins for 1s a pair. The thicker, yet still flexible, rawhide of the buffalo was used in moccasins manufactured for outside travel during the winter – and were better than the European leather boots, which could freeze and cause severe frostbite.

Most of the next day was spent in preparation for their onward journey. As it was intended to hunt buffalo before leaving, the guns were prepared and Milton spent the evening making cartridges. However, word had arrived that two grizzly bears had been seen in the area and it was decided to spend the following day in search of the animals. In the morning, Milton remained in bed to such an extent that La Ronde, and the Métis who had come in with the news of the bears, grew tired of waiting and set off on their own. Even when Milton joined Cheadle and Messiter, they had not gone far when the viscount decided that he was not really interested and turned back. Even the dog Rover lost interest and disappeared, leaving the two remaining hunters fuming at the waste of time spent waiting for Milton. With luck, however, they came across La Ronde and his companion, who soon found the tracks he had seen the previous day but, despite searching over a wide area, the bears were never seen. Disappointed, Cheadle and Messiter returned to the fort. As they grew near, they passed through a group of Indians who looked on with idle curiosity. Just at that moment, a crow flew overhead and Messiter, suddenly realising that he still had a bullet loaded into his muzzle-loading rifle, brought the gun up to his shoulder and fired at the bird – which promptly fell to the ground. The Indians, his companions, and Messiter himself, were all 'astonished' at the demonstration of marksmanship. Such was the effect upon Messiter's reputation among the Indians, that at an Indian camp, many months later, he was regarded with awe by his hosts.

At the fort they were given a meal of bread and cheese by the factor. Cheadle was also given a pair of warm gloves and responded with a slice of tobacco. Milton, they discovered, had already set out on the buffalo hunt and they hastened away to find him and La Ronde. Cheadle's horse was again suffering from saddle sores and he was forced to borrow a temporary replacement. Unfortunately, the animal was very small, making the bulkily built Cheadle look ludicrous with his feet barely off the ground – a sight, according to Milton, which 'excited great merriment'. After a ride of over 20 miles, they found their companions, only to discover that they had been joined by a mixed-race man with a bad reputation. The previous winter he had joined a Cree war party that was responsible for the theft of 130 horses from the Blackfeet, and for the deaths of thirty-five men. The horses had been sold to the Hudson's Bay Company at Fort Carlton. The stranger was not the only one who need to be treated with caution. Messiter greeted the cold and miserable arrivals with news of his shooting two buffalo bulls. Milton exploded with rage to which Messiter responded with full force. Cheadle, however, just pleased to find a warm fire, managed to calm things down, and considered the row to be 'about nothing as usual'.

To the intense delight of everyone, the next day the party came across a small herd of buffalo. Although Milton had hunted buffalo during his first visit to Fort Garry, he had nothing like the experience of La Ronde – consequently, it was agreed by all that the Métis should take charge of the hunt. The buffalo had been hunted for thousands of years and, although the methods had changed, it still remained a dangerous activity. The animals were quite capable of charging at the hunters, both horse and rider were at risk by riding at high speed over ground riddled with holes created by burrowing animals, and the firing of guns from a galloping horse could easily bring down a fellow hunter. La Ronde had the group tighten their harness straps as a loose saddle could be a hazard in the lunging swerves of the pursuit. All guns were to be fully loaded – Milton with a double-barrelled 16-bore shotgun, Messiter with a similar 10-bore, and Cheadle with a single-shot breech-loading rifle. La Ronde used an ancient muzzle-loading flintlock 'trade gun' of the type supplied to the Indians by the Hudson's Bay Company, and worth – according to Messiter – 'seven and sixpence'. The Métis had become so skilled at the hunt that he could, with a musket ball held in his mouth, ride at the gallop, pour gunpowder from his flask down the barrel, placing his mouth over the end of the barrel and spitting the ball out, sending it all the way down by slapping the vertically held gun. As – without wadding – the ball would simply roll out if the barrel was lowered beyond the horizontal, the gun was held with the barrel slightly raised as he put the hammer into the half-cock position, poured powder into the flash pan before closing the frizzen and fully cocking the hammer. He would then select an animal, come up alongside it and lower the flintlock to the level where the ball would begin to roll down the barrel. Then, with the end of the barrel just inches from the buffalo's back, he would squeeze the trigger – usually killing the animal outright. As experience was to show, stopping to reload could not only lead to the loss of the quarry, it could also prove to be dangerous.

With the equipment and weapons in good order, La Ronde then arranged his team, putting Messiter on the left flank, himself next, followed by Milton, and with Cheadle – looking as if he was riding a large dog – on the right. The line advanced slowly with La Ronde making a lowing sound in imitation of the buffalo until, with a nod of his head the pace was increased to a canter. At this, the herd started to take notice and began a lumbering trot to join up with each other. When just 200 yards from the main herd, La Ronde cried out '*Allez! Allez!*' In an instant, all four horses charged in a furious gallop. Milton, raised to hunt foxes, quickly took the lead, with Cheadle bringing up the rear. All were yelling, shouting, and screaming with the exhilaration of the charge as the buffaloes raced away. After charging for half a mile, they were within 20 yards of the herd. Another half-mile brought them to within just a few yards. Cheadle fired two shots, which missed, but caused two of the animals to break off. Bearing down on one of them, he fired three shots from his revolver – all of which missed. Then the buffalo, a large bull, 'looking very vicious', lowered its head and turned to charge. Just at that moment, Cheadle fired a single shot. The bull stopped, walked forward for two or three paces, then dropped to the ground. His excitement now tinged with nervousness in case the animal regained its feet, Cheadle approached the prostrate buffalo. There was no doubt. A perfect shot had hit the animal just behind the shoulder and dispatched it almost instantly. Glowing with pride at his success, Cheadle removed the bull's tongue and cut off its tail before returning to the carts where he found Milton and La Ronde. La Ronde had accounted for one animal, and Messiter had claimed two. That is, until Milton loudly declared that one of the buffaloes claimed by Messiter had, in fact, been brought down by him. The usual 'hot dispute' broke out until Milton accurately described the location of the gunshot wounds on the bull, and La Ronde picked up one of Milton's cartridges close to the dead animal. At this, a sulking Messiter rode off in pursuit of further buffalo as Cheadle, taking the boy, Zear, returned to the scene of his triumph. Wolves had already begun to tear the dead bull apart, but fled as Cheadle and Zear approached. Between them they removed the long bones in preparation for the removal of the highly calorific, nutritious marrow within. As they carried out their work, Messiter was seen riding past at some distance, but no attempt at contact was made.

Finding that they could only remove half of the long bones, as the animal was too heavy to turn over, they began to prepare to return to the carts when Zear looked up and shouted '*Voila! Voila les boeufs!*' Just cresting a low hill, about 300 yards away, nine bulls were charging straight at them. Cheadle dropped his knife, grabbed his gun, and ran forward and fired at the leader. He was close enough to hear the thud of the bullet as it struck and the animal staggered and slowed down as the remainder thundered past him. A second round finished the bull off. Once again, the animal was too heavy to turn over, so only half the long bones were obtained. Zear took the opportunity to instruct Cheadle on the best method of removing a buffalo's tongue. When he had removed the tongue from the first animal he had killed, Cheadle tried the obvious method of removing it directly from the open mouth. This had resulted in the delicacy being three quarters of its full length, and badly hacked about. Zear taught him to roll the head over so that the nose was in the air with the horns resting, or penetrating, the ground. Then, by cutting the skin beneath the jaw, the tongue could be easily removed.

Their next problem was not knowing where Milton had decided to set up camp for the approaching night. Cheadle ranged far and wide in high winds and driving rain, while Zear drove the cart along the track. Eventually, a couple of shots were heard and, on investigation, the lodge was seen in a clump of trees. Warming himself in front of the lodge fire, Cheadle was congratulated on his success in his first buffalo hunt. All that remained was to look out for Messiter. With the darkness now upon them, there was little they could do. La Ronde set off to see if he could find their missing companion, but was soon back, driven in by the cold. They fired guns and hoisted a burning torch to no avail. At midnight they built up the fire and crawled between their blankets, grateful for the comfort, and aware that the best Messiter could hope for was a cold and miserable night, perhaps beneath the shelter of some trees.

At first light, the Métis left the lodge and spread out in search of Messiter, but returned within an hour without success. However, an hour later, five horsemen were seen approaching the camp. To their delight, the party turned out to be Messiter and four Cree Indians. After shaking hands all round, all five were taken into the lodge and given breakfast followed by a calumet being passed around for a shared smoke. During the meal, Messiter told his companions the story of his night on the plain. With the last traces of light, he had made his way in the rain to a small wood where he attempted to light a fire, only to find that his matches and tinder were all wet through and incapable of lighting the driest wood that he could find. Surrendering any hopes of warmth and shelter, he remounted his horse and rode for several hours until sheer chance led him to an Indian camp. The Cree welcomed him onto their site and the chief invited him into his lodge where his clothes were dried and he was given buffalo meat, a drink of 'Indian tea' (a mixture of leaves, flowers, tree bark, herbs, and roots), and a beverage made from animal fat thinned down with warm water. He was then invited to sleep in the lodge. Although this was probably a most welcome proposition, he found it almost impossible as the camp kept up an almost daytime activity. Women, wearing deerskin dresses and with chins tattooed as an aid to beauty, continued to cook, men met to smoke, and dogs barked and fought with each other incessantly. Like their Blackfeet and Assiniboine neighbours, the Cree were a nomadic tribe who lived by hunting the buffalo. Social status was gained by involvement in warfare. Great prestige was achieved by a tally of 'coups' which were obtained by riding up to an enemy, touching him, or stealing something, and escaping unharmed. Each successful coup earned the warrior the right to wear an eagle feather in his headdress. A large collection of scalps also brought honour, as did skill in horsemanship. The braves used a bow of about 3 feet in length, kept, with the arrows, in an otter-skin case. A small, round shield was painted with emblems to provide supernatural powers for the protection of the warrior as he fought using a fearsome stone-headed club. It was not the clubs, however, that had placed the Cree among the most dominant tribes on the northern plains, it was the guns obtained from the fur trappers. When Messiter made it clear that he wanted to return to his hunting party, the chief decided to ride with him, taking three other men.

The Indians had sat and smoked in silence as Messiter told his tale. When he finished, the chief decided he wished to address the assembled company and La Ronde provided a translation. According to the version recorded by Milton, the chief said to them,

I and my brothers have been much troubled by the reports we have heard from the Company's men, who tell us that numbers of white men will shortly visit this country; and that we must be beware of them. Tell me why you come here. In your own land you are, I know, great Chiefs. You have abundance of blankets, tea and salt, tobacco and rum. You have splendid guns, and powder and shot as much as you can desire. But there is one thing that you lack – you have no buffalo, and you come here to seek them. I am a great Chief also. But the Great Spirit has not dealt with us alike. You he has endowed with various riches, while to me he has given the buffalo alone. Why should you visit this country to destroy the only good thing I possess, simply for your own pleasure? Since, however, I feel sure that you are great, generous, and good, I give you my permission to go where you will, and hunt as much as you desire, and when you enter my lodge you shall be welcome.

There then followed an awkward silence. Eventually, Cheadle spoke up and told the chief that they had come to his land 'to hunt, see the country, and visit him'. Gratitude was expressed for his kind permission to travel and hunt over his land, and the chief was presented with ammunition, tobacco, salt, tea, and knives. His response was to ask for a gun, blankets, and especially, for rum. However, rather than prolong the proceedings, in their determination not to give more gifts (it was already one o'clock in the afternoon), the visitors were smilingly ushered to the lodge entrance, hands were shaken, and they left, apparently very pleased with themselves.

La Ronde, however, expressed serious concern about one aspect of the Cree visit. He felt that the visitors had shown a too great an interest in the party's 'méstatém' ('big dogs' – meaning their horses), and his experience suggested that they would make an attempt to steal them. Furthermore, one of the Indians had repeatedly told La Ronde that he had once been drunk – something he clearly believed was a matter of great prestige. Inevitably, the rum the group was carrying was yet another attraction for the Indians, and another reason to attend to their security. Accordingly, the party moved to the bank of a nearby river. The choice of such a site would reduce the directions from which an attack could be expected. In addition, the horses were brought into the camp, and La Ronde and Voudrie took turns to keep watch all night.

Before they retired, Milton and Cheadle discussed the continued presence of Messiter as a member of the party. Not only was he at constant loggerheads with Milton, and not slow in picking a quarrel with Cheadle, but his petulant behaviour in riding off alone after buffalo had placed the entire party at risk. The prospect of spending the winter months with him as part of their company had lost any attraction it may have had. Consequently, they decided that they should part. On being told of this decision, Messiter was 'much cut up', and asked them to reconsider, but there was no going back on their resolution. After a restless night, sleeping fitfully with loaded guns alongside them, they rose to find the district covered in a thick mist. Taking the advantage this gave them, they rapidly struck camp and set out along the river bank. They hoped that not only would they be hidden by the mist but that the Indians would assume they had crossed the river. Such a prospect seemed unlikely with the Indians being expert trackers but, by the time they had covered 20 miles and set up camp once again, the Métis assured them that a stiff wind that had blown away the mist would also have combed through the prairie grass and obliterated all sign of their passing. Nevertheless, having heard strong rumours at Fort Carlton that a war band of Blackfeet was in that particular area in search of Cree, Bruneau and Zear were kept on watch throughout the night.

The following day, taking two carts to carry meat, the party went off in search of buffalo. Seven bulls were encountered and command of the approach was again handed over to La Ronde. The attack formation was as before but this time with Cheadle remounted on Bucephalus. When they reached within 100 yards of the animals La Ronde shouted 'Hurrah! Hurrah!', instantly bringing them to a gallop. Messiter and Cheadle bore down on three of the animals, who tried to break away. After a short distance, one bull went his own way, with Cheadle in hot pursuit. Two shots from his double-barrelled shotgun failed and, having pulled up his horse to reload, he reached into his pouch only to find that, to his fury, the flap had worked loose, and the entire contents had fallen out. Grabbing a spare bullet he had mistakenly put into his pocket, he reloaded one of his gun's barrels. He then looked up, and saw that the bull had turned and was now charging directly at him. Instinctively, jerking at the reins, he hauled the horse to one side as the bull raced past, narrowly missing the hindquarters of Bucephalus. Cheadle raised the gun and fired his last shot. The buffalo, however, continued to charge in the opposite direction, foregoing any further opportunity to attack the horse and rider. Cheadle immediately went back to the camp for more ammunition before returning to the scene. There he found the rest butchering the animals they had brought down. Milton had killed three, Messiter two, and La Ronde, one. Only one animal had escaped – Cheadle's ('Confound it!'). No more herds were to be seen, and the party returned to camp.

Not satisfied that the Indian threat had gone away, once again a guard was mounted through the night. This time the chief part of the task was undertaken by Milton and Cheadle. Much of their time was taken up by rounding up stray horses. Luckily, they were assisted by a bright moon.

The next day being a Sunday, it was decided that there would be no hunt as La Ronde's religious sensitivities would be offended by working on the Lord's Day. 'Work', however, did not exclude the need to keep an eye out for Indians and it was La Ronde who shouted out *'Les Sauvages!'* when he spotted two Indians approaching. They turned out to be two young Cree, aged about 16 or 17, from a camp of 25 lodges that had just been established close by. Earlier that morning, Messiter had decided that he intended to carry out some target practice. He was joined by the Métis who joined in with a will. It was the sound of the protracted gunfire that had not only alerted the Cree but, they were informed by the boys, also frightened off a large herd of buffalo cows that were heading in their direction. If there was even the slightest chance of Messiter staying with the party, it had now evaporated.

The youngest-looking of the two boys told his hosts that he had already been on the warpath ten times, and had stolen six horses from the Blackfeet. All the men gathered in the lodge and stayed up late in the hope that the boys would leave or, at least, fall asleep. Instead, they came into the lodge and joined the rest of the company. La Ronde was very nervous about the situation. He considered the young Indians to be spies and, with the Indian camp nearby, believed the party to be in a dangerous situation. Consequently, a guard was set up once again, and it was decided to leave first thing in the morning.

After giving the boys breakfast, and sending them on their way, the camp was struck. At about four o'clock in the afternoon, they were back at the site they had used on the night of the first buffalo hunt. They were not alone. Also camped in the clump of tree was a Cree family. The Indian woman came out to greet the party and offered to erect the lodge – which she did 'beautifully'. Furthermore, she cooked them a meal of buffalo meat, berries, and watered fat. Messiter and Milton claimed the meal to be 'good', but Cheadle found it 'detestable' and 'nauseous'. As a reward, the father of the family was presented with gunpowder – which he accepted – and tobacco – which he refused, as he had promised his 'Manitou' (a personal spirit) that he would give up smoking. His wife was less fastidious and accepted the tobacco along with a supply of needles and thread. The site was about to become even more crowded. A Hudson's Bay Company wagon train loaded with buffalo meat arrived in the dark and camped overnight. The officer in charge, Cuthbert Sinclair, and the drivers needed no lodge or other type of tent and slept beneath the wagons. By the time the hunting party had risen in the morning, the train had long gone.

At noon the following day, the party caught up with the company train and, sending their own carts on, joined Sinclair for a dinner of buffalo and tea sweetened with sugar. Their host told them that he had met the Indians with whom Messiter had spent the night when he had got lost on the prairie. The two chiefs who had returned with him had been 'vastly smitten' by the party's horses and had determined to steal them. They raised a band of their braves who stalked the party, but lost them in the mist when they turned along the river bank.

4

Goodbye to Messiter, Hello to Fort Milton

Milton, Cheadle, Messiter and Sinclair rode on ahead and reached Fort Carlton at midday on Wednesday 8 October. After lunch with the factor, the carts arrived and the lodge was erected in the same place as before. It was now time to prepare for the approaching winter.

Messiter immediately set about making his own arrangement for wintering outside the fort as the Hudson's Bay Company forts were not allowed to be used for extended stays during the cold weather. He decided to set up camp at Thickwood Hills, some 90 miles to the north-west of the fort. To assist him in this endeavour, Messiter chose a 'villainous looking' Cree half-breed, mainly because the man's father-in-law, Star of the Blanket, was a noted hunter living near Thickwood Hills. However, when the man began to demand his entire pay in advance, Messiter dismissed him and chose a twenty-year-old English half-breed named Badger. His new assistant did not come unencumbered – he also brought along his wife and child. Before the parties went their separate ways, it was decided to have a ball. Milton described the dancers:

> The men appeared in gaudy array, with beaded firebag, gay sash, blue or scarlet, leggings, girt below the knee with beaded garters, and moccasins elaborately embroidered; the women in short, bright-coloured skirts, showing the richly embroidered leggings, and white moccasins of cariboo-skin, beautifully worked with flowery patterns in beads, silk, and moose hair.

The music was provided by Cuthbert Sinclair, who soon had everyone pounding around the dance floor to the tune of his fiddle.

On the following morning, Milton was feeling 'very seedy' so Cheadle was left to organise the final details of their departure. Voudrie and Zear were to take all but three of the carts back to Fort Garry, with the excess horses and letters. Special winter clothing had to be purchased from the fort's store – a very special privilege as cash transactions were usually forbidden. Under normal circumstances, the goods were only exchanged for skins, the basic unit of currency being the beaver skin equal to 2s. The recommended clothing consisted, in addition to lighter summer clothing, of caribou-skin trousers, and three pairs of blanket socks, over which were worn moose-skin moccasins. Next came a pair of cloth leggings, to keep the snow at bay. The neck was wrapped in a woollen shawl ans over all was a double breasted leather great coat, edged with fur and lined with flannel. This was secured around the waist by a thick worsted belt, the neck being closed by a loop of similar material. A pair of caribou-skin 'mittaines' hung from a cord around the neck, and a fur hat completed the ensemble. By the end of the day, all the equipment and supplies had been taken by barge across the North Saskatchewan. That night, everyone slept in the open air as ice formed on the ponds around them. In the morning came the parting of the ways. Messiter, Badger and his family, and an old Indian guide who had frequently crossed the Rocky Mountains, headed off towards the Thickwood Hills as Milton, Cheadle, La Ronde and Bruneau, accompanied by Rover, set a north-by north-westerly course in the direction of White Fish Lake (one of several bodies of water so named).

After four days of travelling over boggy ground with the last of the autumn's warm days shared with increasingly cold nights, Milton's party arrived at the Shell River as it curved south-westerly to join the North Saskatchewan. The steep banks proved to be a difficult obstacle and everyone had to wade shoulder deep into the river to help get the carts and horses into and out of the water. Their fortunes changed dramatically on the following day when they encountered a small stretch of prairie, surrounded by low hills and woods. It had been given the name *La Belle Prairie* by French half-breed *voyageurs* as they had passed through on their northerly fur trapping expeditions. The site, almost idyllic when compared to the previous swamp-like terrain, grew even more delightful when they came across a small lake surrounded by pines, poplars, and aspens. Both Milton and Cheadle agreed that a particular promontory would make a 'very beautiful site for a house'.

Continuing to the north for a short distance, they came across the tight windings of Crochet River (again, a name used elsewhere). This time, Cheadle chose to strip naked rather than get his clothes wet as he had done on when crossing the Shell. Yet again, the water was bitterly cold, but he found his swim 'delightful' – even noting in his diary that he indulged in '2 plunges overhead'. Another few miles found them at the site of two log cabins, one empty, and the other occupied by a large family of Indians led by an old man named Kekekooarsis, or Child of the Hawk, from his prominent hooked nose. La Ronde introduced Milton as Soniow Okey Mow (Great Chief), and Cheadle as Muskeeky Okey Mow (Great Medicine Man). The old man proved to be an affable, even entertaining, host and in 'a weak moment', his visitors offered him a small amount of rum. The Indian nearly exploded with excitement and demanded that the 'isquitayoo arpway' be brought immediately. Realising their mistake, Milton and Cheadle returned to their cart and filled a small keg with watered down rum. This had to be very carefully calculated as the first thing the Indians did on receiving such a gift was to sprinkle a small amount on to the fire to see if it ignited ('isquitayoo arpway' translates as 'fire-water'). A failure of the offering to burst into flame could lead quickly to an unpleasant – and dangerous – atmosphere.

They had just completed the transfer of the weakened alcohol, when the old man turned up with his wife, and his son-in-law, Keenamontiayoo (Long Neck, but referred to by Milton and Cheadle as The Hunter or The Chasseur). All carried skins of beaver and marten – a carnivorous animal related to badgers and weasels – and loudly demanded rum in exchange. When told that the white men were not traders, the Indians alternated between loud and menacing behaviour as if already drunk, and long periods of silence smoking a pipe while staring at the visitors. At last, at midnight, a little more rum was produced, the exchange of goods was made, and the family left the lodge, loudly singing and laughing.

At first light, the family returned with more furs and more demands. Even worse, more Indians arrived from all points of the compass. Soon, the lodge was overcrowded by Indians and half-breeds employed by the Hudson's Bay Company to fish in the nearby White Fish Lake. For hour upon hour, the two Englishmen, supported by La Ronde and Bruneau, sat quietly while suffering a perpetual 'infernal clamour' of demands for rum. At one stage, the old Indian's son arrived in an already drunken state. He took off his coat and shirt and thrust them at Cheadle who simply shook his head. This so outraged the Indian that he collapsed and vomited over his wife. It took the entire day and the approach of night before the unwanted guests realised that they were not going to get their hands on more 'fire-water'. At last, as night closed in, they left in small groups muttering loudly about the appalling lack of hospitality of their unwilling hosts.

When left in peace at last, Milton and Cheadle decided that a plan that had been forming in their mind to occupy the empty log cabin for the winter was no longer realistic. Instead, they decided to return the few miles to the lake on La Belle Prairie and build their winter accommodation there. In the meantime, La Ronde and Bruneau were sent back across the Crochet River to bury the rum barrels in case the Indians returned during the night.

The sun had hardly appeared in the sky the following day before The Hunter appeared with a dressed moose-skin. This time, however, he was not in search of drink. His four-year-old son was ill and he asked Cheadle to look at the boy and to see if he could help. On arrival at the log cabin, Cheadle had no difficulty in recognising the problem. The boy's enlarged head, his constant sleepiness, and history of seizures, could only mean that he was suffering from paediatric hydrocephalus. With no known cure, there was little that Cheadle could do other than advise the parents to apply gentle pressure to the head with bandages. That might assist in closing up the widening skull sutures, forcing the increasing brain fluid to find alternative route to escape. He also suggested fish oil might help, and supplied the family with painkillers. Before he left the log cabin, Milton arrived and asked for hats to be made from the fur they had gained in the trade for rum. He also asked for a supply of stretched and dried skin parchment for the windows of the cabin they intended to build, and for animal sinew for the making of 'racquetes' (snowshoes). All these items were to be paid for in beads. Cheadle's errand of mercy had delayed their departure and was to cost them another night with the lodge, set up less than 2 miles from their lakeside destination. They eventually arrived at ten o'clock the following morning, Monday 20 October, with the temperature taking an unmistakable dip.

The unnamed lake (later to be known as Camp Lake) was approximately half a mile long, about 100 yards across at its widest point, and lay along a generally north-by-north-west to south-by-south-east axis. For the most part, its eastern shore ran in a straight line until a sharp bend resolved itself into a gently curved bay that reached the lake's southern tip. From there the shore bulged out into the waters to mirror the bay on the eastern side before a pair of miniature headlands returned the water's edge to the northern tip. One of these 'promontories' (probably the most northerly one, as it was the furthest from the Indians and Métis just a few miles away) was chosen, and work began before the winter descended in earnest.

Trees were cleared away from the southern side of the headland leaving an open site sheltered by tall pines to the north and hidden from the prairie by other trees fringing the lake. Their efforts to conceal their whereabouts, however, were soon shown to be in vain by the arrival of Child of the Hawk and The Hunter, bringing the goods requested by Milton. The old Indian gratefully accepted the payment of beads for the fur hats and the sinew, but The Hunter demanded payment in rum. This was refused and the two men left with an exaggerated air of dejection. They had not long left when the sound of horse's hooves reached the ears of Milton and the others. It was another Indian who had come to claim a mouthful of rum that La Ronde had promised in order to remove him from the lodge during the day-long clamour. As an incentive, he held in his hand several sheets of parchment – almost certainly obtained from The Hunter. Rather than risk a continuation of the confrontation, a trifling amount of rum was taken from a small keg and given to the Indian. Half-an-hour later rowdy singing could be heard close at hand and, before long, The Hunter and two other Indians were in the camp demanding more rum. This time, a firm stand was taken, and the intruders were ushered off shouting that the white men should not be in 'their country' if they did not want to trade.

Left in peace at last, the work on the log cabin continued and, by the end of the day, an area 15 feet by 13 feet had been lined by trunks of poplars. The following day, the walls were raised to 4 feet as Cheadle went off in search of large stones for the chimney. While searching, he came across a small skunk, which he killed. The arrival of fresh meat delighted the two Métis, but Cheadle was less impressed – 'stunk us out for a week'. Soon the cabin walls were 6 feet high at the front and 5 feet at the rear, thus providing a slope for the roof. As two windows and a door were cut out, Cheadle began to dig out the cabin to a depth of 2 feet to increase the inside height. He then carried sand from the lake shore to provide a substantial floor. By the fourth day, earth had been piled against the lower part of the cabin sides and a pine roof had been fitted. The windows were lined with parchment and a door and basic furniture had been constructed from a damaged cart.

The building work was not a moment too soon – that night 2 inches of snow fell and, in the morning, the lake was frozen over. Later that day, La Ronde discovered a source of poor quality clay several feet beneath the surface of the prairie. A small amount was brought in to act as cement for the chimney. The next day was deemed to be a day of rest as La Ronde and Bruneau would not work on a Sunday, and both retired to the woods to commune with their Maker. On the Monday, however, there was considerable excitement as the cabin's chimney was constructed. In anticipation of the event, Cheadle went off to hunt for partridges and pheasants. On his return, however, with several game birds suspended from his saddle, he learned that the chimney had been built but, once a fire had been lighted, the entire stonework had collapsed. The two Métis – the main builders of the chimney – had fallen into a deep despondency and were incapable of rousing themselves to make another attempt. Milton, displaying an unusual burst of energy (probably prompted by the increasing cold) sent Cheadle out for larger, regular shaped stones while he constructed a number of wickerwork panels that could be used to support the stonework until the clay cement had dried. Between the two of them, the work on the chimney was completed successfully over the next two days, while La Ronde and Bruneau covered the roof with long swamp grass and packed earth, and filled in the gaps between the logs with a mixture of clay and chopped reeds.

There were still the occasional visits from the Indians, but the aggressive demands for rum had died away. When Child of the Hawk arrived with his spouse, he was employed in making snow shoes and dog sledges while his wife patched up their visitor's moccasins and repaired their winter clothing. As a reward, they were delighted with a handful of glass beads. On one occasion, an Indian arrived from Fort Carlton with a copy of the *Nor'Wester* newspaper published at Fort Garry. From its pages they learned for the first time of the horrors of the Indian attacks in Minnesota. They also learned that, as a result of the uprising, they could not expect mail to arrive through the United States.

It was decided that their stock of pemmican should be increased before winter travel became impossible. Accordingly, Cheadle and Bruneau were to return to Fort Carlton while Milton and La Ronde were to complete the final fitting out of the cabin. In addition to picking up pemmican, Cheadle was to see if he could obtain some dogs to help Rover in hauling the sledge. The Fort Carlton party had not gone far when they met up with one of the local half-breeds who went by the name of John Smith. Initially, he had been one of the prime nuisances perpetually demanding rum, but once he had come to terms with the fact that he was not going to get any, he became a regular visitor to the cabin, bringing fish to exchange for pemmican. Smith had with him his 'rather pretty' wife who Cheadle – with true Victorian sensibilities – described as being 'enceinte' (pregnant). Before long, she was riding in comfort on the cart.

Being frozen, the Shell River was passed with relative ease and, by dusk on the following day, Fort Carlton could be seen on the far bank of the Saskatchewan. The group stood on the western bank and fired guns in the hope of attracting someone who could bring the ferry barge over. A man turned up and tried to reach them by canoe, but failed because of the ice which covered much of the river. Eventually he shouted across to them that they would have to wait for the morning when the barge would be sent over. Not far from where they stood, Cheadle could see a lodge and a couple of carts, so decided to walk over to see if the occupants could help.

As he approached, he recognised one of Messiter's dogs – Snuffer. Entering the lodge, Cheadle found it to be empty. With Messiter absent, probably at the fort, a fire was soon started, Messiter's stock of pemmican was reduced, and a comfortable night was had by all.

Their wait extended well into the following day as the barge had difficulty in crossing the ice of the river. Eventually, in the early afternoon, it was approaching the western bank when Cheadle heard a 'whoop' from Messiter – almost unrecognisable in his winter clothing. His winter accommodation at Thickwood Hills (complete with high pitched roof) was almost complete, and he was looking forward to settling in after his visit to the fort to collect supplies. During the time his cabin was being built, Messiter had suffered greatly from the unwanted attentions of the local hunter, Star of the Blanket, and his friends. Unable to hide his rum, Messiter's entire supply was taken by the Indians. On the night prior to leaving for the fort, as he was sleeping, the Indians came into his lodge in a drunken state. One, deciding that Messiter was in the warmest place, tried to climb into bed with him. Messiter kicked him out, but the Indian tried repeatedly to join him beneath the blankets. Eventually, Messiter rose from his bed, grabbed the man and ejected him from the lodge, fully expecting to have his throat cut before the sun rose. Star of the Blanket, however, probably saved him by keeping him awake all night with his singing. Any attempt by Messiter to sleep was met by a jab in the ribs resulting from the Indian's need for an audience.

While at Fort Carlton he had met a Scotsman who had been reduced to such a pitiable state that he was living with old, abandoned Indians existing on scraps they could beg from the fort. In his early forties, James Farquharson claimed to have been a Shakespearean actor, who had travelled to St John's Newfoundland. There, while his acting skills went unappreciated, a newly discovered talent for house-painting provided him with an adequate income. Eventually returning to Scotland (according to his version) he married and had two daughters. When news of the British Columbia gold discovery reached him, he sent his family to live in Iowa, while he spent £40 to join a party of Englishmen who had an agreement with 'The British American Overland Transit Company' to transport them by stagecoaches from St Paul to the gold fields. The arrangement, of course, was a complete fraud (the men that Messiter had observed at St Paul desperately scratching a living by taking on the most menial jobs available had been duped thus). Somehow, Farquharson managed to obtain an ox and cart and made his way to Fort Garry. From there he travelled westwards and reached Fort Carlton, where his ox died. Lacking the aristocratic status of Milton, his pleas for help were rejected by the Hudson's Bay Company and Messiter had found him huddled beneath a blanket as close as he could get to a lodge fire. Although combative and argumentative in nature, Messiter was equally gregarious – so possibly on the grounds that living with a mixed-race family who spoke poor English would not provide anyone with whom to argue, he invited Farquharson to join him over the winter – an invitation eagerly accepted.

With Messiter on his way to Thickwood Hills, Cheadle was invited by the chief factor, Lillie, to stay at his house overnight. While staying with his host, he learned that he, with Milton, had unwittingly been the cause of a rather unsettling incident which followed their departure for their winter site. While transferring some of their rum from one container to another, a small amount had spilled on to the floor. Shortly afterwards, two Assiniboine Indians came into the room and quickly recognised the smell of the alcohol. On their speedy return to their lodges, word not only spread like wildfire, but was also quickly transformed into a fanciful account which claimed that the Hudson's Bay Company had changed its policy, and now allowed alcohol onto its premises for the purpose of supplying it to the Indians. A few days later, Lillie's attention was called to the disconcerting sight of three hundred Assiniboines, dressed in fully feathered regalia and wearing paint, advancing on the fort. The chief at their head lit a pipe and passed it to Lillie before launching into a speech of praise at the Company's new and enlightened policy. The baffled factor had no option but to deny any knowledge of such a policy. At this, the chief demanded that he and his people be allowed to search the fort. Again, Lillie had no option, and the fort was examined in minute detail – even to the extent of descending to the ice cellar where the winter's supply of meat was kept. When it became quite clear that there was no alcohol in the fort, the chief demanded that the factor write to Queen Victoria informing Her Majesty of the 'great regret' that her 'Red Children' felt at the disappointing outcome of their joyful descent upon the fort.

Cheadle failed to obtain any dogs at the fort, but was more successful with the rest of his supplies. The cart was loaded with two 90lb bags of pemmican, 100lb of dried meat, 20lb of fresh meat, and 60lb of fat for cooking. Bidding farewell to the hospitable Lillie, Cheadle and Bruneau reached the bank of the Saskatchewan at mid-morning. The river was iced over for most of its length, but a broad open stretch down its centre required the use of the ferry barge. Cheadle's horse, Bucephalus, was pulling the cart when Bruneau led him on to the ice. Within just a few yards, the ice gave way, plunging the horse into the water. When he emerged, the water clinging to him froze and the two men had great difficulty in getting the animal upright on the surface of the ice. Bruneau began to unload the semi-submerged cart, Cheadle took his horse to the barge, pulled him on board, and took him to the shelf of ice on the other side. He then hauled the shivering animal on to the ice and led him to the safety of the bank. It had been exhausting work but, if his temper had been tested, it was about to be tried even further. The strongly built Bruneau had unloaded the cart, and then hauled the cart back on to the ice. Taking the cart another 20 yards over the ice, the Métis, unseen by Cheadle who was still busy with Bucephalus, decided to reload the vehicle. He had just placed the final bag in its place when the inevitable happened – the cart broke through the ice yet again. Cheadle, in no mood to be tolerant, exploded with rage and brusquely ordered Bruneau to carry the stores across the river on his own, and then retrieve the cart and bring that across as well, while he jogged his horse up and down in an attempt to warm him up.

The delay meant that they did not get away until three o'clock and had only achieved 10 miles when darkness forced them to camp in a small wood. However, the following day they started shortly after the sun had risen, and they spent that night on the south bank of the Shell River. In the morning, the river appeared to be covered in thick ice. Their experience on the Saskatchewan, however, dismissed any foolhardy thoughts of taking risks, and they unloaded the cart, carrying the supplies across. Bucephalus was then uncoupled from the cart and led safely across by Cheadle as Bruneau pulled the cart to the far bank without mishap. Cheadle intended to walk across La Belle Prairie, but had not really taken into consideration the fact that he was wearing leather boots – a poor selection of footwear for use in cold temperatures. About 5 miles from the cabin, his feet were not only very cold, but his Achilles tendons were extremely sore and he had to borrow a pair of moccasins from Bruneau to cover the final distance.

On their arrival they found that Milton and La Ronde had been busy at work constructing two bunks, each furnished with dry grass covered with a buffalo skin. Two crude tables had been built, one for the 'kitchen department', the other for the 'dining end'. The chimney had stayed upright, the windows had been draft-proofed and allowed light in through the parchment panes, while the door fitted snugly into its frame.

The next morning La Ronde and Bruneau were laying split logs as planks on the floor as Cheadle, still limping from his painful Achilles tendons (more correctly referred to by Cheadle as his 'tendon Achilles') arranged the boxes and bags of supplies. Milton supervised until Cheadle had finished his work – and then rearranged everything. A weary, aching, Cheadle noted that the log cabin had also acquired a distinguished name – 'Fort Milton'.

The day was further enlivened by a visit from Child of the Hawk accompanied by his daughter. The old man explained that, a couple of days earlier, he had given his daughter in marriage to another Indian in exchange for a horse. However, the 'husband' had returned a day later and stolen his horse back. The outraged father had retaliated by kidnapping his daughter, and had turned up at the cabin looking to exchange her once again. No one was eager to take part in such a transaction, however, and the offer was politely declined despite the young woman being considered by Cheadle as 'not bad looking'.

With the final touches to the cabin in progress (including the manufacture of candlesticks and a platform outside to keep their meat from wolves), La Ronde walked across the lake ice to search the woods for suitable sites to set traps. Cheadle, having purchased strychnine while in America to protect the horses from wolves and wolverines, laid out bait laced with the poison. He was so successful that, within a week, not only had the wolves disappeared, but he had earned himself the skin of a magnificent white wolf. Milton, in the meantime, taking Bruneau along, decided to check on some work being done on the manufacture of additional winter clothing by The Child of the Hawk 's wife. Cheadle, however, felt that the visit was more likely to be an excuse to 'flirt with la petite sauvagesse'. Sure enough, Bruneau returned alone after dark, explaining that 'milord' was very fatigued and had decided to stay overnight at the old Indian's cabin.

The next day the situation took an unexpected and unwelcome turn. Milton returned at midday in company with Child of the Hawk and two other Indians. When Cheadle, after spending a few hours laying traps, came back to the camp, he found the Indians drunk inside the lodge – Milton had given them a pint of rum in exchange for two marten skins. Not only was it an extremely poor rate of exchange, but it had also informed the Indians that a supply of the alcohol was available. After a night sleeping off their excesses, the Indians were persuaded to leave, their inevitable requests for more rum being ignored. Disregarded by a still fuming Cheadle, Milton spent the next few days moping sullenly and only rousing himself to smoke a pipe while everyone else worked hard in preparation for the coming winter. Already, overnight snowfalls of 6 inches were a regular occurrence, and it was plain to all that the temperature was continuing to fall (they had forgotten to bring a thermometer). Cheadle, tired of Milton's inactivity, handed his fur hat to the languid aristocrat and demanded that he attach fur ear pieces to the headwear. Milton, actually keen to restore his position among the party, chose not to dispute the demand and, shortly afterwards, Cheadle noted 'my ear-caps very comfortable.'

Another way to get Milton moving was for Cheadle to leave him on his own. That way Milton would be forced to make preparations for winter, while Cheadle could be usefully employed on finding buffalo to provide an over-winter supply of meat. Deciding to leave on 18 November ('Hurrah!'), Cheadle took with him La Ronde and a fourteen-year-old son of The Hunter named Nashquapamayoo, (The thing one catches a glimpse of) who, in the cause of brevity, was generally referred to by Cheadle as 'the young savage'. They set off with two horses to drag their sleighs and spent the day travelling towards the low hills. A campsite was found by a small lake whose waters had 'a strong smack of Harrogate' (i.e. smelt strongly of sulphur). Another two days brought them to the edge of the plains where La Ronde immediately spotted five buffalos. A quick meal of dry pemmican was taken before the party – having removed their warm outer clothing because of the onset of balmy weather – set off in pursuit. This consisted of dodging around hillocks and crawling through scrub until, after a final 200 yards on their hands and knees, La Ronde spotted their quarries just 20 yards away behind a screen of bushes.

In great excitement, the Métis issued his plan of attack in a garbled mixture of French and English. Not understanding a word, Cheadle could only grin vacantly and wait to see what La Ronde would actually do. Eventually, when he realised that Cheadle was not going to follow his instructions, La Ronde picked up his musket and peeked over the bushes. At this, assuming that La Ronde was about to open fire, Cheadle stood up and exposed his upper body above the bushes as he brought his rifle up to his shoulder. In a second, the buffalo were up and running, presenting only their rapidly diminishing 'sterns' to the hunters. A fusillade of shots failed to bring any result apart from La Ronde and Cheadle shouting at each other as each accused the other one of being to blame. The squabble did not last long, however, as the need for meat took priority over establishing blame: ('Come for meat & must have it'). The only answer was to remain in pursuit. Again bent double, they hid behind anything that would hide them from their quarry and, after two hours, came up close to the buffalos. By now breathing deeply, the heavily built Cheadle gave his gun to Nashquapamayoo as 'it was a question of victuals'. By the time he caught up again, two bulls lay dead, and one, wounded by La Ronde, was finally dispatched by Cheadle himself.

They now found themselves with a problem. The sun was just about to set, and they were 5 or 6 miles, not just from their camp, but also their warm clothing – and it threatened to be a very cold night. They collected as much of the sparse poplar saplings as they could find to build a fire, before placing a gun and powder flask alongside the furthest dead bull in the knowledge that the smell of humans would keep the wolves away. Stripping the hide from the nearest buffalo, the skin was cut in half with one piece given to

Cheadle as the Métis and the young Indian huddled together beneath the other. The smell from the covering was almost overpowering, but bearable from the warmth gained. All too soon, however, the hide froze solid and turned into a tunnel through which the wind blew with increasing, penetrating ferocity. Finally, the entire party dragged their bitterly chilled limbs from beneath the hides and the night was spent stamping and blowing into hands in an attempt to keep warm as the 'voyageur's clock' (the star constellation Orion) circle over their heads with excruciating slowness. Dawn eventually arrived to a chorus of howls from the surrounding wolves, and La Ronde and the young Indian were soon on their way to the camp to retrieve the horses, sleighs, and warm clothing. The following two days were spent drying the meat and packing the sleighs – but the hunt was not yet over.

The next morning, La Ronde caught sight of a small group of buffalos and they determined to go after them. This time, the Métis told Cheadle that he would take the young Indian with him and circle around the animals. The doctor was to keep his eye on the far side of the animals and, once La Ronde lifted his head above his cover, he was to start firing immediately. This would drive the animals towards La Ronde who would bring down as many as he could before they began to retreat and head toward Cheadle. It was a good plan, but one that did not take in Cheadle's tendency to daydream in situations with little external stimulus ('my fits of absence of mind'). Snatched back from his reverie by the sound of the frustrated La Ronde opening fire, Cheadle looked up to see the buffalos charging past his position. Firing his rifle, he hit one of the bulls, but it continued to chase after the others. In the end, no buffalos were killed and La Ronde was in such a furious mood that he refused to go after them. While stamping the ground in his rage, he even said that he would never take Cheadle on a buffalo hunt again. It took a full pipe of tobacco to calm the outraged Métis down but, eventually, his hunting instincts took over once again and they set off in pursuit of another small group of buffalos feeding on the top of a low rise about a mile away. The chase proved a gruelling trial as the animals moved off every time they approached. Over the next 5 miles of pursuit, Cheadle grew more and more exhausted. Only his 'old boating training' and a determination 'not to give in' kept him going. Finally, approaching from the blind side of a hill, they saw a buffalo emerge from the far side. La Ronde fired first followed by Cheadle who, in his excitement, broke his ramrod. The single dead bull proved to be their only success all day. That night was spent shivering under thick coats or, in Cheadle's case, under the oilskin cart cover where his breath condensed and dripped back on to him. Stiff and cold, but overjoyed with the arrival of daylight, they walked to a small hill to find their bearings – only to find that they were less than half a mile from their camp. During their absence they had been called upon by unwelcome visitors. Wolves had devoured half of the meat stored on one of their sleighs. Nevertheless, with meat from the buffalo shot the day before, Cheadle noted that he 'don't much care'. It was time to return to Fort Milton.

The journey took four days and included crossing an ice-covered lake. The horses refused and La Ronde was forced to drag the sleighs across the ice while Cheadle and the Indian boy hacked a path for the horses round the lake. On another occasion, as it walked across the snow-covered slope of a hill, one of the horses lost its footing and toppled over, ending up with its feet in the air. Cheadle was about to undo the harness when La Ronde took charge. With Cheadle's somewhat surprised assistance, the Métis pushed the horse causing it to roll down the hill until it found its own feet and stood up with the sleigh back on its runners: ('That's the way they do things in this country!')

The nights were spent with La Ronde regaling Cheadle with tales of his frequent fights with the Sioux. According to the Métis, on one occasion he was part of a cart train with sixty men, women and children, which was attacked by 2,000 Indians. The carts were formed into a circle, with a second circle made up of horses. The men made a third circle as the women and children sheltered in the centre. The attacks continued for two days with a priest roaring encouragement from within the circle of carts. When it was all over (again, according to La Ronde), ten Sioux had been killed along with thirty horses, with no casualties among the cart train.

They returned to the cabin twelve days after they had set out. La Ronde immediately announced that he had a dream demanding that he had to get drunk – and promptly went about putting his orders into effect. He had not long begun before The Hunter and several other Indians turned up to provide support. Bruneau, delighted to see his fellow Métis return, joined in the occasion. It was not long before the site echoed to the sound of singing, shouting, and demands for more rum. Cheadle's first thought was for some pancakes as a result of 'an intense longing for some vegetable food after a fortnight with nothing but meat'. His appetite, however, was soured when an earlier suspicion turned out to be true.

Milton had been spending most of his time in the company of Child of the Hawk's daughter. Cheadle, raised with the strict morality of a clergyman's son, nicknamed her 'Delilah' on the grounds that, while Milton did not have the physical strength of Sampson, he did have his moral weakness. After a raucous night in which drunken men prevented both Milton and Cheadle from getting any rest, the latter put his foot down and demanded an end to the abuse of their hospitality ('I say never any more of this!'). The Indians drifted off to their lodges, accompanied by La Ronde and Milton, while Cheadle continued with his preparations for winter. After walking 10 miles in snowshoes, he found himself 'more tired than if 20 without'. Milton returned that evening and Cheadle found himself being introduced to another woman. This time the viscount had no intentions other than the provision of clean clothing, and had hired the wife of an Indian to do the washing. Unfortunately, she was a great follower of the Indian belief that, no matter what the time of day, there was always something that needed doing. Consequently, when Milton and Cheadle took to their beds, she began building up the fire, boiling water, and treating each and every garment to a vigorous scrubbing. With midnight a fading memory, Milton rose from his bed and gently asked the woman to stop working. Utterly baffled by this strange request, the woman ignored him and continued with her work regardless. Eventually, Milton put the fire out and threw the water away. All to no avail. When she considered that he had gone to sleep, she relit the fire and started her labours once more. Defeated, Milton surrendered with little more than a few choice oaths.

Above: Camp on Eagle
River, Cheadle on watch
during the night in case of
an Indian raid.

Right: Messiter's cabin in
the Thickwood Hills.

Sioux Chiefs, with teepees behind them.

Above: The Indian Chief, who has just broken Messiter"s arm with a club, is shot.

Right: Mr O'B at risk of an icy bath; from John McDougle's 1896 book, *Saddle, Sled and Snowshoe*.

Fighting the forest fire whilst Mr O'B sits reading his book.

'Fort Milton', the winter cabin by the lake.

The view from the hill opposite Jasper House.

Crossing the Athabasca

The end of the trail, as it was then.

The end of the trail today, photographed by the author.

View on the Thompson

An 1871 photograph of Assiniboine Bluff on the North Thompson River. The bluff was named after Louis Patenaude – 'The Assiniboine'.

Mr O'B being towed across the river.

Milton, Cheadle and The Boy come across the headless Indian.

Terraces (or benches) on the Fraser River as it was in Milton and Cheadle's day; there is a similar view photographed by the author in the colour section.

The southern slope of Pavilion Mountain.

The Alexandra Bridge, 1872.

The modern Alexandria Bridge, completed in 1964.

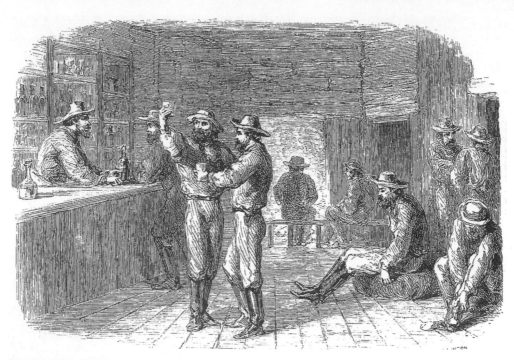

Wayside House. Miners arrive.

Wayside House at midnight.

Above: An Adah Isaacs Menken
postcard.

Right: A postcard showing Adah
Isaacs Menken preparing to
appear on stage.

MENKEN.

A photograph taken in San Francisco of Milton and Cheadle, with their lawyer friend George Walkem.

Top left: Governor Sir James Douglas, often described as 'the Father of British Columbia'.

Top right: Judge Sir Matthew Baillie Begbie, British Columbia's first Chief Justice.

Above: Viscount Milton as a member of Parliament.

Right: Walter Butler Cheadle, 1884.

Barraud, 263, Oxford S. London

A first edition of *The North-West Passage by Land*. This copy was a gift from his mother to William Thomas Fitzwilliam, Viscount Milton's brother.

5

A Wolverine Winter, Starvation and Incontinence

The onset of winter was no excuse for indolent hibernation. It was time to think of the horses. With no fodder or stabling, the only solution available to them was to let the horses loose. With luck, they might survive the winter. The log pile for the fire had to kept supplied and, although there were ample supplies of frozen meat high on its outdoor platform beyond the reach of wolves, opportunities to restock the larder were always to be seized. The skin of a skunk was nailed to the inside of the cabin door as a 'weather-glass'. If it began to smell, it was a sure indicator that the temperature was rising. Furthermore, winter was the season when the fur of the indigenous animals was at its finest. Good quality furs were always a useful medium of exchange for supplies at the Hudson's Bay Company stores and, as Cheadle noted, were always welcomed by their 'dear friends of the fair sex'. Beaver pelts were gradually falling from favour as, in both the USA and Europe, more and more top hats were being manufactured from silk. The muskrat, although noted for its warm fur, was not popular (probably as a result of its unfortunate rodent-linked name), and ermine – the winter fur of the stoat – was uneconomical, in size and effort. The greatest prize throughout North America was unquestionably the fur of the sea otter but, as such an animal was unlikely to be encountered on the Saskatchewan plains, the trapper had to settle for the pelt of the fisher (a strangely named cat-sized animal, which neither hunted, nor ate, fish), the marten, or pine marten, slightly smaller than the fisher; the popular mink; the industrious otter, and the lynx, a fearsomely built wildcat with huge legs and massive fur-covered paws. Greatest of all the prey available to the plains trapper, however, was the much sought-after silver fox – its silver sheen coming from a scattering of black-tipped, grey-white, hairs among the predominantly black pelt.

The greatest competition faced by the trapper was not his fellow trappers, nor the Indians, but the savage wolverine. This animal, looking like a 'shaggy brown dog', was despised in every quarter. Following in the wake of the trapper, the wolverine would make its way along a line of traps, destroying the contents and laying waste days of work. Cheadle employed his American-purchased strychnine against the animals, but found the wolverines either spat it out, or – according to Cheadle – devoured it without ill-effect ('Confound the Yankees!'). Trapping required both strength and determination. Milton could rarely be persuaded to venture out. When Cheadle accompanied La Ronde, he had to carry five or six days pemmican, a tin kettle and cup, tea, salt, and some steel traps, all wrapped up in his blanket and slung across his back. In addition he had to carry a gun, an axe, knife, a pouch containing tinder, flint, and a steel, another pouch holding bullets and tobacco, a powder horn, a shot belt, a gun, mittens, three pairs of socks, leather breeches, a woollen jersey, a flannel shirt, a duffle shirt, a leather shirt, and a tweed waistcoat. Although the crunch of snowshoes could not be avoided, the trapper had to make his way in as near total silence as possible. Whistling and singing was absolutely forbidden as any sound would attract wolverines and drive away the prey. Even the building of 'dead fall' traps to catch martens was carried out in the 'intense stillness'.

After a few days out with La Ronde, Cheadle returned to Fort Milton on 8 December to find several dog trains from Fort Carlton nearby. On investigation, he found that one was driven by Badger, Messiter's English half-breed servant. Messiter arrived shortly afterwards, full of tales of his fur trading activities. Although he had done well, it had not been without incident. One evening, a large, aggressive Indian named Atagakouph demanded a gift of rum. Messiter refused, but told the Indian that he could have rum in exchange for a marten pelt. Atagakouph left and returned shortly afterwards with a marten, which he screwed up and threw at Messiter's face. Messiter retaliated by punching the Indian in the face. Atagakouph drew a knife from his belt and charged at Messiter and Badger, supported by four more of his tribesmen, also with drawn knives. At that moment, Messiter's rescued Scotsman, James Alexander, walked into the room and grappled with Atagakouph as one of the other Indians grabbed the rum barrel. Messiter dashed across the floor, knocked down the rum thief and retrieved the barrel along with a loaded double-barrelled shotgun. Sitting on the rum keg, Messiter cocked the gun and pointed it at the Indians who yelled and gesticulated in return. Suddenly, the door of the cabin was thrown open, and in walked a man so huge that he made Atagakouph look puny. It was Tambout (known as 'Tom Boot'), a Métis who lived with his wife in a lodge close to the cabin. Having fortified himself against the cold of the walk from the lodge with a copious amount of rum, Tom Boot was in no mood for a disorderly house. He strode across the floor to Atagakouph, picked him up bodily and threw him to the floor. No further demonstration of strength was needed – the Indians promptly fled into the night as Tom Boot made himself at home, and Messiter – despite knife cuts to his hand, neck, and chest, – enjoyed an unexpectedly peaceful night.

Milton and Cheadle's former travelling companion had lost none of his capability for bickering at the slightest provocation. His fur trading with the natives cut across the Hudson's Bay Company's self-imposed rules and its own traders frequently found themselves coming away empty handed after Messiter had beaten them to a rum-laced transaction. His excuse that he was only obtaining 'a few furs for his lady friends' soon wore thin, and the factor at Fort Carlton seized one of his dog trains and banned him from the fort. A game of whist with Milton promptly resurrected their old antagonisms, so Messiter decided that he would leave the next day to follow up a rumour of a nearby Indian camp that had yet to be approached by traders. He was determined to get there before 'John Company'.

Foiled by the departure of his sparring partner, Milton turned on Cheadle and demanded all of the furs from the animals trapped during La Ronde's expeditions – including those taken from Cheadle's traps. He claimed that he had purchased La Ronde's share with a quantity of tobacco and, as Cheadle was not a skilled trapper, his efforts did not count. In fact, not only did the doctor pay La Ronde half of his wages, he had personally built twenty marten traps compared to Milton's one. Consequently, he refused to budge on his previously agreed one third portion. The time had come for a welcome break from each other's company. It was decided that Cheadle would remain based at the cabin in company with Nashquapamayoo. The boy would accompany the doctor on trapping expeditions. The Métis, La Ronde and Bruneau, would go to Fort Carlton from where they would join dog trains to Red River, to obtain supplies of flour, tea and sugar. The 1,200-mile round journey would take two months. Milton would accompany the two men as far as Fort Carlton, where he would obtain what supplies he could before returning. Then, he and Cheadle, guided by the young Indian, would visit a Cree Indian camp on the edge of the plain where buffaloes had been reported. Milton and Bruneau left on Christmas Eve, with the former desperate to get there in time to join the factor at his Christmas dinner. La Ronde, delayed by a bad cold, would join them in a few days. Cheadle, however, merely contemplated a Christmas of 'no mince pies, no good things, no family meeting'. In fact, the following day provided a 'merry evening' with a Christmas dinner of galette and hot pot, washed down with a rum punch.

The six months that had passed since they had left Liverpool had seen the continuation of the American Civil War. A dispute broke out between the USA and Great Britain over the building of the CSS *Alabama* in Liverpool. The Indian uprising in Minnesota – narrowly avoided by Milton, Cheadle, and Messiter – ended after the deaths of hundreds of white settlers; 38 Sioux were hanged for atrocities committed during the attacks, their bodies used for anatomical research. Prince Otto Von Bismarck was appointed as Minister President of Prussia, and Jean Henri Dunant published his book on the Battle of Solferino, which led to the creation of the International Red Cross. In England, the balloonist Henry Tracy Coxwell, reached more than 7 miles above the Earth's surface, and Charles Dodgson (Lewis Carroll) sketched out the plot for *Alice in Wonderland*.

After Christmas Day, Cheadle and Nashquapamayoo went on a trapping expedition, but returned after a few days without a single pelt. Within an hour of their return, Messiter and Badger arrived saying that Milton was just behind them, then promptly left in the direction of fur-carrying Indians. When the viscount reached the cabin, he exploded with rage on being told about Messiter and dashed off in an attempt to beat his old schoolfellow to the quarry. But he was too late. Messiter had already done the deal. Milton responded with a threat to use the wolverine-intended strychnine against Messiter – who swiftly drew his knife. Milton then drew his knife. Their companions kept them apart until both stormed off to their cabins. Cheadle, 'very tired of it', was subjected to a long night of Milton's invective against Messiter.

The following day (New Year's Eve) brought a surprise that reduced Milton's rage. A large group of amiable Indians descended upon the cabin, apparently carrying out an Indian custom of taking advantage of their neighbour's hospitality on New Year's Day. To his delight, Milton saw an old friend smiling among the crowd, it was Child of the Hawk's daughter, whom Cheadle had dismissed as 'Delilah'. In a moment of pure gallantry – and much to the 'astonishment' of the visiting Indians – Milton announced that, as the cabin would be crowded that night, he would be camping outside, whereupon the equally thoughtful Delilah decided to share the inconvenience by joining him. The next morning, after much celebratory gunfire to welcome 1863, most of the visitors departed happy with gifts of rum and glass beads. Milton and Cheadle set up the sledges for a buffalo hunt, taking with them The Hunter and his son. The Hunter's wife and another Indian woman remained at the cabin. Cheadle found sledge-driving to be a difficult task with its frequent tumbles and collisions. Milton refused to attempt the task and stumbled on perpetually complaining about his snowshoes. On the second day, Milton became loudly concerned that the two Indians would not stop for dinner. He proved to be right and The Hunter and his son were astonished when he demanded that they stop. Even then, Milton was annoyed when they saw the meal break as a mere chance to eat, rather than as a period of rest. This caused a renewed session of 'groaning and complaint', which Cheadle found very wearing. The following day was no improvement – Cheadle lost his hunter's knife, Milton lost his bullet pouch, and The Hunter lost his pipe. To complete the day, their two axe blades broke, and a sharp drop in temperature was accompanied by a bitter north wind (it was a custom among the trappers never to leave their axes outdoors overnight. The intense cold made the blade extremely brittle). Ice formed on Cheadle's beard and moustache, and even the tobacco oil in the surviving pipes froze, rendering them useless until thawed out by the fire.

On the next day they had expected to find an Indian camp, but it had moved on. By now short of food, they followed the tracks made in the deep snow. Milton, feeling unwell, had taken to riding on the sledge. Cheadle took a look at his face and noticed that he had frostbite. The doctor showed the aristocrat how to massage the spot and was successful in reducing the effects.

In the morning, The Hunter decided that, with their supplies very low, he would go out and look for buffalo. Milton stayed at the camp smoking his pipe while Cheadle and the boy gathered wood and mended moccasins. Scanty meals were made of the remaining pemmican and flour while the dogs not only had to go without, but also had to undergo the indignity of being judged on the basis of which would make the next good meal. As the evening's darkness deepened, the boy became fretful at the nonappearance of his father and persuaded Cheadle to fire shots in the hope of a reply – but none came. Nashquapamayoo then stood aside staring into the darkness listening for any sound. Without moving, he stood for hours despite being invited to join the others around the fire. Just before midnight, the boy suddenly twitched and leaned forward. Far away, but approaching, he had heard the sounds of feet upon snow. It was his father, bearing on his back a pack containing a buffalo heart and tongue. Having given up any hope of finding such an animal, The Hunter had started his return when, by the last of the day's light, he came across a solitary bull. Once shot, the bull – minus its heart and tongue – had to be buried to such a depth that it was safe from wolves.

After a good night's sleep on a full stomach, the party set off the next day to retrieve the rest of the bull. The temperature continued to fall, and Milton's face showed a slight swelling that Cheadle took to be evidence of a gumboil. The next day, Milton and the boy stayed at the camp while The Hunter and Cheadle went off in search of more buffalo. Two were found but, despite their best efforts, both bolted before they could be brought down. On the morrow, The Hunter and his son set off to see if they could find the two animals as Cheadle stayed at the camp. Milton's face continued to swell with the affected area turning red. That evening the two Indians returned with a good supply of meat. One of the buffaloes had been brought down by wolves, but had remained largely intact as the bitter cold had frozen the animal. This had meant that the two had to build a fire to warm the bull before it could be butchered.

In the morning, Cheadle found that one of Milton's eyes had swollen dramatically. Clearly, it was not merely a gumboil – but erysipelas (widely known as 'St Anthony's Fire' or 'Holy Fire'). The bacterial infection could have arisen from a wide range of sources, but generally enters the skin through cuts and abrasions. Once established, the infection can cause vomiting and fever. Cheadle, 80 miles from the cabin, could see no other course of action than to get Milton back to their camp as quickly as possible. It took three-and-a-half days of travelling to reach Fort Milton. The Hunter had led, followed by his son pulling the supply sledge. In the rear, Cheadle hauled on the sledge bearing Milton tied on board 'like a sack of flour'. The dogs were almost utterly useless and individually described as 'thin and weak', 'aged and asthmatic', and 'lame and lethargic'. Time and again, Cheadle's sledge toppled over, leaving Milton buried in the snow. Eventually, Cheadle persuaded an unwilling Milton to lie on the sledge unsecured so that he could roll off when difficulties were encountered. The viscount responded by 'grumbling loudly' when he had to walk up the occasional steep rise.

The last night was spent 10 miles from the cabin and The Hunter suggested an early start the following morning without lighting the fire and cooking breakfast. Cheadle agreed, but Milton lost his temper and demanded both. When they managed to get under way the following morning, Milton – with his ailment now appearing to be considerably better – wearied the doctor by his constant refrain of 'whether we are nearly there?' They arrived at the cabin in the early afternoon to find that the two Indian women had not only made the cabin 'much neater than it had ever been', but had a hot meal of fish and bread waiting for them. There was, however, little food remaining, so the buffalo meat was shared with the Indians as they prepared to leave for White Fish Lake, giving them enough food to last for two weeks. The Hunter and his son would then return in a week's time and lead an expedition in search of more of the animals. Milton and Cheadle could live on the remaining fish and flour and, with Milton already 'quite lively', there was a good chance that he would be fit and well enough to take part in the hunting trip. Both, however, were surprised just three days later when The Hunter, his son, and Child of the Hawk turned up once again on their doorstep. It seemed that the Indians had gorged on the two weeks supply of meat until there was none left. They wished to set off immediately on another buffalo hunt, but Cheadle disagreed on the grounds that it was pointless to set out on a hunting trip without an ample food supply. Instead, he decided, they would leave Milton at the cabin while he and the Indians made a dash for Fort Carlton to obtain a supply of pemmican. They set off the next day, leaving Milton thirteen fish and some desiccated vegetables on which to live until their return.

The three Indians and Cheadle were delayed by heavy snow and, on their first night, it was so cold that the doctor shivered violently despite a covering of two blankets and a greatcoat. The next day the Indians were reluctant to move, and could not be urged to move until midday. On the following day, Cheadle rose early, demanding that they had to be at the fort before that nightfall. They set off after a breakfast of two small fish – the last of their food. By midday, the realities of the situation struck Cheadle with alarming force. Bent double, and almost fainting with hunger, he suggested that the party stop for a rest and a pipe of tobacco. The Hunter, however, refused, pointing out that if they stopped, they would be unlikely to reach Fort Carlton that night. Cheadle plodded on in pain from his snowshoes vowing that henceforth he would view people forced to commit crimes through lack of food with a far more benevolent attitude ('they deserve the utmost pity'). The fort was reached just before dark that evening. When they had come across the road, Cheadle pulled off his snowshoes and ran the last mile reaching the fort gates well ahead of his companions. Having seen that the Indians had food and shelter, he then settled down to a huge meal of buffalo, potatoes, bread, and butter, before retiring to a warm bed.

After a day's rest (during which The Hunter drank copious amounts of rum), Cheadle sent the Indians back to Fort Milton with the supplies. He, on the other hand, decided to wait for the arrival of the mail packets. The first was from Fort Edmonton in Alberta, with the sledge announcing itself with the tinkling of harness bells and the waving of coloured plumes. It was driven by a 'yellow-haired Scotchman ... a very pleasant fellow indeed and very obliging' who surprised everyone by announcing that there was no snow at Edmonton. There was, however, great consternation the following day when an emaciated Indian arrived at the fort with news that smallpox had broken out at Fort La Corne, the most westerly of the originally French forts on the Saskatchewan, and north-east of Fort Carlton. Cheadle vaccinated everyone against the disease – only to find out that the whole thing was a false alarm. He celebrated the following day with a special 'treat' – rice pudding made from boiled rice, sugar, and butter.

Two days later, the packet arrived from Red River. The wait had been in vain. There was not a single letter or package for him, or for Milton. Cheadle blamed the 'rascally Sioux' for the presumed failure of the mail through Minnesota, and had to settle instead for some out-of-date newspapers. At last, after more than a week behind The Hunter and the other Indians, Cheadle decided he had to get back to the cabin. The problem was that he had no means of transport. He was offered a horse-drawn sledge (a 'cariole'), but the snow proved to be too deep. However, Jemmy Isbister – an English half-breed at the fort – heard of Cheadle's difficulties and offered to take him back using a sledge and his train of dogs. When Cheadle tried to negotiate a price for the service, Isbister refused any payment on the grounds that Cheadle was a doctor who had helped his child.

The journey proved to be afflicted by a bitter cold. The overnight temperature was so low that sleep was almost impossible. Setting off early, Cheadle found that he not only had frostbite on his face and neck and a bleeding nose, but that the area around his thighs was badly affected. Not only was his 'Johnson' (a Victorian euphemism) frozen, but the bladder sphincter muscle would not work, causing embarrassing – and inconvenient – incontinence. Fortunately, Isbister proved to be an experienced and capable dog driver, and they arrived at the cabin just after dark on the second day. With Milton nowhere to be seen, Isbister set about looking after Cheadle, lighting a fire, and chopping wood before setting out on the return journey in the dark just two hours after their arrival.

Cheadle awoke the next day aching violently throughout his body. After 'anointing' his damaged parts with medication, he decided on a quiet, restful, day, limiting himself to chopping wood for the fire, smoking his pipe, and manufacturing 'kinnikinnick' – a tobacco substitute used by the Indians made from the dried shavings of wood from the willow tree and mixed with leaf tobacco. His peace was interrupted during the early evening when the door of the cabin opened, and in walked a Métis. The man turned out to be Mahaygun (The Wolf) who joined Cheadle in front of the fire and accepted a pipe of tobacco. After two hours of general conversation, The Wolf told Cheadle that he had not eaten for two days, and that his wife was in their lodge, a short distance way. Moreover, he had entered the cabin a couple of days earlier, helped himself to some water, but did not touch a packet of pemmican laying on the cabin table. Cheadle knew this to be true as the packet remained unopened. The Wolf had held to his Indian heritage in this matter. Firstly, it would have been considered bad manners to have raised the question of food immediately on his arrival and, secondly, it would have been a great discourtesy to have entered someone's home and stolen their food. On realising the situation, Cheadle promptly cooked his visitor a large plate of 'rubbiboo' (fried pemmican and mashed potatoes) before he departed for his wife and lodge clutching a supply of pemmican and tea.

In the morning, Cheadle – assuming that Milton had set up a liaison with 'Delilah' – left for Child of the Hawk's camp, 10 miles away. He found it very difficult, and his legs 'gave in' during the last mile. Eventually, he was spotted and Milton emerged from the cabin to help him over the last few hundred yards. The doctor soon recovered after a serving of pemmican. Milton, it transpired, had gone to White Fish Lake in search of 'society'. Food at the site was scarce so he helped out by shooting the odd rabbit and partridge until The Hunter and his son returned with the pemmican dispatched by Cheadle. After a day or so, The Hunter decided to go out in search of moose, but soon returned empty handed. To seek divine aid, The Hunter then organised an invocation to the Great Spirit or Manitou. This took the form of dressing in wolf skin belts, and ermine and muskrat skins covered in glass beads. He then danced to the beat of drums and the rattle of dried, pebble-filled bladders; sang songs he composed himself; or made long speeches promising the best of the moose meat would be sacrificed to the Manitou. Despite being a sacred animal among the Wood Cree Indians, the Manitou prevailed and The Hunter returned having killed not one, but two of the huge animals. The bulk of the carcasses had been cached for later retrieval, but tradition demanded that the best portions – the heart, liver, kidney and tongue – had to be eaten as soon as possible. A great feast was had that night with some of the tastiest morsels being thrown into the fire in gratitude for the Manitou's help. All present joined in with the exception of the women who (again traditionally) were not allowed to eat the tongue. This may have annoyed one of the women present, but she was soon to be doubly annoyed. The chief, Child of the Hawk, took Cheadle on one side and suggested that he might like a closer, more intimate relationship with his daughter. The doctor was outraged and turned the offer down, noting that 'Delilah' was 'very much offended' by his rejection. What Milton thought of this proposed infidelity (if it was ever revealed to him) is unrecorded.

The two Englishmen returned to their cabin the following morning to find that The Wolf had kept his promise and brought his wife along to wash their clothes and carry out any necessary repairs. The next day, with the woman still busy at her chores, The Hunter and his son arrived with a supply of moose meat. Milton rewarded The Hunter and The Wolf (who turned out to be old friends) handsomely with a pint of rum. The Métis behaved amicably repeatedly raising his tin cup and shouting loudly '*Je vous salue!* Good luck!' The Hunter, however, after an interminable phase demanding more rum, annoyed Cheadle to the extent that he shouted at the Indian telling him to behave himself. The Hunter dropped his tin cup, grabbed Cheadle by the arm, and drew his knife, placing the tip at the doctor's chest. His face inches from Cheadle's, The Hunter then screamed – 'If I were an Indian of the Plains, I would stab you in the heart for saying "No".' Cheadle, remaining outwardly calm, replied in a level tone, 'You are not a Plains Indian, the Indians of the Woods know better.' This confused The Hunter, causing him to lower the knife and step back. Complaining that he was disgusted with their meanness, he staggered out of the cabin and began to harness his sledge dogs. His son, terrified by the display of aggression, begged his father not to leave, but to no avail. Within a few minutes, both had left. Two days later, The Hunter returned in a very contrite mood. His life had probably been saved by his son who, after his father had collapsed unconscious in the snow, dragged him to the shelter of some trees, lit a fire and stayed up all night keeping it blazing to ensure his father remained warm. After a barrage of apologies, Cheadle made no more of the matter and spent the night entertaining The Hunter and his son with card tricks.

With the cold weather continuing, the desire for animal skins diminished to be replaced by the need for food. Cheadle, accompanied by The Hunter and his son, went after buffalo and, after twelve days returned with the meat from four they had managed to shoot. But they had been extraordinarily lucky. While out on the frozen prairie, a large group of Indian families staggered and limped past their camp. Gaunt and thin, they had been unable to find any buffalo. Unable to help so many, Cheadle was pleased to be able to provide sustenance to an Indian and his wife who had clearly undergone a terrible period of starvation. Carrying nothing but what they wore, they had traded everything they had for scraps of food. The man was more than 6 foot tall and very thin with clear evidence of an unfortunate episode at some recent stage of his life. His left eye was hidden behind a patch, he had not a single tooth in his mouth, and his nose had been flattened against his face. The injuries had been caused by a fight with a bear. Nevertheless, both he and his wife ('rather good looking') showed a remarkable ability to eat non-stop when offered food. On departing for Fort Milton, Cheadle left the man a pipe, some tobacco, and the entire head of a buffalo.

Cheadle had also learned that 40 miles to the south of their cabin, Messiter and his Scots companion, Farquharson, had also been starving. Messiter had sent his English half-breed trapper, Badger, to Fort Carlton for supplies, but the man had been refused on the grounds of Messiter's private fur trading activities. Now Messiter had set off for the fort himself to see if he could persuade the factor to help him.

On his return to the cabin, Cheadle was met by Milton and a cheery 'Hello Cheadle, devilish glad to see you back, all alone here for four days and getting very down in the mouth.' His loneliness on the other days had been tempered by a visit from 'Delilah', but some sort of squabble had seen her return to White Fish Lake.

With a reasonable supply of meat available, and the imminent return of the Métis, La Ronde and Bruneau, from Fort Garry at Red River, Milton and Cheadle decided that the spare time could be usefully employed in giving the cabin a 'spring clean'. This had been one of Milton's tasks while Cheadle was away hunting buffalo, but his task of entertaining Delilah had probably been too much of a distraction. As it was, with Cheadle quite used to the employment of domestics to help around the vicarage, and Milton with an army of servants at his command, the sight of each other imitating housemaids often reduced them to outbursts of giggling as they swept the sunken floor with brushes made from pine branches, and used tin dinner plates as dustpans. With the rest of the building dusted down, it was time to move on to the next domestic task – the production of a plum pudding. When Messiter made his Christmas visit, he had presented Milton and Cheadle with a small quantity of raisins and currants. Despite Milton's plea to him to make a plum pudding, Cheadle, doubtful of his own abilities, and knowing Milton's shortcomings in such a skill, refused, and merely put the dried fruit to one side. Upon later investigation, Cheadle discovered that the precious commodity was mysteriously shrinking in quantity, and so locked it away with the remnants of flour and sugar in his personal strong box. Unfortunately, however, after about three months, the box was opened only to find that the paper bag containing the dried fruit had fallen apart allowing the contents to fall to the bottom of the container – where it joined an assorted collection of loose gunpowder, buckshot, tobacco, and soap. Undeterred, Cheadle picked and scraped up what he could, mixed it with the flour and sugar, and wrapped it in a cloth before placing it in boiling water. After several hours boiling, and the preparation of a brace of prairie chickens to provide the main course, it was decided that the cooking was complete. The pudding 'proved delicious beyond all anticipation', despite the frequent spitting out of gun caps, buckshot, and lumps of tobacco leaf. What had not been anticipated was the size of the pudding – it was so big that a sizeable portion remained for breakfast and, assisted by indigestion, both men remained awake, keeping an eye on the other in case he surreptitiously helped himself to an extra slice.

Philip Tait, an English half-breed (and a 'civilised person') in the employ of the Hudson's Bay Company at Fort Carlton, arrived by cariole and bought news that the winter had been unusually severe, and food was scarce throughout the region. At one of the smaller forts, the occupants had been reduced to boiling buffalo hides for sustenance. Two men, sent for supplies to Touchwood Hills, arrived in a starving state yet could not be helped and, even at Fort Carlton, men sent out to hunt only survived by eating their dog. Milton and Cheadle also learned from Tait that the Hudson's Bay Company was beginning to consider seriously the establishment of cattle and cereal farms in Saskatchewan – the days of living by hunting and fishing were clearly coming to a close. Hearing that Tait was on his way to visit Messiter at Touchwood Hills, Cheadle decided to join him as their former companion owed him some marten pelts in payment for a gallon of rum. Tait's main task was to obtain skins from the Indians and Cheadle did not want to see his furs sold to the company leaving Messiter with no means of settling his debt. Cheadle rode on the sledge whenever he could, but a sudden rise in the temperature meant a difficult journey over thawing snow. Whenever he tried to light his pipe he had to loosen his grip on the sledge, repeatedly falling off as a result. They arrived just before dark, and Cheadle was surprised to find Messiter and Farquharson dining on meat stew with macaroni and bread – a meal in which they were delighted to join.

Messiter was suffering from losing a nail and part of a big toe to frostbite, but was otherwise well. He told Cheadle to choose the furs he wanted from a large pile, and served his guests with a supper of sardines and coffee before they retired to bed.

The following day, Cheadle learned that Messiter intended to leave within a day or two. Both he and Tait argued against this as the warmer weather would inevitably bring rain, making a journey far more difficult. Cheadle advised him to try and get Jemmy Isbister and his train of dogs to come from Fort Carlton to collect him. Messiter thought this was a splendid idea and asked Tait to try and arrange matters for him. On leaving after breakfast, Farquharson presented Cheadle with two pairs of white trousers, a bottle of quinine, and two cakes of Brown Windsor Soap (made from exotic oils, spices, and herbs; a favourite of Napoleon Bonaparte's – despite being made in England). Tait gave him a ride on the cariole until he had to branch off towards another group of Indians, leaving Cheadle a walk of about 20 miles. The distance was not far, but the thaw had turned his snowshoes into 'great lumps of frozen snow'.

On arrival at the cabin, Cheadle found Milton in a depressed mood. Child of the Hawk had brought his family (including his daughter Delilah) over in an attempt to get food. Milton refused despite Delilah's attempts to get him to co-operate. Eventually, the family – taking Delilah with them – stormed off. When Cheadle heard that Milton had 'discarded' Delilah, it was to his great 'delight'. With the end of winter just a few weeks away, there was little more to do than wait for the return of La Ronde and Bruneau – already several days late. The Hunter turned up with a good supply of moose meat, leaving his son to stay at the cabin while he went after more supplies. Cheadle noticed that, with a sharp drop in temperature, the boy began to shiver, so he lent him his 'Inverness cape' – a long great coat with a cape covering the shoulders and arms down to the waist. The boy was transported with delight as he swaggered around in a coat many sizes too large for him. In the meantime, Cheadle smoked his pipe and read Shakespeare aloud while Milton listened ('attentive and pleased').

After a day setting traps with the young boy, they returned just before dark to be told that their young companion would be returning to his family the following morning. Before leaving, he had one last message to give – a message that he had put off for as long as possible out of embarrassment. On his return to White Fish Lake, a great feast was planned around the best parts of a moose. He had been told to invite Cheadle to the event – but not Milton. As it was, Cheadle was not over-enthusiastic about the idea as he was still suffering from sore feet, but Milton was very keen. When it was confirmed that Milton was not to be invited, he descended into a raging sulk. Cheadle, with a large measure of relief, turned the invitation down. Delilah, it seemed, had, at last, done him a service.

Two days later, La Ronde and Bruneau arrived after their 1,220-mile round trip to Fort Garry. La Ronde was in a poor state, suffering from bronchitis and 'mal de Johnson' – a condition brought on by the cold. He was consigned to his bunk while Bruneau unloaded the sledge. The two men had brought half a sack of flour, 20lb of tea, 5 gallons of rum, and pemmican (having left a sack of flour at Fort Carlton to make room on the sledge). Most importantly of all, however, was a batch of letters and newspapers for Milton and Cheadle. The mail was devoured as eagerly as the abundant pancakes and the tea. The journals revealed that the American Civil War remained the dominant feature in the news, with President Lincoln's anti-slavery 'Emancipation Proclamation' leading to the hanging of forty-one 'Union sympathisers' in Gainesville, Texas. La Ronde also told Milton and Cheadle that the situation at Fort Garry was tense, with many people fearing for their lives. Two thousand Sioux Indians were camped 2 miles outside the fort, intending to get their hands on ammunition to fight the Americans in the coming spring. The Sioux bristled with swords, rifles, revolvers, and Bowie knives taken from American soldiers, glittered with necklaces of gold coins, uniform epaulettes, and bright scarves plundered from women, and even drove around in looted horse-drawn buggies. The local militia was on its way and many of the Métis were being organised into military formations, with some even being paid an astonishing guinea (£1 1s) a day to guard the fort. Even closer to home, Milton and Cheadle learned that all but two of the horses sent back with Voudrie and Zeal had died through lack of care. Apparently, the horses were tied up all night to save the Métis the trouble of rounding them up in the morning. This had resulted in a lack of nutrition, and they had died of starvation. Both Messiter and Milton had paid high prices for their horses, and one had been given to La Ronde as a reward – all had gone. Cheadle, on the other hand, had released his horse, Bucephalus, along with two other horses, on to the surrounding prairie in the hope that they would survive the winter.

In the early hours of the morning, the residents of the cabin were woken by the opening of the door. In walked The Hunter followed by Child of the Hawk and his family – including Delilah. Clearly, word of La Ronde and Bruneau's arrival had travelled quickly. Cheadle, in no mood to be hospitable, simply turned over and went back to sleep, but Milton got up and persuaded the visitors to camp outside and wait for the morning. Quite apart from the possibility that La Ronde had brought them something back from Fort Garry, the Indians were at the cabin to settle up their accounts. Now that the winter was drawing to a close, they knew that Milton and Cheadle would be moving on. The Hunter was to be paid one skin a day (the vast majority of which he had already traded for rum); his son, half a skin a day and Child of the Hawk owed Milton and Cheadle forty skins for everything from pemmican to gunpowder. His reaction to this news was to storm out of the cabin, followed by his wife loudly accusing the two Englishmen of only coming into their country to starve them. No record remains of Delilah's comments on the situation. Later that day, Child of the Hawk returned with a silver fox pelt he wished to trade, but La Ronde immediately declared the skin to be merely a red fox dyed to look like the silver version – a trick commonly used to fool the gullible. Undefeated, Child of the Hawk sold the fur to another Indian who gloried in the name Crooked Nose.

During the last few days of March, Cheadle – mainly in the company of Bruneau – checked his traps. It turned out to be a poor harvest with only a couple of martens recovered. He then decided to delay his return to the cabin by destroying the remaining traps 'in order not to kill things uselessly'. The result was that his snowshoes fell apart in the slush, and he had to complete his journey wading through waist-high snow. Even then, just a few miles from Fort Milton, he had to sleep on the soggy ground to recover his strength. In the meantime, La Ronde had shaken off the worst of his bronchitis, and had added to their stock of meat by spearing numerous muskrats (which Cheadle described as 'balls of fat, almost too rich').

The next morning, La Ronde was sent out in search of the three horses let loose shortly after their arrival. He found them about 8 miles from the cabin. Astonishingly, they were in superb condition, probably through having learned to dig through the snow to reach the grass beneath, and to take shelter at night beneath any available tree cover. Milton considered that they were 'nearly in as fine condition as the stall-fed cattle of the Baker Street Show'.

Much to the doctor's delight he had managed to trap a silver fox, but, in company with The Hunter's son, had taken too long to retrieve the animal, finding that carrion crows had wreaked their destruction on the carcass. Fuming at his misfortune, he wrote,

> My disappointment and chagrin were unbounded at the provoking result of all the ingenuity and toil with which I had laboured to secure the great prize – nay, my devices had better failed altogether to deceive the ill-fated animal, and I felt unfeigned regret at the useless destruction of the dainty fox ... My only chance of obtaining the skin of a silver fox was gone for the season, and we plodded our way home to the hut disgusted and disconsolate.

On the following morning, Friday 3 April, they set off for Fort Carlton with Bucephalus hauling the Red River cart, packed with their belongings, Milton riding one of the smaller horses, and Cheadle walking ('leaving the house, without a tear'). They arrived on the following Monday, having safely crossed over the still-frozen Saskatchewan River. Messiter and Farquharson had already arrived, and the former was soon regaling Milton and Cheadle with an unhappy incident, which happened just before their departure. On returning from their final trapping expedition, Messiter and Atagakouph found that their cabin had been entered and several articles had been stolen. The thief could not have been Badger or Farquharson, who were still out hunting together. Every deduction led to one conclusion – it had to be Tom Boot, the giant who had humiliated Atagakouph. With Atagakouph very keen to be involved, Messiter ensured the Indian was not carrying a weapon, and secreted a small revolver in his own pocket. It was a 20-mile journey to Tom Boot's lodge and when they arrived, their target was seen to be sitting outside. Hiding in nearby trees they waited until dusk when Tom Boot and his wife retired for the night. Desperate to avoid the sound of snow crunching beneath their moccasins, they crept forward, burst into the lodge, and fell upon the sleeping giant. A mighty struggle ensued, made worse by the screeching of his wife as she fizzed with rage. Eventually, the assailants were able to tie Tom Boot's hands and feet and he lay quiet upon the floor of the lodge. Sure enough, all the stolen goods were scattered around the inside of the tepee. While Atagakouph gathered the items together, Messiter drew his revolver and pointed it at Tom Boot's head, telling him that if he ever came anywhere near them, or the cabin, he would be shot on sight.

Messiter had had enough of the Saskatchewan wilds for the time being and decided to return to England. He would be accompanied as far as Red River and Fort Garry by Badger, the half-breed leaving his wife and child at Fort Carlton. Messiter and Badger's journey proved to be fraught with danger. They narrowly escaped being burned alive by a prairie fire that Badger was convinced had been started by Indians in an attempt to obtain the horses by panicking them. Then they stumbled into an Indian camp, the occupants claiming to be Cree, but were, quite plainly Sioux, and were probably a band that had crossed the border from Minnesota to escape the repercussions rising from the Indian war. Standing outside the chief's lodge, Messiter was joined by the chief himself who demanded his gun and horse. When Messiter refused, the chief took the reins of the horse and began to lead him away. When Messiter demanded he stop, the chief pulled a club from beneath a blanket he was carrying, and struck out at him, breaking his left arm. Messiter then pulled out his Tranter revolver (a single-trigger, double-action, revolver made in England) and fired two shots. The chief fell, instantly dead. This act was followed by a three-day chase. Messiter and Badger's horses were more powerful than the Indian ponies, but had less endurance. Several times the pursuers closed with the pursued but, eventually, they reached settlers' accommodation on the outskirts of Fort Garry, and a large group of armed men caused the Sioux to retreat.

The reception at Fort Garry was kind, with accommodation being offered and accepted. Despite the bishop, Dr Anderson, offering a carriage and horses, travel by horseback was preferred, and arranged. Badger was paid off and prepared to return to Fort Carlton as the services of a very tough guide were obtained. The new guide was a French half-breed named Isadore Maronde. Despite having 'a bad character', and proving to be very expensive ('£50 in money, a fine double gun of mine, and the three horses, which we would use on the road'), he was, unquestionably, the most highly recommended man for the job. Messiter and Maronde set off at 5pm on 2 May. As it was well known that Sioux bands were marauding over northern Minnesota, it was decided that they would travel by night and hide during the day. At night, fires could be seen and avoided and, during daylight, plumes of smoke were likewise circumvented. While concealed behind river banks and trees, shots were heard during the day, but the saddest sight was several burnt-out farmhouses with rows of graves in the front gardens. After several long nights and uncomfortable days, they reached St Cloud where they joined a group of lumberjacks sleeping on the floor of a bedroom. The single bed was unoccupied, and Messiter gratefully accepted the opportunity to get between the sheets. Just as he was about to drift off to sleep, he was awoken by a movement across his neck followed by the eruption of a blister. Lighting a candle, he discovered that the pillow, the rest of the bed, and even the log walls, were covered in bedbugs. He ended up having a more comfortable night on the hay of an adjoining stable.

Late the next evening the two men rode into St Paul. After stabling their horses and finding accommodation for Maronde, Messiter invited his companion to join him for dinner at the hotel he was booked into. The Métis took one look at the elegant ladies and gentlemen enjoying their dinner surrounded by porcelain and crystal glass and decided to make his own arrangements. After washing his hands, Messiter took a seat at a table, fully conscious of his appearance ('leather shirt, leather trousers, and moccasins, and a fur cap, all of them being very much the worse for wear'). Several of the ladies looked aghast at their new dining companion and complained to a US Army general who had also come to the opinion that Messiter was a 'half-breed scout'. Consequently, an officer on the general's staff came over and told Messiter that the general wanted a word with him immediately. With the innate courtesy of an English gentleman, Messiter replied that he would be delighted to meet the general – after he had finished his dinner. The meal completed, Messiter introduced himself to the general who told him that he was to command 1,200 infantrymen with orders to march into northern Minnesota and drive out the Sioux. Messiter replied that he would be far better if he sent for enough half-breeds from Fort Garry and organised them into a corps of rangers. Their experience of Indian fighting would be invaluable when compared to the inexperience of the infantrymen. The Indians, he explained, 'would hang round his line of march, cutting off stragglers and shooting his sentries, they themselves being always invisible'. The general chose to ignore Messiter's advice, and the expedition (according to Messiter) '...saw a few Indians in the distance whom they failed to catch, remained out about three months, harassed in every way by the Indians, and returned having done nothing'. While strolling around the town a few days later, Messiter came across an exhibition of photographs. Several were of Indians, one of whom he recognised immediately. It was the Sioux chief whom he had shot. The man's name was 'Ki-chi-ma-ka-ses', or Little Fox. As if the damaged arm was not enough (it was already stiffening up, and would never work properly again), there was a reward of a $1,000 for anyone who killed Little Fox; but Messiter's only witness was Badger, and he was probably hundreds of miles away on the Saskatchewan plains. There was nothing left for him to do but to return to England.

Messiter's companion over the winter, James Farquharson, had made great play over his intention to reach British Columbia and to get involved with the area's gold mining (Cheadle frequently referred to him as 'The Columbian'). Whether he did so or not is uncertain, but he clearly became involved with the opposition to the Red River Rebellion of 1869–70 when the Métis feared for their lives and their property. Allying himself to John Christian Schultz (who married one of Farquharson's daughters, and later became Lieutenant-Governor of Manitoba), Farquharson earned a reputation as a political agitator and leader of rioting mobs. He was particularly known for firing his pistol at random into crowds of protestors – fortunately without any degree of success. Farquharson continued with his agitation after the rebellion, earning himself the label 'Old Depravity'. He died in November 1874, unlamented in many quarters.

After just two nights at Fort Carlton, Milton and Cheadle left for Fort Pitt. They had said their farewells to Messiter, Farquharson, La Ronde, and Bruneau, and hired a French Métis named Baptiste Supernat at £12 a month to guide them over the Rocky Mountains. Baptiste's qualifications amounted to being 'very civil and handy, and gives a favourable account of shooting in the mountains'.

6

Joined by the 'Assiniboine' Family, Burdened by Mr O'B

The three men, Milton, Cheadle, and Baptiste, travelled westwards with two carts and two horses. For most of the 155-mile journey towards Fort Pitt, Milton and the Métis drove the carts while Cheadle chose to walk. The land was generally gentle prairie undulations streaked with remnants of the winter snow, dotted with emerging blue flowers and clumps of trees growing on low hills. Baptiste proved to be an engaging, if garrulous, companion who entertained the others with his tales of the discovery of gold in the Rocky Mountains. Such accounts were entirely believable, but neither of the two Englishmen could quite accept his stories of the stones that rattled when shaken (the rattling apparently coming from diamonds trapped inside the stones), and of the lump of iron found by an Indian that was taken to a mountain top – only to grow to such a size that no man could pick it up. The iron was later shown actually to exist and turned out to be a meteorite, worshipped by the Cree and the Blackfeet as Pi-wa-pisk-oo – Cree for Iron Stone. Three years after Milton and Cheadle passed through the area, the 386lb stone was removed to the Royal Ontario Museum – an act leading to a twentieth-century war of words between Alberta and Saskatchewan as to who had the right to ownership. The matter was settled after a conference with the tribes concerned, and the meteorite ended up in the Provincial Museum of Alberta.

The worst obstacles on their journey proved to be the rivers. Usually swollen with melted snow, some were still surfaced with decaying ice. Where the ice could be broken, a raft was constructed and paddled across – usually by Cheadle. The raft was then hauled back across the river and used to transport Milton, who was then set to work building a fire for drying clothes and cooking, while Cheadle and Baptiste dragged the carts and luggage across. On one occasion, apart from a gap at the river's centre, the ice had remained solid enough to bear the weight of the men. The wheels were removed from one of the carts and pushed across the ice until it bridged the ice gap. With everything across, just as the 'bridge' was hauled on to the far bank, the ice broke up and was swept away with the current. The day, however, was not over. Cheadle noted tersely – 'Milton set the prairie on fire.'

A couple of days later, after having crossed another river, four Indians were seen approaching on horseback. The rum was hastily hidden, but the new arrivals turned out to be Gatchi Mokamarn (Big Knife), a frequent companion of The Hunter during the winter trapping expeditions, and three Wood Cree. All four were treated to a 'drop of grog' before two departed to hunt buffalo. Big Knife and the remaining Wood Cree joined the party overnight at Jackfish Lake (named after the fearsome pike that could be caught in its waters). Cheadle bartered a large lens he had used to concentrate the sun's rays when starting a fire, known as a 'burning glass', in exchange for a stone-carved pipe such as favoured by 'mountaineers' – men who lived and traded as fur trappers in the Rocky Mountains. Before setting off in the morning they were approached by a party of ten men led by two old Métis acquaintances – The Wolf and John Smith. They were on their way to Fort Pitt to take charge of Hudson's Bay Company barges that would be poled and towed back to Fort Carlton filled with furs, pemmican, and dried meat. All the party were in poor condition, having been given just six days supplies of pemmican and a small amount of gunpowder and musket balls. Their baggage was carried by dogs dragging 'travois' (Cheadle referred to them as 'travailles') – long poles attached to the dog's backs and held apart by crossbars. No food had been supplied for the dogs. Consequently, Cheadle and Baptiste were hard put to supply the greatly increased party with food. Fortunately, the air overhead was full of ducks and geese flying north, and the mating antics of the prairie grouse – massing in large groups and stamping their feet while rattling their tails and inflating their neck pouches – made them an easy target.

Fort Pitt was situated on a flat area of the north bank of the North Saskatchewan, and was overlooked by a low hill (bluff). The fort consisted of a few buildings surrounded by a 15-foot-high stockade and, being at a juncture of the Cree and the Blackfeet territories, was ideally situated for trading with the local tribes. Unfortunately, both tribes had a tendency to engage rapidly in conflict over anything from the most insignificant slight to outright murder. There had been the recent signing of a peace treaty between the two sides, but no one took it for granted, and there was a continual tension in the air. The onerous task of keeping the peace between the tribes in the interest of the Hudson's Bay Company fell to Louis Chastellaine (Cheadle spelled his name 'Chantelaine', and the Hudson's Bay Company had a further alternative – 'Chatelaine'). A Métis, he had been appointed to Fort Pitt as the postmaster in 1853, before being appointed as clerk-in-charge six years later. On the evening of Monday 20 April, Chastellaine entertained Milton and Cheadle to a supper of fresh meat and potatoes washed down by milk. The latter upset Cheadle's stomach, but he still managed to sleep 'like a top'.

The next morning, with Cheadle busy with numerous requests for his medical skills, Milton sent Baptiste to look at the Indian horses that were on offer from both the Blackfeet and the Cree camped in the area. Chastellaine persuaded Milton that Baptiste should be accompanied by a French-Assiniboine Métis named Louis Patenaude. The man's life was in a state of disarray. His youngest child – eleven-year-old Theresa – was extremely ill and was being looked after by Cheadle, but with no expectation of recovery. He had been involved in a drunken brawl with another Métis ('a notorious bully'), which had resulted in the other man's death and his own dismissal from the Hudson's Bay Company employment; and he had been maimed when a gun exploded as he was firing it, leaving him with just two fingers on the left hand. In view of the death in the brawl, Chastellaine had no option but to eject him from the fort, and was grateful that Milton could – at least in the short term – put the man's undoubted skills to good use. Cheadle approved of the arrangement. He spelled the man's name as 'Battenotte', and always referred to him as 'the Assiniboine' as he had been raised by that tribe and had all the appearance of a full-blood Indian. Sadly, however, Baptiste and Patenaude could not set out immediately as the young girl, Theresa, died that night. Consequently, Milton traded his Reilly hammer 12-bore shotgun with its beautiful damascened barrels for a horse supplied by Chastellaine. The horse remained within the security of the company's stable yard where it was joined by a number of other horses belonging to a party of Blackfeet Indians, newly arrived at the fort. Chastellaine knew from experience that the local Cree would not hesitate to steal the Blackfeet horses. The theft of horses had been continuing for some time on both sides despite the peace treaty and, on the following day, a rumour arrived at the fort that a Cree woman had been stabbed to death by the Blackfeet. The clerk-in-charge immediately prevailed upon the Blackfeet chief to leave the fort. Before they could depart, a lone Blackfeet arrived breathless and dressed only in a loincloth. He carried a message from the tribal camp urging their fellow Blackfeet to leave immediately. The situation was on the edge of disaster. Cheadle, however, was unresponsive to the threatening atmosphere and was 'ennuyeed' and 'tired of the slow life' at the fort. He was also pestered by both Métis and Indians for his opinion on the fragments of 'gold' they had found. Much to their disappointment these, inevitably, turned out to be sparkling splinters of mica or grains of granite. Eventually, however, much to his delight, accompanied by Milton, Baptiste, and Patenaude, and with their carts packed, they left Fort Pitt on the morning of 28 April. Baptiste had arranged to meet a party of Cree and Saulteaux Indians some distance from the fort to negotiate the sale of some horses (probably recently stolen from the Blackfeet). Patenaude went along to assist.

They had hardly reached a mile from the fort when a party of about twenty Indians rode up. Baptiste and Patenaude were soon at work. Two horses were each purchased for 'one gallon of mixture (watered down rum), forty trade balls (musket balls), 2 pints of powder (gunpowder), 2 yards tobacco (a lightweight cotton fabric), & a yard of red cloth'. The same, plus half a gallon of mixture, was paid for a 'weedy chestnut' and a snorting, fidgety, 'roarer'. With everyone seemingly happy with the purchases, and with the Indians disappearing over the horizon, Patenaude suggested that he would like to join the party as they crossed over the Rocky Mountains. Despite the damage to his hand, the Métis had proved both hard working and trustworthy, and so an agreement was made that he would be paid £3 for the first month, and £5 a month thereafter. He then left to make the necessary arrangements with his family, and with the intention of rejoining the party on the morrow. They had not gone far when, after hauling the carts out of a bog, Cheadle was thrown off the newly purchased chestnut. With the wind knocked out of him, it was decided to set up camp and they spent an unquiet night with loaded revolvers at hand and Baptiste on guard through the darkness. It was not at all unknown for the Indians to attempt to steal back the horses they had traded earlier in the day, so no one had a peaceful night's rest. Eventually, with the approaching light, Cheadle got up, relieved Baptiste on watch and lit the fire. The sun had not long been over the horizon when a young 13-year-old boy walked into the camp. It was Patenaude's son, and he announced that he would be joining his father on the journey west. Cheadle provided him with a couple of horses to help 'the Assiniboine' and his son return to the camp. Patenaude arrived at midday accompanied by his wife and son. He had decided that 'Mrs Assiniboine' (as Cheadle referred to her) would join them on the journey. A somewhat startled Milton and Cheadle were, at first, reluctant to take on two 'supernumeraries', predicting problems with the supply of food when they encountered the mountains ahead. However, Patenaude's undoubted skills weighed heavily in the balance, and both men agreed that the boy and the woman could join them. Those skills were soon clearly evident. While passing through a country of gently rolling hills, scattered birch and aspen woods, gentle streams, and stretches of prairie, they again came across the wide Saskatchewan at Snake Hills. At this point it was necessary to cross the river to reach its southern bank, which carried a well-worn horse track. The problem was, however, that there were no trees in the immediate neighbourhood to provide timber with which to build a raft. Patenaude set to work immediately constructing a flimsy canoe of buffalo hide stretched over a frame of green willow. Six feet long, the vessel was 2 feet in the beam with a draft of 1½ feet. First across was Baptiste, ferrying the baggage. When this was completed, he was joined by the bulky Cheadle whose considerable weight almost proved to be disastrous. In the fading light, the canoe not only began to leak, but began to sink slowly, the water creeping higher and higher up the sides. Within feet of the southern bank, the frail craft was on the verge of capsizing and Cheadle scrambled ashore, just in time to avoid an unwelcome soaking. With Milton brought across with little difficulty, it was decided that it was too dark to continue with the ferrying, and Baptiste was sent back to the northern bank with a measure of rum in reward for his and Patenaude's work. The carts, horses and the rest of the party would cross in the morning.

The subsequent crossing the following day proved to be a similar mixture of initiative and luck. A cart shaft was tied to the tail of a horse, and the horse was then led into the water as the cart was pushed in from behind. Being entirely made of wood, the carts floated in an upright position and the horses towed them across without difficulty. The southern shore, however, provided its own problem. Once the carts were loaded, it was discovered that the bank was too steep for the horses to haul their load to the top. The answer was to put a horse between the cart shafts and then, again, hitch another horse's tail to one of the shafts. To control the horses (particularly the horse at risk of injury when pulling with its tail) the two lightest members of the party – Milton and 'The Boy' – rode 'postilion' as the remainder gathered at the rear of the cart and pushed it up the slope. Their problems did not end there. Once the track had been gained, they could clearly see the red glow and heavy black clouds of prairie fires at several points on the near horizon. They had not travelled far when they encountered wide swathes of land blackened by the fires as it had passed over the area. With no pasture to feed the horses, they were forced to continue until they found a site to camp on marshy ground, which also provided poor but adequate nourishment for the animals. By now short of food themselves, a duck hunt was organised. It brought in not just wild fowl, but also their eggs. Milton and Cheadle were very particular in selecting the eggs they intended to eat. They were shocked, however, when they saw Baptiste's and the Patenaude family's delight in coming across eggs containing a developed duckling. The contents were lifted out by a leg or wing and dropped whole into their mouths, 'as we should eat asparagus'. Six days later, after a journey accompanied by bitterly cold winds and a snowfall that extinguished the prairie fires, they arrived in sight of Fort Edmonton, high on a bluff on the north side of the Saskatchewan. They had known they were getting close to the fort when Baptiste and Patenaude had a wash and put on their best clothing. Apparently, it was important to create a 'swell appearance' upon their arrival. They did not have to wait long before a barge came across the river to pick up Milton and Cheadle while the rest of the party brought across the horses, carts, and baggage.

The Hudson's Bay Company fort was an impressive feature in that part of British North America. Surrounded by an 18-foot high wooden wall and guarded by four watchtowers, the fort contained several buildings including a church, a blacksmith's forge, a carpenter's workshop, and a windmill. Its largest building, the chief factor's house, had been constructed in 1842 by the then chief factor, John Rowand. A hugely unpopular man, Rowand had once appalled a visiting clergyman who pointed out that one of Rowand's men appeared to be ill. The chief factor replied: 'Any man who is not dead after three days sickness is not sick at all.' When Rowand dropped dead himself during a confrontation with his men, there were few mourners and his body was taken to Fort Pitt for burial. The corpse was disinterred after a while and boiled to remove the bones, which were then taken to Montreal for re-interment. A legend grew that the boiled flesh was taken by local Cree women and used to make soap. The four-storey building erected by Rowand remained the largest building in western British North America for several years.

The chief factor greeting Milton and Cheadle's arrival at Fort Edmonton was of a wholly different nature. The red-haired Richard Charles Hardisty's father had fought against Napoleon at Waterloo and had served the Hudson's Bay Company as a chief factor for many years. His mother was part-Scottish, part-Indian. Trained at the Company's Red River Academy, Richard Hardisty remained in the Red River district as assistant post master before being sent to Cumberland House as clerk-in-charge. It only took a year to impress his superiors, who sent him first to Carlton House before promoting him to chief trader. In 1862, at the age of 31, he was promoted to acting chief factor for the District of Saskatchewan and was moved to Fort Edmonton. Having made Milton and Cheadle at home in his huge house (which, in addition to accommodation had offices, a meat store, a large hall for social events, a kitchen and cellar) Hardisty suggested that they might like to take part in a bear hunt the following day. Five bears had attacked a herd of horses belonging to the priest at the nearby community of St Albert (referred to by Cheadle as 'St Albans'). Two men were also attacked – both narrowly escaped, with one avoiding death by throwing his coat at the bear, which proceeded to tear it to shreds. The opportunity was taken up, but before they could retire, Cheadle went to check on the condition of the baggage they had left in the care of Baptiste and Patenaude. He was not best pleased to find both men had broken into his supply of rum and were 'very screwed'.

If the first day at the fort had ended on a sour note, the next morning proved to be no better. Baptiste had been told to ensure that Milton and Cheadle were up early, but had overslept. Cheadle tried to wake Milton, but the viscount refused to get out of bed and felt the rough edge of Cheadle's tongue. Eventually, having intended to start on the road before breakfast, they decided to use the delay both to join Hardisty over the meal, and to calm their frayed tempers. After an easy, pleasant journey they arrived at St Albert, a community of about twenty houses, half a mile from a lake. Cheadle was greatly impressed with the place, considering it the 'most civilised place since Fort Garry'. They soon encountered the priest, thirty-six year-old Father Albert Lacombe – the same priest who had caused the reaction about 'sickness' from John Rowand. Father Lacombe came from French stock and, after being ordained a priest in 1849, entered the Order of Missionary Oblates of Mary Immaculate six years later. The Oblates were a nineteenth-century version of the medieval friars, living and working in the communities in which they carried out their missionary duties. Father Lacombe had earned a high reputation among the Cree, the Blackfeet, and the Métis. He was said to speak the Cree language better than the Métis, and was later to translate the New Testament into the Indian's language. Nevertheless, it was with some disappointment that the priest told his visitors that no date had been fixed for the bear hunt. In consolation, however, he invited Milton and Cheadle to his house for lunch. After smoking a pipe of birch root, they sat down to a meal of soup, meat, potatoes, and turnips, followed by pancakes and sugar. Beneath portraits of the Pope and the Bishop of Red River, and a large image of angels rescuing various saints from the fires of purgatory, Father Lacombe told them of the convent attached to the building where the nuns taught the local girls in French (the boys were sent to Fort Edmonton where they were taught in English), and of the construction of a new mill nearby that was driven by a horse sauntering around in circles. Father Lacombe had also built a 200-foot bridge across the nearby River Sturgeon. Every able-bodied man turned up to help, and the priest rewarded them by granting them free passage across the bridge for life – everyone else had to pay a penny. Milton considered the priest to be 'intelligent' and 'agreeable', but Cheadle – brought up in a Church of England vicarage – thought it worthy of note that, having refused to bury an unconfessed man, Father Lacombe accepted a fine black horse from the widow in exchange for a grant of absolution.

At Fort Edmonton that evening, Milton and Cheadle were joined by Hardisty, who introduced them to Andrew Pambrun (referred to by Cheadle as 'Pemberton') and Aulay Macaulay. The latter was in charge of Jasper House – a trading post on the Athabasca River, south-east of Edmonton – and was at the fort to collect supplies. He, and his predecessors at the post had all experienced the perils of running short of food during the winter months. The occupants were expected to camp in the nearby woods during the summer in the hope of being able to shoot as many moose as possible to provide for their winter existence. However, none had survived a winter without eating his horse. Macaulay had even stocked up on squirrels to provide cold weather sustenance. Pambrun, the son of a French-Canadian chief factor of the Hudson's Bay Company, had followed his father into the company and had also achieved the position of chief factor. He was responsible for the 'brigade' of men and barges travelling eastwards towards the company post at Norway House, on the Nelson River, in Manitoba. Ever conscious of the rarity of French-Canadians serving in the higher ranks of the company, and despite have a French-speaking father and an Indian mother who spoke only her own language and French, Pambrun perfected his English and always claimed that he only spoke 'very poor French'. Of greater interest to Milton and Cheadle was the fact that Pambrun had frequently passed through the Rocky Mountains using the Athabascan Pass and Jasper House. Although far to the south of their own intended route, they were keen to learn what they could from the experienced traveller. Pambrun explained that he used dogsleds as his usual means of transport. The sledge he used was 8 feet long and 1 foot wide and was expected to carry 400lb of supplies made up of buffalo tongues, the biscuit-like cakes known as galettes, buffalo bladders full of grease (for cooking), and bags of pemmican. Once that was secured, provisions for the dogs had to be added, with an axe, a kettle, a change of 'duffels' (thick, warm, clothing), and spare moccasins.

Hardisty entertained the group with stories of the clashes between a local French Roman Catholic priest and a visiting Methodist minister – Thomas Woolsey (Cheadle calls him 'Wolsey'). The priest spoke no English, while Woolsey knew not a word of French. Latin was tried, but Woolsey wasn't up to the challenge. Consequently, the knowledge of a few mangled Cree words that they shared in common proved to be the only means of communication – much to the hilarity of those present during the exchanges. The chief problem was that when the priest, or the minister, converted an Indian, his fellow Christian would promptly reconvert him to their side. This, in turn, provoked a retaliatory baptism leading, once again, to another reconversion. Before long, the poor convert had no idea whether he was a Roman Catholic or a Methodist. The situation was brought to an end when the pair erupted into a violent squabble over who should say grace at dinners. At this stage, Hardisty stepped in and demanded that they gave grace on alternate attendances – if they could not agree on such a scheme, they would have to leave the fort. Faced with eviction if their behaviour did not improve, the fort's population was able to enjoy a continued, if surly, silence.

Over the next days, as the opportunities for the bear hunt gradually fizzled out, other visitors to the fort were encountered. Several were gold miners, including Timolean ('Charlie') Love from Kentucky. He had crossed the Rocky Mountains via the

Athabascan Pass and was now working at White Mud Creek, 50 miles west of the fort. He told Cheadle that the roads were 'pretty bad in the mountains, and worse on the other side'. Nevertheless, the effort had been worth it as Love and his fellow miners claimed to have found £90 each already that season. For some, it had taken two weeks, for others, just four days. Gold could be sold at $17 an ounce, and Love claimed he had done so well as a result of searching mainly for gold dust, which usually provided a steady supply, rather than the random search for nuggets. The miners also told tales of a man named Perry (there are several contenders for the origin of the following story, but none can be identified with certainty). According to Cheadle, Perry was a 'downright down-east Yankee' – in other words, someone for whom nothing could be the best in the world, unless it was American. Apparently, intending to get rich from gold mining, Perry had crossed the continent from eastern America, through the Rockies to California, pushing all his belongings in a wheelbarrow. Having failed to strike it rich, he made his way to Minnesota with nothing but a gun, some ammunition, and the clothes he stood up in. There he borrowed an axe, chopped down a tree and hacked the trunk into a canoe, which he used to paddle 600 miles down the Red River to Fort Garry. He set out for Fort Carlton and eventually crossed the Rocky Mountains through the Athabascan Pass. On his way through, he met Andrew Pambrun at Jasper House. The chief factor was so impressed that he described Perry as 'the most determined fellow he ever knew.' Having staked a claim west of the Rocky Mountains in the Cariboo region, Perry stormed off after discovering that although he was finding gold, it was a tiny amount compared to his neighbours. He had not been seen since.

When not being entertained by new acquaintances and their succession of anecdotes, Milton and Cheadle succumbed in a very minor way to gold fever. Under instruction from Hardisty and Baptiste, they used their tin plates to 'pan' for gold and succeeded in obtaining a very small amount of the precious gold dust with a large proportion of sediment. On their return to the fort, the two Englishmen were so keen to find exactly how much gold they had obtained that they used the 'mercury amalgamation' method to retrieve it. This entailed washing the combined gold dust and sediment through with mercury resulting in the gold dust combining with the liquid metal to form an amalgam. Then the mercury was burned off, normally using a long handled iron spoon, leaving just the gold behind. However, in their eagerness to get a glimpse of their precious metal, they used their tin plates directly over the fire. The result was 'bad manipulation', the red-hot plates spilled, and all the tiny flakes of gold disappeared for ever into the flames – thanks to their 'stupidity'. Even the loss of hard-won gold dust was as nothing compared to the disaster that happened on the evening of Sunday 22 May.

As the shadows lengthened that day, Milton and Cheadle were taking a slow stroll around the fort when they were approached by a tall, thinly built, unshaven man of about 60 wearing a long alpaca coat ('of ecclesiastical cut'), a 'black wide-awake' (a wide-brimmed hat with a low crown), and 'fustian' (made of heavy woven cotton) trousers. He wore 'high-lows' (footwear – too high for shoes, and too low for boots) tied with string, and carried a substantial, rough-hewn stick. Advancing upon Milton, and speaking with an Irish accent, the long-faced man with a prominent nose and 'retreating mouth' ('almost destitute of teeth'), introduced himself as 'Mr Eugene Francis O'Beirne' (Cheadle spelled his name 'O'Byrne', but he became known to all and sundry as 'Mr O'B'). Speaking in a rapid manner that employed frequent Latin phrases and allowed no pause for interruption, O'Beirne explained that he was a grandson of the well-known Bishop Thomas O'Beirne who, coincidentally, had been chaplain to the 4th Earl Fitzwilliam – the great-grandfather of Milton. Mr O'B said he was also a 'Cambridge man' and, consequently, he was delighted to meet two equally well-educated Cambridge men with whom he could have an intelligent conversation. After impressing them both with his knowledge of Cambridge University and a succession of acquaintances familiar to all of them, he proceeded to inflict his life's story upon them. Apparently, on leaving Cambridge, Mr O'B served for a year or so as the editor of a newspaper in Lahore, India, before moving to the United States of America where he settled in Louisiana as secretary to a cotton planter. Unfortunately, the American Civil War broke out and, much to his horror, Mr O'B was elected as captain of the Home Guard. Managing to flee north of the combat, and with the recommendation of the Bishop of New York, he obtain employment as a Professor of Classics at Jackson College, Columbia, Tennessee. However, the financial effects of the war led to the college closing down. Mr O'B then made his way to Fort Garry to work at another school, which promptly 'broke up'. Having made his way west to Portage La Prairie, and declaring that he wanted to make his way to British Columbia, Archdeacon Cochrane sent him towards the Rocky Mountains with a Métis – but his new companion ate all the rations and abandoned him at Fort Carlton. From there, with the help of Richard Hardisty, he obtained passage in the Hudson's Bay Company boats to Fort Edmonton, a good deed for which the newly installed governor of the company, Alexander Dallas, charged Hardisty £16 10s. The combative Methodist minister, Thomas Woolsey, took pity on Mr O'B and gave him accommodation over the winter. By spring, however, the former editor-secretary-professor and would-be gold miner, was utterly destitute and living in a squalid miner's shack near the fort.

When more became known about Mr O'B many years later, he turned out to have been born in County Longford in Ireland sometime around 1809–11, thus making him about 53 years old when he met Milton and Cheadle. At about the age of 16, he was sent to St Patrick's College, Maynooth, County Kildare, to study for the priesthood, only to be expelled on the grounds that he was 'a nuisance by his idleness, malignant fabrications, and general irregularity'. He then spent about six years at Trinity College, Dublin, but left without graduating, having completed just two pamphlets attacking St Patrick's – publications that the *British Critic and Quarterly Theological Review* considered to have been written 'not only in the temper of exasperation which may have been inspired by a sense of wrong, but also, for the most part, in a style of dictatorial arrogance, and sometimes, of coarse, but vapid and feeble jocularity'. The *Dublin Review* thought the first pamphlet to be 'bigoted and unfair in the last degree' and the second 'all insolence, bluster, and abuse, from the beginning to the end'. The attacks on his old college continued for the next three years while travelling around England giving anti-Roman Catholic lectures. At Northampton, he claimed he had been expelled from

St Patrick's 'for reading the scriptures'. On another occasion, at Thetford, Norfolk, he packed the town hall with drunken youths who drowned out the speaker, the Reverend Charles Brigham, and ignored the mayor's threat to have him removed. When the speaker left the hall in defeat, Mr O'B harangued the audience and 'notwithstanding the presence of a number of females, continued for some time to indulge in the most obscene and disgusting language'. At Worcester, in 1837, he claimed that, when in the confessional, both married and unmarried women were asked 'obscene, licentious, and disgusting questions', and had the answers 'wrung from them'. In 1842 he managed to be accepted by St John's College, Cambridge, transferring to Clare College a year later, but left 'struck off' without graduating. It is believed that he moved to Louisiana sometime in the 1850s, arriving in Minnesota in 1861 where he tried to obtain a teaching position or ordination into the Episcopal Church – but failed in both. He arrived at the Red River Settlement in September of that year where his story is taken up by John McDougall in his 1896 account of his travels – *Saddle, Sled and Snowshoe: Pioneering on the Saskatchewan in the Sixties*. McDougall was the son of the Methodist, Reverend George McDougall, who had removed the 'Iron Stone' held in great reverence by the Indians. His version – since confirmed by other sources – did not start off very well with regards to Mr O'B, whom he described as a person 'whom I do not feel justified by naming at length'. McDougall explained how Mr O'B, having failed to find employment as a teacher, had managed to insinuate himself into the social circle of Bishop David Anderson, who took it upon himself to provide Mr O'B with food, accommodation, and spending money.

Soon known as 'The Irish Schoolmaster', it was widely believed that Mr O'B had attended the university at Oxford (as had the bishop). He claimed to have been in India and had a great skill in convincing everyone that he not only knew people with whom they were familiar, but also many leading public figures in England. He also tried to convince a large number of people that, if he could borrow some money from them, he intended studying for the clergy as 'his ordination at the hands of the bishop was certain'. Nevertheless, his efforts in that direction soon failed and he took to reducing his expenses by calling on a succession of clergymen in the area as a means of obtaining food and shelter. When this source dried up, he raised money for a room at the Royal Hotel by teaching children for an hour a day – only failing to turn up at the requisite hour. McDougall encountered him for the first time at a dinner with the bishop. They next met when Mr O'B limped into Fort Garry with a frostbitten ear – caused through his wearing a 'miserable apology for a fur cap'. Shortly afterwards, he came across the Irishman loudly berating a man 'in the outrageous tone he ordinarily assumed when speaking to servants'. The man had refused to play the fiddle for him. It urned out that the person in question was a cultured gentleman who had just picked the instrument up out of curiosity – and was certainly no fiddler.

Mr O'B was also noted for his loud disdain for Americans when he was in solely British company. With international incidents threatening to bring the possibility of conflict between the two nations ever closer, he would noisily demand that the United Kingdom should refrain from going to war – 'Britannia would only soil her knuckles in hitting Uncle Sam.' In private, however, he very quietly requested that McDougall refrain from repeating his views on Americans as he 'did not want his ribs tickled with a Bowie knife'. Having expressed an interest in increasing his opportunities for finding a livelihood, Mr O'B was given money and letters of introduction by Bishop Anderson. He was only away for a few weeks before he returned having outraged gentlemen by demanding in an 'imperatively insolent' tone that they should 'fill his tumbler', humming loudly to himself at a Roman Catholic funeral, and getting into 'royal rows' when servants refused to clean his boots. Before long, all and sundry were praying that he would 'relieve them of his company'. On his return, the Archdeacon gasped with 'unfeigned dismay' – 'You cannot mean he has returned!' Unsure what to do, Mr O'B simply established himself in the Archdeacon's private rooms with the true tenant and his family left to stare in stony silence at the intruder. Relief came when Mr O'B talked with a group of men heading westwards towards the Cariboo goldfields. Suddenly, the same urge to seek his fortune fell upon him, and he determined to head in the same direction. On his departure, the kindly bishop held out his hand, but Mr O'B refused to take it shouting 'Never, never! No, sir! No sir! No sir! You have deceived me, you have deceived me, I shall see you no more!' McDougall noted that 'It is probable that these words were the most gratifying the bishop had ever heard from O'B.'

Having made his way west of Fort Garry to Portage La Prairie, Mr O'B managed to worm his way into the home of Archdeacon Cochran, a clergyman described by a company historian as 'a man of gigantic form and of amazing bonhomie'. It was not long, however, before the archdeacon was urgently negotiating a passage westwards for Mr O'B with a section of the 'Overlanders' – a large group of men and one woman intent on reaching the Cariboo goldfields. The particular section Mr O'B joined as 'chaplain' was led by the artist William Hind, the English-born brother of Henry Hind, a geological surveyor who had taken part in several expeditions on the Plains and along the important river valleys. His artistic skills, which produced the first illustrated account of a journey westwards from Fort Garry, were abundant, his toleration of incompetence was limited. Accordingly, the 'useless and troublesome' Mr O'B found himself abandoned at Fort Carlton. He next found employment as a boathand on board one of a fleet of company boats heading up the Saskatchewan to Fort Edmonton – only to be set ashore at Fort Pitt thanks to his 'insolently overbearing manner'. He still managed, however, to join a cart train heading for Fort Edmonton where he found refuge with the Methodist Reverend Woolsey. Woolsey soon observed that his new guest 'lived in a chronic state of bodily fear. Beside the wild animals, of which wolves and grizzly bears were the object of his special dread, he stood in much fear of the Indians'. Eventually, after the household had been increased by the arrival of John McDougall, two friends – Messrs Steinhauer and Erasmus – arrived en route to Fort Edmonton, Woolsey took McDougall on one side and said 'John, I am about tired of Mr O'B. Could you not take him to Edmonton and leave him there. You might join this party now going there.'

McDougall jumped at the chance to relieve Woolsey and himself of Mr O'B and, within a few hours, he had joined Steinhauer and Erasmus with Mr O'B wrapped up warmly on a cabriole sledge pulled by dogs and with himself directing the driving from the rear. The route plan was to take the party down the still frozen

Saskatchewan – a plan that went well until they came across a section where the surface ice disappeared under 1½ feet of flood water, its own surface frozen with half an inch of ice. There was nothing for it but to drive on through the flood and reach the opposite bank. For McDougall, it was a precarious passage, often wading in the freezing water while fighting to keep the sledge and its passenger upright. The situation was not helped by Mr O'B loudly swearing and blaspheming while shouting that McDougall was deliberately trying to tip him into the water. The idea suddenly had a great attraction for McDougall and, irritated beyond control, he rolled Mr O'B off the sledge and told him to make his own way to the river bank. When the dogs and the sledge were secured ashore, McDougall looked back and saw Mr O'B standing up to his knees in the water pathetically trying to fend off lumps of ice with a stick. Taking pity on him, McDougall waded back in and dragged his shivering passenger out while telling him that he 'would not stand any more swearing'. After two days, the flood water subsided and allowed them to return to the river ice. There were more delays with flood water and a succession of outrages from McDougall's passenger. On one occasion, in an attempt to lighten the load, McDougall was about to throw off a soaked, undressed, hide only to find that Mr O'B had suddenly decided that he had a special affection for the object and demanded that the heavy, and valueless, hide be retained. McDougall responded by ordering Mr O'B to walk on up the river ice while he repacked the sledge – minus the hide. The task done, and on catching up with his passenger, Mr O'B suddenly began to pull the stores off the sledge in search of the pelt. Unable to find it, Mr O'B – according to McDougall – 'began to rave at me, using the foulest and most blasphemous language'. McDougall looked directly at his raging passenger and said, slowly and deliberately, 'Get in, or I will leave you here.' At this, Mr O'B climbed on board the sledge, wrapped himself in blankets, and sat sullenly refusing to apologise to the gravely offended McDougall.

Revenge was not long in coming. Just as they were within hours of reaching Fort Edmonton, McDougall saw a wide crack in the ice with water flowing fast beneath. He steered the sledge towards the crack, saw his dogs leap across safely on to the far side followed by the forepart of the sledge. At this moment, he ordered his dogs to stop and lie down while he hauled on one of the rear sledge lines, taking the weight of the sledge as it lost its momentum. Mr O'B suddenly found himself with the rear part of the sledge over the deep, rushing, water. He could not step out of the sledge as the ice would not take his weight at the edge, and the only thing stopping the sledge from falling backwards into the water was McDougall hauling back on the rope. Mr O'B, clutching the sides of the sledge in terror, cried out 'For God's sake, John, what are you going to do?' McDougall stayed silent for a moment or two before replying, 'Well, Mr O'B, are you ready now to apologise for, and take back the foul language you, without reason, heaped on me a little while since?' There was no delay in Mr O'B's reply, and even a herd of charging buffaloes could not had stopped his outpouring of fulsome apology. When he had drained himself of expressions of regret, McDougall allowed the rope he was holding to slip a little causing a squeal of terror from Mr O'B who, in response, promised never to misbehave in such a manner again. At this, McDougall ordered his dogs up and set off once more with a much subdued passenger. Just as the ground began to rise towards the fort, McDougall ordered Mr O'B off the sledge, and left him holding his baggage while he continued up the hill and through the fort's gate, delighted to be rid of 'the old fraud'. That evening, the chief factor, Richard Hardisty, said to McDougall, 'So, you brought Mr O'B to Edmonton. You will have to pay ten shillings for every day he remains in the fort.'

'Excuse me, sir,' replied McDougall, 'I brought him to the foot of the hill, down at the landing, and left him there. If he comes into the fort, I am not responsible.' McDougall would later be ordained as a Methodist minister, appointed as a commissioner at the Department of Indian Affairs and, against the general opinion expressed by the local press, supported the Indians in their desire to wear ceremonial costumes when taking part in sun dances and other traditional events.

Mr O'B, on the other hand, managed to find a space in a miner's shanty outside the fort but, when the miners departed for their seasonal search after gold, he left the lonely accommodation for fear that bears might come to eat the willow shoots growing just outside. He managed to borrow a buffalo hide lodge, which was erected for him, only to have it blown down. Utterly incapable of putting it back up, he made his way to the fort's stockade where he found a sturdy Red River cart. Pulling the collapsed lodge over the cart, he camped underneath its shelter, unaware that the cart belonged to two new arrivals – Viscount Milton and Walter Cheadle.

Discovering that the newcomers were on their way through the Rocky Mountains, he chose his moment to introduce himself, and 'nearly knocked [Cheadle's] head off with Latin quotations'. Cheadle, nevertheless, thought him to 'a great humbug and ne'er do well' in addition to being a 'dead weight'. Mr O'B soon made it plain that he would like to accompany them in their travels to the west. For the next two weeks, Mr O'B tried every means that he could to ingratiate himself with Milton and Cheadle. His most novel tactic was to turn up every day as Cheadle tended to the fort's sick. Claiming to afflicted by a number of ailments, he continued with the charade for several days before admitting that he was really only looking for further opportunities to put forward his case in favour of joining the party as they headed for the Rocky Mountains. However, much to his shock and dismay, Cheadle assured him that he really *was* ill and that he would have to swallow a very large dose of rhubarb and magnesia – a particularly potent laxative. Eventually, after much discussion, usually centred around the fact that Mr O'B had studied at Cambridge University, and ignoring the fact that Cheadle considered him 'the most helpless fellow in the world' and 'an ungrateful dog' – and both of them knowing that 'it would be foolish to burden ourselves with and extra mouth' – Milton and Cheadle agreed that they 'could not find the heart to refuse him'.

Both Baptiste and Patenaude, almost certainly having heard about Mr O'B from other sources, came close to rebellion when they heard the news. Mr O'B, on the other hand, assured Milton and Cheadle that they had acted wisely. After all, he would be useful on the trail, had not asked for any wages, and had only asked to join them for their own interest. Having sold the carts, and in addition to their well-tried horses, they assembled a collection of pack horses, some of which they would ride, others which carried the baggage. Mr O'B was given a horse and saddle by some of the men at the fort, along with a gift of £12 (contributors included Milton and Cheadle), but their new companion rather spoiled the moment by asking Cheadle if he would take the horse back to the stockade and quietly exchange it for a better one. Cheadle refused and 'felt rather disgusted' at the mean-spirited suggestion. They left the fort in the early evening of 3 June, in fine, hot weather. They also left slightly embarrassed considering that Milton's father was the sixth richest man in England. Their bill at the fort came to £23 3s 4d – and all they could muster between them was £23. 'Not a sixpence between us,' noted Cheadle, predicting 'Starvation in Cariboo!'

7

Bears, Mosquitoes, a Forest Fire and the Athabasca

Over millions of years, strong-flowing rivers have cut their way through the towering Rocky Mountains, creating passes that allowed human passage between east and west. Several had been used by the tribes as trade routes for thousands of years, others were too dangerous. With the arrival of the fur trading companies, the passes were obvious targets for the transportation of furs, skins, stores and supplies, from source to market. By the time Milton and Cheadle arrived, the Peace, Leather (Yellowhead), Athabasca, Howse, Vermillion, Kicking Horse, and Simpson passes were all in regular use. Only one of the passes, however, met the requirements of the reason for their journey across British North America – only the Leather Pass provided a direct route between the Cariboo goldfields and the east of the country. The pass had received its name from the fur companies using it to transport moose hides to the east – mainly for the manufacture of moccasins. Although in use previously, it was first surveyed in 1820. Amongst the surveying party was a French Métis named Pierre Bostonais who set up a cache – a collecting place for stores and skins (sometimes in a raised cabin to keep the contents safe from animals). Bostonais' nickname was *Tête Jaune* (Yellow Head) and the site became known as *Tête Jaune Cache*. Gradually, the English version of his name began to spread eastwards until, by 1859, the whole pass was named The Yellowhead Pass.

The chief factor of Fort Edmonton, with his officers, had tried to dissuade the two Englishmen from using the Yellowhead Pass.

Hardisty stressed that the early season would catch the rivers en route in full spate with the melting of the winter's snow. Deaths resulting from attempts to cross the rivers were commonplace and voyageurs from the Hudson's Bay Company had abandoned the route as a link between the Athabasca and the Fraser rivers as a consequence of the many casualties – particularly on the raging Fraser. Milton and Cheadle also spoke to a French Métis, André Cardinal, who had escorted the Overlander parties through the Yellowhead Pass. Some of his advice was useful, but most was insubstantial and contradictory and, even when added to that of the company's officers, failed to deter them from their initial decision – it was to be the Yellowhead Pass.

Although the proximity to the goldfields remained the key influence on their decision, there was also the fact that the Overlanders had gone through the pass during the late summer and early autumn of the previous year. Inevitably, with so many people on the move together, the trail they had left would still be evident and easy for Baptiste and Patenaude to follow.

With little chance of resupply along the route, the party of seven – Milton, Cheadle, Baptiste, Patenaude ('The Assiniboine'), Mrs Assiniboine, The Boy, and Mr O'B – required six horses, The Boy riding behind Patenaude or Mrs Assiniboine. The remaining horses carried, amongst them, two 100lb sacks of flour, four 90lb bags of pemmican, and a supply of tea, salt, and tobacco. They also had to carry a 40lb bag of pemmican and a small amount of tea and tobacco given to Mr O'B by men at the fort to ensure that they were finally rid of him. Unfortunately, they also departed with a degree of simmering discord. Even before they had left the fort, Baptiste and Patenaude both expressed their dislike for Mr O'B – and he was not long in retaliating. During the final hours of preparation, Mr O'B approached Milton and Cheadle with a serious face and a high level of urgency. Speaking in a conspiratorial tone he (according to Milton) said, 'My lord, and Dr Cheadle, I am sure you will thank me for a communication which will enable you to escape the greatest danger. I have been credibly informed that this "Assiniboine" – the man you have engaged – is a cold-blooded murderer, a villain of the deepest dye, who has been excommunicated by the priest, and is avoided by the bravest half-breeds.' An attempt at reassurance failed. 'What! You don't mean to tell me that you really intend to trust your lives with such a man?' A further attempt at reassurance failed. 'Then, in the name of your families, I beg to enter my most solemn protest against the folly of such a proceeding.' Although still intending to join them on their journey to the west, he remained convinced that they would all 'fall victims to the bloodthirsty Assiniboine'. With the fort some short distance behind them, Mr O'B soon began to show symptoms of distress at the possibility of not just being murdered by Patenaude – but also of being eaten by bears. Even on the first day, he tried to counter this fear by retreating further and further behind the remainder of the party, causing an almost universal irritation when they were delayed in waiting for him to catch up. Two days later, he was some distance behind the group when he heard the loud – and close – growl of a bear. Mr O'B instantly fled to catch up with the rest while Patenaude rose from his hiding place shaking with glee. That night, Cheadle wrote in his notebook,

O'Byrne's assistance is nil; most helpless fellow I ever saw; frightened of a horse, & shews very little disposition to help in anything without I ask for it. Tells the men to do little things for him, as if they were his servants & he an emperor. Does not even attempt to pack his own horse. I fear trouble with the men on his account. He is the greatest coward I ever saw.

Four days after leaving the fort, the party arrived at Lake St Anne, a 'pretty' lake surrounded by dense forests. The main sustenance for the approximately thirty houses was the fish caught from the lake. These were white-fleshed members of the salmon family, sometimes known as 'lake herrings'. Farming, on the other hand, was restricted to a few open spaces cleared with great difficulty in the closely packed woods. Before the arrival of the European fur traders, the lake had been named 'Lake of the Great Spirit' or 'God's Lake', but the Hudson's Bay Company, possibly because of a legend that the lake contained a monster, changed the name to 'Devil's Lake'. The name was changed again by an energetic French Roman Catholic priest who not only built a mission, but also renamed the lake *Lac Ste Anne* after the patron saint of the French

Métis. The local Indians may have known more than is realised. In the late nineteenth century, Christian pilgrimages to the site began, which have continued into the twenty-first century.

Milton and Cheadle paid a visit to the company's local officer, Scotsman Colin Fraser, who not only greeted them warmly, but also provided a welcome meal of fish, potatoes, and milk. Fraser had been with the company for thirty-eight years, for part of which time his talent with the bagpipes obtained for him the position of piper to George Simpson, the governor of the company. However, for reasons undisclosed, Fraser was eventually sent to the lonely company post at Jasper House, where he lived in general isolation for seventeen years. When Simpson closed the post in 1857, Fraser was transferred to Lac Ste Anne. During the discussion around the table, Fraser assured his guests that, although they would be travelling through Blackfeet country, they would not be at risk from the Indians. According to him, in his many years of service in the region, he never knew of an Englishman being killed or injured by them. Several Americans on the other hand, had lost their lives. Fraser illustrated the point by a story in which he had been involved. When visited by the then Fort Edmonton chief factor, John Rowand, they went out into the country for the day. Resting at noon, they were taken by surprise by a large band of about 200 yelling Blackfeet wearing war-paint and rushing down upon them. Rowand jumped to his feet, held up his hand, and cried 'Stop – you villains!' The Blackfeet promptly stopped in their tracks, just long enough for one of the chiefs to recognise Rowand. After much apologising and other expressions of regret that they had 'taken them for Yankees', Rowand and Fraser spent the night in secure and peaceful company with the Blackfeet.

The following day, Milton and Cheadle's intention to depart was hindered by the horses straying overnight and having to be rounded up. The job took most of the morning, and so it was decided to wait until after lunch before setting off. Milton went for a swim in the lake while Cheadle visited Fraser again to give him some advice on the medicines suitable for his medicine chest. When he returned, he found Baptiste requesting to spend the rest of the day visiting some members of his family who he had not seen for twenty years. This was agreed with reluctance, and only on the grounds that to have refused permission would have seemed unnecessarily churlish. As a consequence, both Milton and Cheadle returned to Fraser's house where they had a drink of milk with a bonus lesson in fly making. Using worsted woollen yarn, silk, and speckled duck's feathers, Fraser had them producing flies that Cheadle considered to resemble 'no live fly I had seen', but, nevertheless, assured them that Rocky Mountain trout would find them irresistible. While they laboured over their fishing lures, Fraser told them that, in his time with the company, he had spent twenty-seven years in charge of posts, but had never been promoted, and his pay was a paltry £100 a year. He had not visited Fort Garry for thirty years, and the nearest he had come to 'civilisation' in the past fifteen years had been a visit to Fort Edmonton. His main problem was that he lacked 'interest' (the social contacts needed for advancement). Cheadle was sympathetic, but felt that the answer was simple – Fraser should have married a chief trader's daughter.

While the fly making continued, and the conversation continued to flow, Milton suddenly 'had a severe symptom'. After returning to their camp, he had 'two more not quite so strong'. Whether or not these 'symptoms' were full-blown fits is not clear. Still very 'seedy' the following morning he, with Cheadle, called again upon Fraser who served them a meal of fish, potatoes, and barley flour galette, which they 'enjoyed amazingly'. Fraser also told them of the time when the Palliser Expedition passed through his area during the British North American Exploring Expedition of 1857 to 1861. The Irishman, Captain John Palliser, led a small – but highly successful – expedition investigating the passes through the Rocky Mountains. Fraser particularly remembered a fellow Scotsman, Dr John Hector, the expedition's surgeon, botanist, and geologist. Hector was the cause of one of the expedition's most enduring legends. While investigating one of the passes, he was kicked in the chest by his horse, and rendered unconscious for a couple of hours. This incident gave rise to the pass being named Kicking Horse Pass. The subsequent part of the legend, however, where Hector was assumed to be dead and was just about to be buried when he regained consciousness, may be considered as rather fanciful. Such was their admiration for Fraser that, before finally going on their way, Milton and Cheadle presented him with a Dean and Adams revolver. Such a weapon would have been greatly prized. With its hammer being automatically cocked and released when the trigger was squeezed, the pistol was a great favourite among soldiers, both of the North and South during the Civil War then in progress south of the border, and considered far superior to the American Samuel Colt designs with which they had been issued. Cheadle considered Fraser to be 'a very fine old fellow indeed, and of Highland hospitality as well as birth'.

Mr O'B, Baptiste, and the Assiniboines were reached after a gruelling 7 miles, wading through boggy ground and clambering over fallen trees. The tent (favoured by Patenaude over the native lodge they carried) was erected and the horses were being fed on a good patch of pasture. Mr O'B was eager to tell Milton and Cheadle about the problems he had encountered while travelling, but had difficulty finding a sympathetic ear. The following morning, Cheadle upset Milton by waking everybody up just as the sun rose. While the doctor was keen to start on their way, the viscount's early call caused him to be 'very sulky'. Nevertheless, Cheadle's urging paid off and, after passing most of the day walking along the shore of a lake, they had travelled 'a very fair journey'. Instead of disappearing with pipe in hand, Mr O'B surprised everyone by helping to unpack the horses – probably as a result of overhearing Baptiste and Patenaude loudly commenting on his abundant inadequacies. Unfortunately, however, the party had ended up by a swamp, and the resident mosquitoes proved to be so irksome that Cheadle was forced to smoke out the tent even as the sun broke the horizon, grabbing just a little sleep afterwards.

Later that morning, he set off on foot to shoot ducks. To his surprise, he was overtaken by the party and eventually found them on the far side of the Pembina River which, despite its often steep banks, had been crossed with ease. Of particular interest were the exposed strata of coal, plainly visible in the river bank. Of generally poor quality, Cheadle still recognised the fuel as being good enough for 'engine coal'. Milton, in the meantime, caught a bout of gold fever again, but succeeded in only obtaining a few, unusable flecks of 'the colour'. They were further delayed by an encounter with two 'freemen' (independent trappers not working for the company) who had had only modest success in trapping twenty-four beavers and shooting a black bear. While in conversation with the two men, Milton decided he wanted lunch – a decision resulting (much to Cheadle's annoyance) in the two men 'kindly giving us their assistance in consuming our provisions'. The next two days were little more than a succession of scrambling over fallen trees and wading through deep bogs of sphagnum moss, decayed pine needles and leaves, known as 'muskeg' (an Algonquin word meaning 'grassy swamp'). The only light moment was provided by Mr O'B once again fleeing from the sound of an animal passing through the undergrowth.

The morning of 14 June began with the distressing sound of Mr O'B discovering that the boots he had left out all night had frozen solid. The morning continued as a monotonous trial as the muskeg meant the horses sank up to their stomachs and the party endured a wearying trudge through continuous, knee-deep swamps. Cheadle kept everyone going in the hope of finding better ground as Milton grumbled at the exhausting pace. After a late lunch, the ground improved considerably and it was decided to make camp to give everyone a rest. Patenaude chose to take the opportunity to hunt beaver, and was about to be joined by Cheadle when the doctor came across a small stream, which showed the promise of containing trout. Returning to camp, Cheadle was disappointed to find that he had lost his grandfather's small brass box ('the one with burning glass as a top') along with the flies he had made under Fraser's tuition. Determined not to be thwarted, he promptly set about 'whipping' a new fly and returned to the river where, after some considerable time, he landed himself a rather disappointing 2oz trout for supper. Just as darkness crept over the camp, Patenaude returned in a state of great agitation and alarm. After a pipe of tobacco, handed to him by his son, the Métis calmed down enough to gasp out his story. Having shot a beaver, but failing to recover the dead animal, he was within a quarter of a mile from the camp when he stumbled upon a grizzly bear ripping rotten wood apart in the hope of finding insects for a meal. Seeing the Assiniboine at the same time, the bear charged at the man as Patenaude raised his gun. He squeezed the trigger, but the gun misfired. Then, as he stood absolutely motionless, the bear made repeated feints at him while growling ferociously. The situation was not improved with the arrival of two more large bears coming to see what the commotion was about. For a time, all three bears, with bared teeth and accompanying roar, made mock charges at Patenaude until, tiring of the sport, they returned to the prospect of an insect meal. At this, the Assiniboine slowly edged out of the clearing, but, instead of taking to his heels, Patenaude reloaded his gun and silently worked himself into a position downwind of the bears. Quietly reappearing in the clearing once again, he aimed at the largest bear only, yet again, for the gun to misfire. The largest bear promptly charged at him, while the other two fled into the woods. This time, when within just a few feet of him, the remaining bear began to parade up and down while growling. Once more, Patenaude edged himself out of the clearing, and made his escape – the bear evidently considering a supply of ants and beetle larvae a more attractive proposition than mounting an attack against the Assiniboine. Of course, Patenaude's story affected one person with far greater terror than anyone else. Milton, knowing that Mr O'B could not understand the Assiniboine's mixture of Cree and French, said to him, 'Mr O'B, the Assiniboine has been attacked by three grizzly bears, close to camp.' With eyes wide open with the shock of the news, Mr O'B turned to Cheadle and pleaded, 'Doctor, it's no use shutting our eyes to the fact; we are in a most serious position – in very great danger. *Jamdiu expectans expectavi!* (I waited a long time). This is a most terrible journey; will you do me a great favour, and lend me your revolver? For I am resolved to sell my life dearly, and how can I defend myself if the bears attack us in the night? I'm an unarmed man.' Cheadle took his revolver from its holster, cocked the hammer with his thumb several times, and replied 'very maliciously' – 'Oh, certainly, with the greatest pleasure; here it is: oh, yes, if you like: perhaps, under the circumstances, you had better take it; but I ought to tell you that you must be extremely careful with it, for it is in the habit of going off of its own accord.' For Mr O'B to place himself at such a risk would have been unthinkable. He rapidly withdrew the hand he had stretched out and responded by making his bed up next to Cheadle's tent and taking a large axe to bed with him.

The following morning, with the exception of Mr O'B, the men of the party set out in pursuit of the bears. Mrs Assiniboine and The

Boy left to try to find the beaver Patenaude had shot the previous day. Mr O'B, in the meantime, complained loudly about being left alone in the camp, convinced that the bears would attack the site in the absence of the rest of the party. When his remonstrations failed to have any effect, he retreated to the lodge with his large axe, built up the fire, and sat awaiting his fate. The main party had no difficulty in finding the truth of Patenaude's account. The tracks of the three grizzlies were plain for all to see, and even the wreckage of a bee's hive pointed out their presence. By noon, the trail led to part of the pine forest packed with dense undergrowth, which had to be approached with the greatest of caution for fear of a bear ambush. Baptiste and Patenaude went ahead to survey the route, only to return saying that they had come across a section of hard ground that had made further tracking impossible. Cheadle felt that the two Métis might simply have lost interest. With nothing further to be done, there was no other option but to turn back towards the camp. As they grew near to the site, by now in the hands of The Boy, Mrs Assiniboine, and Mr O'B, they came across the track of a moose. Eager to gain some return from an otherwise wasted day, it was decided that Milton and Baptiste would return to the camp to oversee the packing of the horses, while Cheadle and Patenaude set off in pursuit. It did not take long for Cheadle to become 'astonished' at the speed with which his Métis companion travelled over the ground while, at the same time, spotting evidence of the passage of the animal – evidence which Cheadle freely admitted he 'could only discern by carefully stopping to investigate'. It was all, however, to no avail. Defeated by an outbreak of heavy rain, muskeg, empty stomachs, and a moose 'evidently bent on a long walk', they gave up the hunt and rejoined the rest of the party, by now searching for an overnight campsite.

After an uncomfortable night adjacent to a swamp, and ignoring a lecture from Mr O'B to have both barrels loaded and his gun fully cocked, Cheadle set off early, keen to find a suitable route – only to lose his direction and be overtaken by the others. Inevitably, Milton was treated to a lengthy sermon by Mr O'B who told him,

My lord, you may depend upon it the doctor has met those bears. I've warned him repeatedly against the rashness of walking alone in this way. It was only this morning, as you heard, I advised him to be careful, and load both barrels with ball. But he only laughed at me, and walked off with his gun on half-cock, carelessly thrown over his shoulder. And now you see the terrible consequences. *Medicus ipse mortalis* (He is a mortal doctor).

Finally, Mr O'B added with an air of almost smug satisfaction: 'There is not the slightest doubt that he has been surprised by those three bears, and torn to pieces, poor fellow!' However, Cheadle, on realising his mistake, fired his gun several times to attract the attention of the party, and to let them know that he was behind them rather than ahead. The signalling, nevertheless, failed, and he had to suffer several hours of hard marching in pursuit of the party. When he eventually caught up with them, they had set up the camp for the night and Milton was in a foul mood brought on by the belief that Cheadle had pushed on far ahead with the aim of making them (in Milton's opinion) walk much further than was necessary. The mood was lightened, however, by the discovery of some newly made bear tracks, which were used to bring on a quaking terror to Mr O'B.

The camp had been set up on the eastern bank of the McLeod River, a broad, gently flowing but shallow river with clear water and banks laced with large grey rocks. Pine and poplar forests reached down almost to the water's edge. The peaceful scene was interrupted the next morning when Milton was very reluctant to rise from his bed. After a lot of shouting, first by Cheadle and then by the two Métis, he eventually got up and, to everyone's delight, an early start was made. However, once the river had been crossed, gold fever again descended on Milton. Cheadle sent the rest of the party on with the intention of joining them as soon as Milton decided that he had had enough of his amateurish panning for gold dust. With little return for his labours, the viscount soon gave up, only to find that both his and Cheadle's horses had freed themselves and departed in pursuit of the main party. At this, Milton became 'very unhappy at the prospect of a long walk', but fate lent a hand when they found his horse with its bridle caught up on a fallen tree. Cheadle took the horse to check on the party ahead leaving Milton happily searching for gold in a small stream they had come across. Finding no trace of the elusive gold, Milton looked up from the stream bank and saw a horse making its way through the dense trees on the far side. Believing that the rider was one of the party about to play a trick on him by pretending to be a bear, he started shouting and whistling to let the rider know he had seen him. The horse jumped at the commotion and revealed itself to be a large moose – a supreme prize, especially to Milton who had grown weary of eating small fish from the rivers they encountered, and the pine partridges, wood partridges, and pigeons that usually fell to Cheadle's shotgun. Nevertheless, even if Milton had kept silence, there was little he could have done to secure an evening's feast of moose steak as – much to Cheadle's irritation – he 'as usual had given someone else his rifle to carry'. Clearly, the traditions of aristocratic game shooting on the home estate were well ingrained. The day did not improve when it was discovered that Cheadle's horse, during its brief break for freedom, had shaken the party's only large, timber-felling axe out of one of the packs it was carrying. Nor did the swampy campsite add to the group's pleasures. Swarms of mosquitoes hovered, waiting for the opportunity to strike, only to be joined by deeply unpleasant horse flies, which drove the horses wild with their attacks. The humans soon found that they were not immune from the detested insects (known to the Métis as 'bulldogs'). Greenwood fires were built in an attempt to drive the insects away. The horses, however, continued to suffer greatly as they roamed in search of pasture, their hunger taking them away from the protective smoke. The campsite also had clear indications that they were not the first to rest there. Amongst other indicators, a note, written in pencil, was nailed to a tree. It was from the lyrically named Aulay Macaulay, the trader in charge of Jasper House, the company's trading post on the Athabasca River. They had met him at Fort Edmonton during his visit to collect supplies for the following winter. His note informed them that he had reached the spot in just ten days' travel from the fort. Cheadle was modestly pleased with the fact that, despite the stop at Lake St Anne, they had done the journey in twelve days. The path by the river and through the woods proved to be consistently difficult. Passing between a 'thick wall of timber' and boggy ground was especially difficult for the laden horses. Milton described a day's passage through the country as 'floundering through bogs, varied by jumps and plunges over the timber which lies strewn, piled, and interlaced across the path and on every side'. Following the bend of the MacLeod River as it swung sharply to the south, they decided to have a day of rest where the horses could graze at ease, the river and its tributary streams could be fished, and a meat supply could be sought among the local wild life. Setting up the camp by one of the tributary streams proved to be a trial. Milton told Baptiste that he wanted the lodge erected in a certain position but the Métis, probably for good reason based upon his experience, chose a different site. Once again, Milton demanded that he erect the lodge where *he* wanted it. This time, exhibiting 'a most discontented and rebellious spirit', Baptiste stormed off and began to pack his bags. Eventually, he calmed down and left to try his hand at fishing.

At daybreak the next day, Cheadle and Patenaude set off in search of moose. They returned with no sighting of their prey, but with an eagerly anticipated meal of fish being prepared for that evening. Milton had tried his hand at fishing with modest success, the largest of the catch – two trout of about 2lb each – being taken by The Boy with partridge feathers. Mr O'B caused an alarm by sitting idly by the fire and allowing the flames to set the nearby underbrush on fire. Fortunately, the fire was brought under control very quickly as the risks to all concerned, including the horses and the baggage, were very severe from being trapped in a dense, burning, forest.

Setting off the next morning along the MacLeod's western bank, Cheadle went ahead in case there was any game to be had. He was followed soon after by Milton, who had left Baptiste and Patenaude to bring on the pack horses. Cheadle was found by Milton on the trail after about a 4-mile ride from the camp, and both were soon joined by Patenaude and his family. Baptiste was missing. Patenaude told the others that he had last seen Baptiste as he had left with the horses. His fellow Métis had waved him on as he stopped to light his pipe – and he had never been seen again. It did not take them long to come to the conclusion that Baptiste had 'deserted' taking with him Milton's best horse, one of Mr O'B's saddlebags, and a small supply of pemmican and tea.

Milton fumed over the loss of his horse, but Cheadle reasoned that, as they owed Baptiste £10 in wages, the loss of the horse was 'not much'. A meeting was held at which Patenaude claimed he could find the trail without too much difficulty. In this, he was supported by Cheadle, who remained deeply impressed with his hunting skills. After Patenaude had democratically consulted Mrs Assiniboine, it was decided that he should be promoted into the now vacant office of guide, and should be paid the same as had been agreed with Baptiste. In return, he promised to stay with the party until their journey had been completed – calculated by Milton to be 600–700 miles. The loss of Baptiste had presented the party with the difficulty of loading and unloading the pack horses every day – especially with their 'only man being a one-handed one'. Cheadle soon found that, with thirteen horses to load, it was 'no joke lifting 180 pounds over the back of a tall horse'. Under such circumstances, Mr O'B 'represented a minus quantity', frequently retiring to sit on a fallen tree and read his copy of Paley's *Evidences of Christianity* – a book not to be read with the risk of interruption.

Two days were spent following the river bank as it passed through a shallow valley lined with low, well-wooded hills. Stopping at one of a number of small open spaces, they decided to spend some time fishing for trout seen rising in the water. Two were caught by The Boy before both he and Cheadle fell headlong into the river. The day was not improved when it was discovered that all the men, with the exception of Mr O'B, had lost several of their pipes. Cheadle had started out from Fort Edmonton with six, but now found that only two remained: 'A great misfortune'. The next day, the state of the track they were following suggested that they might be going in the wrong direction. Earlier, Patenaude had seen a track that branched off to the west, but had preferred to continue on the track they were following on the grounds that bullock-tracks indicated that a considerable number of people had passed that way. However, he came to the conclusion that the route had been used by American gold miners looking to find gold on the MacLeod. It was decided, therefore, that Patenaude should return along the trail and investigate the western track he had seen. When their guide had departed at about noon, two small clearings were cut among the closely packed trees. One was for the horses, and one for the party. Small fires were lit at both sites as the horseflies and mosquitoes had begun to gather. In the meantime, Mrs Assiniboine and The Boy had gone to the river bank to wash clothes. Before long, pemmican was being cooked on the camp fire as Mr O'B removed his boots and puffed away contentedly on his pipe.

Suddenly, a roaring sound attracted their attention and, looking up they were horrified to see that the fire in the horse's clearing had spread to the surrounding trees and had taken hold very quickly. Cheadle ran towards the flames and began pulling the panicking horses clear. When Milton arrived on his heels, Cheadle grabbed a hand axe and began cutting down the trees surrounding the fire to create a barrier over which the flames could not pass. After a while, straightening up to catch his breath, Cheadle noticed Mr O'B, still sat on the ground, trying to pull on a boot. He roared above the flames, 'What on earth are you doing! Why the Devil don't you bring some water?' With the air of someone deeply offended by such a question, Mr O'B shouted back – 'I can't, I've only got one boot on.' Again, Cheadle bellowed, 'Are you a fool, staying to put on a boot, when the forest will be on fire in a minute and you burnt to a cinder?' Milton joined in with, 'For God's sake, come and help us, or we shall all be burnt to death!'

The realisation that he was in very real peril suddenly took hold of Mr O'B and, wearing just one boot, he hopped down to the water's edge and filled a half-pint tin mug before returning to face the flames. Milton, in the meantime, having dragged all the horses clear, had grabbed a bucket and ran back and forth between a nearby pond and the fire. Slowly the fire was dampened down, as Cheadle's barrier prevented its further spread. One of the horses had been singed, but the damage was slight.

Eventually, Mr O'B managed to pull on his remaining boot as Patenaude returned with the welcome news that he had found the trail for which they were searching. They camped that night in an open area near to where the tracks diverged. A two-day passage through the wetlands to the west of the MacLeod River saw them and their baggage soaked by a continuous thundery downpour. On the third day, the weather had improved greatly and they covered the final half a mile to the Athabasca River with ease. But they were to meet with disappointment. Brown with drained rain and melt-water, the river was up to the highest point of the bank. It was unquestionably a mighty river, 200 yards wide and bearing huge pine trees that surged past on the heavy current. There was no chance of crossing the river until the flood had subsided.

Cheadle blamed his closest companion's tardiness in rising in the mornings for not having brought them to the spot before the river had chance to flood: 'Will Milton never learn the value of time?' They had no other option but to continue along the eastern bank of the river. Led by Cheadle, they pressed on until they reached a knoll rising amidst the trees lining the bank. This they climbed and saw beyond the far bank the first welcome sight of the Rocky Mountains. Behind the pine-clad foothills rose the lofty peaks, some blue in the weak sunlight, others still capped and streaked with the remnants of winter's snow. A cleft in the formidable barrier, guarded by the high peak of what could only be the Roche á Miette, was the signpost to their next destination – the Yellowhead Pass and Jasper House.

8

The Yellowhead Pass and the Naming of Mountains

On the morning of Saturday 27 June 1863, the party awoke to a sharp frost, which not only froze their water supplies but also presented Mr O'B' with an iron-hard, unwearable pair of boots that he insisted upon thawing out before they left. He would not wear wear moccasins – the best footwear in such circumstances – and the delay he caused infuriated Milton who was already fuming at Cheadle for waking him up at the unconscionable hour of five o'clock. Ignoring Milton's 'crabbed and vicious' attitude, Cheadle stuck to his view that an early start was always preferable to the extended indulgence of a warm bed. With their immediate destination, the Roche á Miette peak, frequently in view (looking remarkably like 'half of a sponge cake cut vertically'), they plodded on along the eastern bank of the swollen Athabasca through boggy ground that almost cost them one of their horses as it became stuck in the treacherous mud. In hauling the animal clear, Patenaude and Cheadle were watched with idle curiosity by Mr O'B, who showed a complete lack of concern when Cheadle vented his wrath upon him for not helping. The trek, however, was lightened by the occasional burst of colour from a wide variety of flowers including the firewheel (also known as the 'Indian blanket', or the 'sundance') with its 2½-inch flowers of red petals tipped with bright yellow. Roses and orchids joined blue borage flowering amid the red and white vetches and, of particular, personal nostalgic value to Cheadle, the marsh violet, which he had last seen when walking in the Yorkshire Dales with his sister, Sarah Jane, near Bolton Abbey. The night was spent in a deserted cabin that had probably served as a cache for trappers and hunters supplying Jasper House. The next day saw the party waiting at the cabin as Patenaude reconnoitred the path ahead that continued along the eastern side of the Athabasca. Milton busied himself manufacturing kinnikinnick to augment their supply of leaf tobacco, while Cheadle spent a fruitless day fishing in the 'heavy' water of the river. Patenaude returned with the news that they could be within a day's march of Jasper House, once the river had been crossed.

Before the sun rose the following morning, the party were woken by Milton suddenly sitting up in his bunk and shrieking 'Hello! Hello! What's the matter?' This unconscious outburst woke a terrified Mr O'B who sat bolt upright with the tremulous query, 'Oh, dear! Oh, dear! This is perfectly horrible – what has happened. It's only me – O'Beirne – don't shoot, my lord!' Cheadle in the meantime, used to such erratic behaviour from Milton, huddled beneath his furs, shaking with laughter. The Irishman, failing to receive an answer to his – not unreasonable – question, was far too alarmed to return to sleep, and chose to sit outside the cabin to wait for the morning light. When, later that morning, the party moved off, Cheadle and Patenaude, leaving their horses behind, climbed the lower slopes of Roche á Miette in search of mountain goats or sheep ('miette' was an adaptation of 'maya atik' the Cree words for the bighorn sheep that were abundant in the mountains). As they did so, Milton, taking the hunting party's horses with him, led the remainder of the party along the trail which, much to Mr O'B's dismay, suddenly began to climb upwards. Before long they were at a height of 500–600 feet above the river, which was now at the bottom of a sheer face. It was all too much for Mr O'B, who dismounted from his horse saying 'Poor fellow, my weight is too much for him.' The animal, sensing a chance for freedom, and not liking the height any more than his rider, immediately began to descend, prompting a chase by Milton and The Boy while Mr O'B proclaimed that he was 'far too exhausted'. With Mr O'B eventually re-united with his mount, the struggle to the top of the steep slope was completed. There, from west to east, a magnificent panorama was revealed to the party – a spectacular view across snow-capped mountains underlined by the Athabasca's rushing torrent. The river widened for a couple of miles as it curved towards the south, narrowed again under the pressure of the silt brought down by the Snake River tributary, and expanded into a long, wide stretch (Jasper Lake). Just before the eastern end of this broadening, the Athabasca was joined by the Rocky River from the east. Almost opposite the confluence of the two rivers, on the western bank, could be seen the tiny speck of Jasper House. Milton considered the view to be 'one of the most beautiful it has ever been my fortune to behold'.

With the descent of the equally hazardous slope down to the valley floor behind them, the party set up camp on the sandy river shore opposite Jasper House, described by Milton as a 'little white building, surrounded by a neat palisade, and situated in a perfect garden of brilliant colours'. Their intended destination, however, was 'seemingly without inhabitants'. In the meantime, 800 feet above the valley floor, Cheadle and Patenaude had managed to shoot one of the mountain goats, along with a kid. On reaching the valley floor, and finding that their horses had gone, they cut up the goat, keeping the head, two of the legs, and the brisket (a cut of meat from the chest of the animal). They then strung the butchered meat and the complete kid onto a pole, which they carried between them. Cheadle considered that the climb up the slope that had defeated the horse-riding Mr O'B to be 'the most awful grind in my life' and that 'coming down was nearly as hard work', as they slipped on the wet grass and 'uva ursi' (bearberries). While regaining their breath at the top, Cheadle had fired shots in the hope that the forward party would send horses to pick them up, but none arrived until they had almost reached the camp site when Milton and The Boy were seen setting off to find them. Although desperately tired, Cheadle and Patenaude stayed awake long enough to enjoy the fruits of their labour. The goat meat (referred to by Cheadle as 'mutton', using its nineteenth-century name) was 'strongly flavoured' – probably as a consequence of his not having had fresh meat for two months. The next day, after a breakfast of fried goat cutlets, the main task of the day was to build a raft that would carry them across to Jasper House. Clearly, the raft would have to be substantial as the river remained in full flood, and there was a significant amount of baggage and personnel to be ferried across. Due to the loss of their heavy axe, the tree cutting would have to be done using just two small hand axes. Despite being very tired after their exertions on the previous day, this work was handed to Cheadle and Patenaude. By noon, there were enough tree trunks cut and trimmed for the work on assembling the craft to begin. Cheadle and Patenaude were detailed to carry the heavy timber, while Milton and Mr O'B, and Mrs Assiniboine and The Boy, would provide another two parties to carry the lighter wood. It was soon discovered that the two parties intended for the lighter loads were needed to help lift the heavy tree trunks up onto the shoulders of the 'heavy' party. Help was willingly provided – with the exception of Mr O'B who concentrated on reading his book, or giving advice from the sidelines. When it came time for him to assist with the actual carrying of the lighter timbers, Mr O'B persistently chose the lighter end of the wood, and dropped his load without warning causing acute discomfort to the smaller-built Milton. At one stage, Cheadle and Patenaude met Milton dragging a heavy log by himself as Mr O'B sauntered along to the rear giving instructions to the gasping viscount. Patenaude let fly with a volley of French invective before snatching up the log from Milton, lifting the entire load onto his own shoulder and running off with it. Milton, instead of rounding on Mr O'B, complained bitterly to Cheadle. At this, Mr O'B loudly complained that it was 'all very well' to pick on him, but Cheadle had shoulders like 'the Durham ox' (a particularly strong, early nineteenth-century prize bull). On the other hand, he (Mr O'B) 'was not so strong', and that such labour would 'soon kill a man of my delicate constitution'. He then raised his hand to show Cheadle a minute scratch, but the doctor replied by showing his hands, both of which were 'perfectly raw with blisters'. At this, Mr O'B skulked away.

Before work on the raft's construction could get underway the next morning, a stranger rode into the camp. He proved to be a Hudson's Bay man belonging to a party of hunters led by Aulay Macaulay, the squirrel-eating man in charge of Jasper House. The visitor had been despatched by Macaulay to hunt down moose and had been ordered to rejoin the party further upstream. Clearly, it made more sense to place themselves under the guidance of a man who had intimate knowledge of the area. Consequently, they packed up and followed the hunter for about 5 miles to where there was a small lake containing a good stock of fish. En route to the new site, they had to cross a number of streams, several of which required a cautious crossing. The most obvious answer was to ride the horses across, but Mr O'B, still smarting at his horse's reluctance to pass the heights at the foot of Roche á Miette, refused to ride across and insisted on wading the streams. With almost comic inevitability, when crossing one of the streams on foot he fell into a hole up to his neck. His shouts of 'I'm drowning! Save me! Save me!' were ornamented by a quotation from the works of the Roman poet, Ovid, *'In medio tutissimus ibis'* (approximately – 'The middle ground is the safest.'). Cheadle watched as he floundered about, before shouting at him to 'Get back'. Giving up the 'middle ground', Mr O'B splashed his way back to the bank where he was eventually brought across the stream hanging on to the stirrup of the Hudson's Bay man.

A short distance further brought them to a sandy area where, on the suggestion of the company man, they set up camp. His local knowledge proved its accuracy when they were joined by other Hudson's Bay men and their families awaiting the return of Macaulay. Other arrivals came in the form of a pair of Secwepemc Indians (known in English as 'Shuswaps'). A few Shuswap families lived among the mountains, surviving on mountain sheep, deer, dried fish and berries. Their contacts with Europeans were rare, but where contact had been made, the Indians had suffered devastating losses through contracting smallpox. The two Indians promptly set about catching fish in a nearby lake and river, which they traded with the others for ammunition and tobacco. As they did so, they were joined by their families. At night, the men speared fish by the flare of torches – 'a very pretty sight'.

Settling down to wait for Macaulay, Milton swam in the lake, only to suffer one of his 'symptoms', and retired to his tent under Cheadle's direction. The 'symptoms' re-occurred several times over the next two days, preventing the party from advancing further along the river bank to the point where the company's men expected Macaulay to cross the river. Apart from the fish, food was in perilously short supply. Cheadle could see quite clearly that both the company men, and the Shuswap, were starving. Inevitably, they were soon 'honouring us with their company at meals'.

On the evening of Friday 3 July, just after the party had finished a meagre dinner, Macaulay rode into camp bringing with him ten bighorn sheep and forty-two large trout. Sending a quarter of a bighorn over to the company men and the Shuswap, he invited Milton and Cheadle over for their second dinner that evening. Mr O'B also turned up having wheedled an invitation, as he earlier scrounged some tea almost before Macaulay had dropped from the saddle. Cheadle was concerned that Macaulay's hospitality would leave him with 'short commons' during the approaching winter, but the trader brushed aside his concerns and told the group an anecdote from the previous winter. On returning from a hunting expedition, Macaulay had returned to Jasper House to find that all the window parchment (made from local sheep or goat skin) had vanished. On entering the hut, he found a parchment-gorged wolverine fast asleep – a prize that provided several substantial meals.

The next day saw a further journey along the river bank, along the slopes of mountains, through lakes, and several streams and small rivers. Mr O'B, quite incapable of commanding his horse, fell behind and became lost. His cries for help alerted the group and Milton, Cheadle and Macaulay rode to the rear. There they found their wailing companion leading his horse, fearful of even getting into the saddle. Cheadle told him that if he fell behind again, he would be left at the mercy of the grizzly bears. Such a thought soon had Mr O'B pleading for assistance in getting back astride his horse. The doctor was beginning to lose patience with their fellow traveller and recorded that, 'I never saw such an old woman in my life, or such a nuisance.' That evening the party arrived at 'a nice still place' on the river. It was the best place they had found for a crossing, which they intended to make on the following day. As they began to organise the raft building and manner of the crossing, Cheadle approached Milton over a matter that was concerning him. He had decided that he had 'no confidence' in Patenaude. Despite their guide's crippled hand, he had shown strength and energy all the time he had been in their company, but Cheadle felt that he was becoming increasingly aggressive in his manner. If the man took it into his head to abandon them, Cheadle felt that 'to be left alone with Milton and O'Byrne to haul to Cariboo (the goldfields), would be too great an undertaking'. As a precaution, he had decided to take along an elderly Métis who 'bore a good character'. His name was Louis Carapontier but, as he had grown up among the Iroquois Indians, he was simply known as 'The Iroquois'. Cheadle had agreed with the man that he would be employed as an interpreter and guide, and if he successfully guided them to Tête Jaune Cache, he would be rewarded with a small pony that had been used to carry the rum. Milton, still recovering from his 'symptoms', was in a hyper-sensitive frame of mind and began to rage at Cheadle. The doctor decided against a riposte and after stating that the deal was done, walked off.

Their raft was built by the company men, but all were involved with the transporting of the timber once it was cut. All, that is, with the exception of Mr O'B who stood aside until the work was completed and then approached Cheadle, saying, 'Oh, Doctor, can I be of any assistance?' The Yorkshireman replied by snapping back, 'You are a great deal too late, Mr O'Beirne!' This was an almost conciliatory gesture compared to the reaction of Patenaude. Their guide, furious with Mr O'B's laziness, demanded that he should not be taken across the river unless he started working, or paid the raft-builders. Cheadle stepped in and eventually Patenaude stormed off, while the Irishman beat a hasty retreat. A short time later, Cheadle was talking to Macaulay about the problems associated with Mr O'B when the trader offered to give him a 'good talking to'. There is no record of what Macaulay said, but whatever it was, it had a good effect. Mr O'B was soon almost overwhelming in his desire to be seen in his efforts to assist in the loading of the finished raft. Cheadle may also have mentioned his recent difficulty with Milton with the question of hiring the Iroquois as, shortly afterwards, Macaulay persuaded the viscount (who was due to inherit one of the biggest fortunes in England) that taking the Métis along was worth the price of a small Indian pony.

The river crossing proved to be straightforward and without incident, marred only by the accidental leaving of one of their two hand axes behind. On their safe arrival on the northern bank, the company men were given the remainder of the rum, and Milton presented Macaulay with the barrel. Cheadle gave him a 'telescopic' cup, which could be collapsed when not in use. Mr O'B's gift was the news that he had already eaten his way through his entire supplies. After pointing out that the pemmican that had been supplied to him should have lasted, at least, until Tête Jaune Cache, Cheadle gave him a 'good lump' of pemmican, while tea and tobacco was provided by Macaulay (who probably dreaded the thought that Mr O'B would be left behind). The party, now numbering seven with their new guide, set off with their backs to the Athabasca River on 6 July along the banks of the Miette River, a route strewn with fallen rocks and trees. Cheadle compared it to 'walking among a game of spillikins, a child's game where straws – 'spillikins' – were removed from a pile without disturbing the remaining straws. Due to the river's meanderings on the first day, they were required to cross it several times – much to the alarm of Mr O'B. Deep and fast flowing in places, the Miette reminded Cheadle of the dangerous Strid, a narrowing of the Yorkshire River Wharf near Bolton Abbey. The following day, with heavy rain and no improvement in the chaotic route, they found themselves at the site where the Overlanders had crossed, leaving their raft secured to the far side. At this point, the river was about 30 yards wide, and Cheadle suggested that he throw a weighted rope across. His suggestion was ignored, and The Boy whipped his horse into the waters carrying the end of a rope; but after a hazardous crossing, the animal panicked at the steep bank on the other side and returned of its own accord. Patenaude crossed the river, but lost the end of the rope. Then, someone advanced an entirely practical idea. With Patenaude on the far bank, and his dog, Papillon, panting eagerly on the eastern bank, the dog could be sent across to his master with the rope around his waist. Without any further ado, the dog, trailing the rope, completed his mission, and the raft was hauled over. With all safely across, they pressed on, only for Cheadle's saddle to slip causing him severe bruising where he fell on his back.

After a night at a site that provided good grazing for the horses, the route began to improve. The day, however, proved to be a tiresome one concerning the horses. When harnessing the cantankerous Bucephalus, Cheadle examined the girth and found that the buckle holes had perished and torn, the cause of his fall the previous day. After attending to the necessary repairs, he went on ahead with the Iroquois guide, only to have his horse stumble and fall. Luckily, the horse was uninjured and continued forward until they heard a bellowing to their rear. It was Milton galloping up and clearly in a foul mood. His 'awful passion' was nothing more than an annoyance that Cheadle had advanced so far ahead, leaving him behind. The doctor explained quite roughly that he was riding the worst of the horses. The animal needed his close attention just to keep it going forward – and if anyone else wanted to ride it, they were welcome to take over. The offer was not taken up. Milton's bad temper was the result of one of the horses being left behind at the river. Patenaude and The Boy returned to find the animal, leaving Milton and Mrs Assiniboine to look after the other horses – not a situation to Milton's liking. The day did not improve when Mr O'B allowed one of the horses to wander off. Patenaude descended into a rage, and Mrs Assiniboine had to return and find the stray. The party was restored to good humour when it was noticed the streams they encountered, instead of flowing towards the east, were streaming westwards. This could only mean that they had passed the high point of their route, and were now on the Pacific watershed. To complete their day, they found themselves a good campsite at the eastern end of the unattractively named 'Buffalo Dung Lake' (later, Yellowhead Lake).

The following day dawned with bright, clear weather to a backdrop of high, snow-capped peaks reflected in the lake. Those closest to the north marched line-abreast to the very edge of the lake itself; to the south and west, the mountains vied for dominance in the sky. Someone (Milton says it was the Iroquois, Cheadle implies that it was Milton), suggested naming mountains after the two Englishmen. Milton chose a dignified mountain to the south (Mount Fitzwilliam), while Cheadle chose the westernmost of the northern peaks, naming it Mount Bingley after his father's parish. He also took the opportunity to copy Alexander the Great (who named a town after his horse) to name another peak, just to the south of Mount Fitzwilliam, as Mount Bucephalus, in honour of his own irascible mount. The morning march started well but by midday descended into a chaos of swamps, deep streams, and fallen trees. Mr O'B contributed amply to the confusion by lagging behind, getting lost, and being pitched over the head of his horse. His horse then fell on top of him. A threat from Cheadle to leave him to the bears, persuaded him to ride to the front of the column – where he promptly led the party off the track. Cheadle, now realising his mistake in allowing Mr O'B to the front, sent him to the rear where he was later seen with his saddle beneath the horse's belly and, with him too frightened to mount his horse, leading him by the reins through the clinging muskeg and over the piles of tree trunks. Neither Milton nor Cheadle escaped unscathed. Milton ran into the bough of a tree, which swept him to the rear of his horse, but the viscount 'scrambled on again like a monkey without stopping'. Bucephalus (no doubt in pleasure at having a mountain named after him) suddenly 'buck-jumped' into the air ramming Cheadle's head against a pine tree – and later, kicked him on the shin. They had hoped to reach the southern shore of Moose Lake (to the west of Buffalo Dung Lake) but the delays and conditions caused them to spend the night at a very damp site short of their target. They had, however, reached the bank of the Fraser River and knew that their route to Tête Jaune Cache was assured. The uncomfortable situation, was not improved by their supper of vegetable soup and bread being enlivened by Mr O'B regaling them with tales of the 'fearful perils' he had encountered throughout the day.

Cheadle's horse, Bucephalus, set the pattern for the next two days by swimming across the Fraser and having to be rescued by Patenaude. Forced up the steep slopes of the towering mountains, the horses frequently fell and rolled down the slopes. They became trapped when trying to clamber over piles of fallen timber and occasionally wedged themselves between close-packed trees. The provisions were soaked several times.

When Moose Lake was reached, it was found to have flooded, and huge stretches of water had to be waded through. A patch of dry ground was used to dry the soaked pemmican and flour, with the sun also melting Cheadle's gutta-percha (a natural solid latex) fracture splints. Mr O'B gave up attempting to ride when his saddle continually slid from his animal's back. Milton's temper grew more and more aroused as the difficulties increased, and Cheadle decided that his companion 'had neither the patience, activity or constant attention necessary to drive horses in the woods'. Even their eventual arrival at the Fraser Grand Fork, where another river (later named as The Robson) joined the main stream, did nothing for Milton's tendency to 'kick up a bobbery' (create a noisy commotion). The situation grew even worse when Milton's saddle slipped and he was thrown head first into a deep pool of muddy water – a state of affairs made woefully embarrassing when he realised he was being pulled from the water by none other than Mr O'B. Consequently, his main targets were Mr O'B or the Iroquois, or anyone who suggested an early start in the morning. Cheadle, however, refusing to retreat before the viscount's rages, did manage to record the spectacular scenery around them:

> The Grand Fork … is certainly the finest scene I have ever viewed. To the right Robson Peak, a magnificent mountain, high, rugged, covered with deep snow, the top now clearly seen, although generally covered with clouds. Ranges of other mountains and pine-clad hills run along the Fraser on each side, and in the blue haze were quite fairy-like.

The next day, 15 July, brought an answer to the seemingly perpetual squabbles. One of the horses, Gisquakarn (a native word for 'Fool'), carrying much of Milton's personal effects and a large quantity of flour, jumped into the Fraser followed by Bucephalus – who was carrying the medical supplies and some of Cheadle's clothing. Patenaude and The Boy raced after the horses while the Iroquois galloped off in an attempt to reach Tête Jaune Cache where Indians with canoes could help if the horses and supplies were swept down the Fraser. When Cheadle told Milton of the situation, the viscount immediately began to rage at his companion as if everything was his fault. The doctor, in no uncertain manner, seized the moment and replied sharply that the men 'were discontented, and the best thing, and wisest for us to do is to give up quarrelling and wipe out all that has passed, and do our best to work together or we shall be left in a most unpleasant fix'. The brusque response worked. Milton agreed, and the pair set off in pursuit of the horses.

When they reached the horses, Bucephalus appeared to recognise Cheadle and began to make for the bank on which he was standing.

Gisquakarn, on the other hand, continued to paddle downstream, so Bucephalus, in a display of equine loyalty, rejoined his fellow escapee. Eventually, with the two horses a mile ahead, Milton and Cheadle gave up the chase and set up camp by the river. In the meantime, Patenaude and his son continued to gallop along the bank and caught up with the horses. This time it was Gisquakarn who recognised the neighing of The Boy's horse and managed to stop, but Bucephalus, carried on by the powerful current and at risk from the rock-strewn river, was swept further down until he managed to touch bottom and halt his chaotic progress.

On reaching the bank close to Cheadle's horse, Patenaude dismounted and leapt into the river, only to lose his legs in the current and was carried beneath the horse's belly. Grabbing one of the horse's legs, he held on until he could regain his footing and, pulling at the horse's reins, dragged him to the side. Bucephalus was too exhausted to scramble up the slope, so Patenaude had to pull the bags off the horse's back and throw them onto the bank before he could get Bucephalus clear of the water. After securing the horse to a nearby tree, and spreading the bag's contents out to dry, Patenaude then noticed that Gisquakarn was standing in shallow waters near to the far bank. This time with little difficulty, the Métis retrieved the second horse and led them both back to the camp. Flour, pemmican, clothing, guns (including Milton's revolver), gunpowder and wads had been lost, the medicines had been soaked, but were recoverable. Cheadle particularly mourned the loss of a small botanical collection that he had assembled ('utterly rotten and spoilt'). For his part in the rescue of the horses, Patenaude was promised a handsome extra £5 on top of his wages. The disasters did not end there.

Just as the Iroquois arrived in company with two Shuswap Indians, it was discovered that another horse had gone into the river, and no trace of it could be found. One of the Shuswap was persuaded to search the far bank, but returned without result. Once again it was personal belongings that were lost. Milton suffered greatly, having lost his greatcoat, best suit, moccasins, shirts, socks, silk handkerchiefs, letters, notes, cheque book and passport. An additional loss of tobacco left Milton with just six plugs of chewing tobacco with his tattered canvas trousers, a single pair of worn-out moccasins, and a buckskin shirt. He had no boots or coat. Cheadle lost his sextant, revolver, all his gunpowder and percussion caps, his cash box containing matches, watch, ring, cravat pin, souvenirs, and all his papers and letters. He also lost most of his tea, and all of his tobacco. Milton and Cheadle reacted as only two Englishmen could under such circumstances – they both 'had a good laugh over it', a reaction that 'restored good feeling among us'.

Mr O'B had not escaped the losses. In his case, he had lost some letters of introduction, his reading glasses, and his kettle. He was reduced to using his only remaining 'pair' of spectacles, which had only a single lens remaining. He was also very agitated about the general loss of tobacco as he had intended to plead for some of Milton's. Matters the following day did not improve for Mr O'B. On their way to Tête Jaune Cache, Cheadle, at the rear of the pack horses, heard a commotion behind him. It was Mr O'B, running up to catch him. As Cheadle stopped, Mr O'B gasped out 'Doctor! Doctor! You had better go back directly, something's happened; don't you hear someone shouting for assistance? I expect it is Mrs Assiniboine with one of the horses fast in a bog.' Cheadle demanded 'Why on earth did you not stop and help her?' Mr O'B, astonished by the need for an answer to such a fatuous question, replied: 'I ran away as fast as I could, afraid of losing you.' Cheadle boiled over: 'You miserable old woman, to leave another in such a fix.'

He then ran back to Mrs Assiniboine and helped haul the animal out. By the time they had caught up with the party, they had set up camp opposite Tête Jaune Cache and Cheadle lost no time in seeking out Mr O'B to give him a severe 'lecture' on his shortcomings. Patenaude, his wife, and his son, all joined in assuring Mr O'B that they would never give him any help in the future.

Tête Jaune Cache was situated on the south side of the Fraser where the Shuswap 'bark slants' (shelters with sloping roofs made from silver birch bark) could be seen. Arrangements were made for the two Shuswap who had accompanied the Iroquois to transport them across on the following day. In the meantime, Milton and Cheadle took stock of their situation. The viscount thought that the view to the west with its profusion of mountain ranges was 'the most wonderful in the world'. Cheadle, however, while an ardent admirer of mountain views, was looking forward to a change of scenery. He wearily noted, 'We are supposed now to be on the other side of the mountains, but we see nothing but their snowy tops on every side still.' The crossing of the Fraser proved to be a bumpy ride through the fast-flowing stream. Mr O'B was ordered to lie down in the Shuswap's small dugout canoe in case he took it into his mind to stand up and jump overboard. As the craft bucked and reared, he raised his hand and frantically waved while shouting for someone to loosen his cravat and shirt neck; it appeared that he had reached the conclusion that he would stand a better chance of escaping drowning with his neck unencumbered.

Once safely ashore on the southern bank, needles and thread were exchanged for an enormous amount of the local species of serviceberry, a small but delectable fruit. Milton also obtained some roots from what appeared to be lilies, to add to their rubbiboo. Cheadle thought the added ingredient 'quite spoilt' their meal, while Milton 'of course' declared it to be delicious. The local population consisted solely of the two men who had ferried them across the river, their wives, the wives of two older men who were on the trail guiding a group of gold miners, and numerous small children. The chief food supply came from dried chinook salmon (the community was situated close to the end of the salmon's 800-mile journey upriver from the Pacific Ocean), wild goats and marmots. The latter were cat-sized squirrels that lived in burrows, and were greatly prized for their skins. The Shuswap women wore marmot robes – large, blanket-like, squares or rectangles made up of between thirty and fifty marmot skins. Less concerned about feminine preferences, and attracted by the warmth of the garment, Milton obtained two, and Cheadle swapped a blanket and an old flannel shirt for another. The Shuswap men, on the other hand, preferred coats ('capotes') made from blankets worn over moose-skin breeches. Discussions with the Shuswap revealed that they were just 100 miles or so from the Cariboo Goldfields. The route, however, lay across a series of mountains which, without a guide, map, or Cheadle's sextant, would face the party with unacceptable risks. In addition, Milton and Cheadle were desperately short of equipment and clothing, neither of which were available prior to their departure from Tête Jaune Cache.

The obvious alternative was to head south to the fort, and newly booming town, of Kamloops at the confluence of the North and South Thompson rivers. Kamloops (from a Shuswap word meaning 'the meeting of the rivers') was on one of the routes taken a year earlier by the Overlander gold prospectors on their way to the Cariboo Goldfields, and could be expected to have the sort of provision needed by Milton and Cheadle.

Deserted by their Métis guide, the Overlanders had split into two groups. The larger group headed up the Fraser to its most northerly point where it arced down to Fort George (modern Prince George). From there they continued on to Quesnel, situated in the goldfields. It was a difficult journey, supplies were lost in the river rapids, and four men died from exposure or drowning. The other group – a party of between fifty and sixty, including the sole (and pregnant) woman – attempted to reach the goldfields by crossing the land, taking more than 100 cattle and horses. They reached the North Thompson River after great difficulties and decided to let the horses loose, slaughter the cattle, and descend the river by rafts.

Neither of the two Shuswap men would agree to take the party to Kamloops, although one of them offered to spend the first day on their journey with them – in exchange for which service he wanted one of Cheadle's white shirts. This was agreed. The other Indian gave Milton a couple of interesting, gold-coloured crystals the Shuswap used as gun flints. Additional help was provided by the wife of one of the absent older men. She had come from Kamloops many years before and drew them a map, while assuring them that their journey would not take longer than eight days. From Kamloops, the route to the goldfields was well-known and indicated.

Monday 20 July 1863 was a dull day that threatened rain. Most of the packing had been completed when Mr O'B noticed that his horse was missing. The Iroquois – who was about to begin his return to Jasper House that day – while complaining about the small grey pony he had agreed to take in payment for his services, claimed he had brought Mr O'B's horse back to the camp, but had no idea where it was at that particular time. As the animal belonged to Mr O'B, Patenaude refused to help search for the horse, but agreed that The Boy could help in searching for it. As the Iroquois bade them farewell, the party began the journey south to Kamloops down a long, wide, valley. They had barely reached half a mile from Tête Jaune Cache when The Boy returned, empty handed.

Milton and Cheadle slowly began to realise that they had been 'done', and they both felt that Patenaude had a hand in the loss. Nevertheless, to risk a breakdown in their relationship with the Métis at this stage of the journey seemed too great a gamble. Accordingly, Mr O'B set out on foot with his saddle and blanket being carried by Cheadle.

9

Disaster on Canoe River – a Headless Indian and Hell's Gate

On the grey morning of 21 July, the overnight guide received his payment of Cheadle's white shirt, with the bonus of four fish hooks ('very good pay for an easy day's work'), and returned to the comfort of his bark-roofed hut. The trail from Tête Jaune Cache had been along a dry, sandy valley, thinly forested with spruce trees. A small river (later named Swift Creek) had been crossed with ease and, that morning, about a mile to the south of their overnight camp site, the party encountered the Canoe River. Although not as wide as the Fraser and other great rivers, the Canoe River ran swollen and fast and very deep. Both banks were cluttered with rocks, large pieces of driftwood and overhanging trees, and it proved necessary to move upstream to find a good crossing place. Eventually, a place was found and the horses sent across. Patenaude and Cheadle then took it in turns to wield the single small axe in their possession and by the middle of the afternoon, enough substantial logs had been cut down to start building a raft that would take them and their baggage across. With Mr O'B's spectacularly poor effort at raft building when preparing to cross the Athabasca, Cheadle decided that he would partner the Irishman in transferring the tree trunks to the bank. Inevitably, although always taking the lighter end, Mr O'B persisted in groaning 'Steady, steady, Doctor,' as Cheadle forced the pace. After two journeys, Mr O'B was finished ('another would kill me'), and his place was taken by The Boy. As their companion rejoined the work by dragging small poles along while groaning in agony, Patenaude constructed the raft. Boarding the unsteady craft proved to be no easy task due to the speed and turmoil of the current. As soon as the last of the party stepped on board, the raft raced away down river at an extraordinary rush. An overhanging tree was only just avoided through Patenaude's captaincy and by pushing clear of the obstacle with poles. Unfortunately, their actions also forced them across the river where the current appeared to gather strength and raced them toward another tree that had fallen into the waters. Unable to control the craft with the poles, Patenaude, shouted '*À terre – á terre avec la line!*' He grabbed a rope and leapt for the bank, followed by Cheadle grasping another rope. Both men reached the bank, scrambled up and took a turn around the nearest tree – but Patenaude's rope snapped instantly, and Cheadle's was wrenched from his grip. Joined by The Boy, who had also leapt into the water, they could only watch as the raft swept beneath the fallen tree. With the raft drifting well beyond the obstacle, the two men and The Boy raced along the river bank in pursuit.

As he reached the fallen tree, Cheadle heard a cry to his immediate left. Turning that way, he spotted Milton and Mrs Assiniboine hanging onto drooping tree branches. Jumping into the water, he hauled himself onto the tree trunk and made his way along its length. On reaching Milton first, the viscount shouted to him 'Never mind me, help the woman.' Cheadle continued on towards Mrs Assiniboine, but, when he arrived above her, he realised that she was too far below the trunk to reach by himself. Instead, he made his way back towards Milton and dragged him onto the trunk. They both then returned to the woman and, finding her too heavy to pull to safety, held on to her while shouting for Patenaude. The Métis and his son had run down river in pursuit of the raft and came up with it as it was held up by a tree just short of the bank. There, still on board the craft, was Mr O'B holding the end of a rope – itself still attached to the timbers. Patenaude shouted to Mr O'B to throw him the rope, but received in reply just a shaking of the head and 'No, no, no.' The situation was recovered when the current suddenly lifted the raft and drove it closer to the shore. Mr O'B promptly leaped on to the bank and ran off into the bush as Patenaude struggled to secure the violently rocking vessel. Looking to the shore, and still shouting for assistance,

Cheadle saw The Boy running about in great agitation. Gaining the thirteen-year-old's attention, Cheadle told him to get his father and a rope. The Boy sprinted off, eager to comply. As he did so, Mr O'B emerged from the trees, walking along as if in a state of 'perfect imbecility'. Cheadle shouted to him, 'For God's sake, try and bring us a rope, or the woman will be drowned.' Mr O'B took off his cravat and handed it to The Boy who was running ahead of his returning father. Eventually, with Patenaude's help, the woman was lifted out of the bitterly cold water.

Although Mrs Assiniboine survived her ordeal, all her possessions, and those belonging to her husband, were lost. The party's sole frying pan had vanished, along with all the tea, and the matches. The only means of starting a fire was the flint and steel Patenaude was carrying in his pocket. Milton had lost his cap, and Cheadle felt obliged to give him his – as Milton had given it to him in the first place, ('I go bareheaded'). A camp was set up 2 miles south of Canoe River after a walk through a continual downpour, and a fire could be started only with the greatest of difficulty as little dry tinder could be found. The only person with the slightest semblance of cheerfulness was Mr O'B who was delighted to be out of sight and sound of the river. He explained that he could remember nothing after the raft had been swept beneath the fallen tree – except for '*Heu me miserum! iterum iterumque, strepitum fluminum audio.*' ('Alas, poor me! Again and again, I hear the noise of the river.').

The next three days were spent heading south over difficult, rocky ground. For much of the time they seemed to be travelling towards a 'magnificent mountain covered with glaciers'. Eventually, the trail veered off slightly to the east, taking them away from what had seemed to be a terrible obstacle. So impressive was the snow-covered mountain that it was decided that it should be named Mount Milton. A small lake, from which issued a south-running stream, was named Albreda Lake by Milton after a favourite aunt – Lady Albreda Lyveden. Later, when the stream grew to the size of a substantial river, it was named Albreda River. In addition, the spectacularly favoured aunt had a fine mountain to the east of the trail named in her honour. The valley along which they were travelling had become more heavily forested, mainly with pines, but they came across several magnificent examples of the western red cedar. The latter tree, which can grow to 200 feet high, was measured around the base, and found to be around 39 feet in circumference. With the floor of the forest encumbered with piles of fallen trees interspersed with swamps and muskeg, the horses found progress to be very difficult. Several deep streams had to be crossed, often placing the party's meagre supplies at risk.

On the morning of Saturday 25 July, (five days after leaving Tête Jaune Cache) the Albreda River – by now a substantial watercourse, 30 feet in width and swollen with melt-water from glaciers – turned sharply to the south-east, cutting directly across their path. Fortunately, a beaver dam, crumbling in parts but still useable by the horses, remained, linking the banks. To reduce the risk of damage to the provisions, the packs were removed from the animals as they were led safely across. The packs were then brought across and reloaded onto the horses. They had only gone a few yards when one of the animals – carrying the very limited flour supply – fell into a shallow gully and soaked the precious commodity. After a rest at noon to recover from their exertions, they continued southward for about two hours and found themselves on the north bank of the North Thompson River. Looking towards the east, just a couple of hundred yards away, they could see where the Albreda River joined the Thompson and, a little further on, the wide river curved gently towards the south. Patenaude crossed the Thompson in the expectation of finding the Overlanders' trail on the far side, but returned without success. In the hope that a narrower crossing would be found upriver, they followed the bank to the west and came upon the place where the Overlanders had camped before crossing. From there, it was plain to see where they had actually crossed the river.

Continually pestered by mosquitoes and sand flies, they set up camp on the northern bank. Patenaude would not cross a river on a Sunday, but agreed to prepare the timber needed for a raft. Cheadle helped, and Mr O'B – who was delighted with Patenaude's superstition – dragged along some small branches while appearing to be on the point of collapse. During times of rest, they searched the bank for gold – without success. Eventually, Milton and Cheadle had to address the question of which path to follow, now that they had reached the North Thompson. Milton declared that he was very keen to follow the river to the Cariboo goldfields. Cheadle, however, pointed out that they were very low on provisions, the horses were desperately weak, they had very little ammunition, and their clothing was in an extremely poor state. After some debate, it was agreed that once across the river, they would pick up the Overlanders' trail and, whichever way it led, they would follow it.

The following day was Milton's 24th birthday. Cheadle insisted that there was no time for celebrations, and was already considering instituting a system of rationing. Mr O'B then tried another method of delaying the river crossing. Approaching Cheadle, and – after complaining about the crossing of the Canoe River ('What an escape I had!') – he explained that he had a 'most fearful presentiment that if we make the attempt today we shall all be lost – every one of us drowned, Doctor.' Cheadle explained about the shortage of supplies, suggested that Mr O'B was just nervous, and went to assist Patenaude to assemble the raft. First the horses were sent across without mishap, then the raft, carrying the whole party and the baggage, was poled from the northern bank. All went well until they neared the opposite bank when Mr O'B jumped overboard in an attempt to reach the shore. Cheadle, annoyed at the Irishman's thoughtless risk of upending the raft, reached down and hauled him back on board 'and made him wait'.

With the relief of a successful crossing, and with Mr O'B's forebodings 'happily unfulfilled', the party untied the raft, rolled the logs into the river, collected the horses, and ate a lunch. On completion of the meal, Patenaude walked off to see if he could find a trail left by the Overlanders. He did not take long before returning 'in great disgust' to inform the rest that they were not on the southern bank – but on an island. There was an immediate dash to the landing place where they were able to recover a few of the logs from their previous raft (the others had floated well out of reach). An attempt to find the trail used by the Overlanders to leave the island failed, by which time night was approaching and they retired to their tents.

The next day dawned beneath a clear blue sky, and much of their gloom disappeared when Patenaude returned from an early morning exploration to say that he had found a bridge to the south bank made up of driftwood piled up against an old beaver's dam. The horses were sent through the waters as the bridge was crossed by the party carrying the baggage – all, that is, except for Mr O'B who, exhibiting great terror with the water rushing beneath his feet, carried no baggage, not even his own. Once on the far bank, he pulled his favourite book from his pocket and sat down to read while refusing to recross and claim his baggage. Giving up trying to persuade Mr O'B to help, Milton and Cheadle returned to bring the remaining baggage across. As they did so, they were amazed to see Mr O'B almost sprinting across the rickety bridge, eager to lend a hand. It turned out that Patenaude had advanced on the studious Mr O'B with a heavy stick raised like a club that he was about to bring down on the Irishman's head. Preferring to risk the crossing rather than have his brains dashed out, Mr O'B suddenly discovered a willingness to work, and actually crossed four times.

With Mr O'B playing his part, the main problem turned out to be an equine mutiny. Having waded as far as the middle of the river, the remaining horses had found themselves, not just a shallow sandbank, but a refuge from the clouds of biting insects. There they determined to stay regardless of the shouts from the party and even the shower of stones and sticks which were propelled their way. Probably led by the belligerent Bucephalus, Gris, Petit Noir, Sauvage, Grand Rouge, and Petit Rouge, all stood their ground. Eventually, the answer was found by The Boy, who returned to the beaver dam and log bridge and sent large pieces of timber racing in the fast current towards them. The onslaught caused the horses to leap into the deeper waters and swim across to the southern bank.

There was also another problem, one that had been developing over the past few days. Milton's expectations since the departure from Tête Jaune Cache had been severely frustrated. The loss of supplies, the antics of Mr O'B, the occasional friction between Patenaude and the other members, Cheadle's opposition to striking out towards the goldfields, and his threat to ration the remaining supplies, had a marked effect upon Milton's enthusiasm. His instinctive response was to cause squabbles whenever the opportunity presented itself. The greatest test of patience came after the river had been crossed. The path cut by the Overlanders had been found after a struggle up a steep slope. The trail was followed to the west as it climbed the bases of hills that sloped down to the river's edge, and turned into swamps where the river had flooded into the intervening valleys. By the time they set up camp for the night, even Patenaude was exhausted. In the morning, Milton decided that his disintegrating moccasins had to be replaced and insisted that he would not move until Mrs Assiniboine had produced a pair for him. Cheadle, desperate to find grazing for the horses, offered him a pair of his own – but Milton insisted on a new pair. At this, Cheadle 'completely resigned all share in management', thus handing Milton a victory that he did not want.

In the meantime, Patenaude had pressed on ahead, and came back after two hours with some disconcerting news. Not only had the trail run out – it had disappeared into the river. With his feet clad in his new moccasins, Milton and the others set off in the wake of the Métis. If the previous day had been difficult, the dense forest, with its floor of fallen trees, and the steepening slopes of the riverside hills, continued to wear down the starving horses. They stumbled, fell, and rolled down the slopes where the men needed to lift them back onto their feet.

As early evening approached, the party came across a wholly unexpected sight that Patenaude was eager to show them. An area on the river's bank had been cleared of a large number of trees. Animal bones littered the ground, and piles of horse harnesses and saddles were scattered throughout the clearing. In one corner, the posts and frame of a 'churrasco' (a South American construction for smoke drying meat) could be seen. Nearby, part of a tree had been stripped of its bark, and a pencilled message written onto the exposed wood – it read, 'Slaughter Camp, Sept. 22nd, 1862.' At the site, the Overlanders had released their horses into the woods, slaughtered their remaining cattle, and dried the meat. As this was being done, trees were felled, and rafts built that would take them down the Thompson to the fort at Kamloops. The conclusion from the remains of the year-old activity was obvious, even to Milton. If about fifty well-fed men, equipped with an ample supply of large axes, were unable to cut their way any further through the seemingly perpetual forest, how could two active men, a man with the use of just one hand, another man with no inclination to work, a woman, and a boy – with just a single hand axe between them – and assisted by utterly worn out horses, get through? The option of constructing a raft was barely credible. Not only was their tiny axe useless for the construction of the substantial sort of craft necessary for the long voyage down the fast-flowing river, even with a larger axe, the time taken would outstrip the meagre provision that remained. Their stock had been reduced to 10lb of flour and 10lb of pemmican – not enough for three day's food for the six members of the party (although Cheadle felt the food could stretch to ten days if strictly rationed). Despite signs that there were caribou deer in the vicinity, wildlife of any sort was rarely seen, and their ammunition and powder had almost disappeared.

After a further reconnaissance to the west confirmed their fears, it was decided that they would have to cut their way through the forest. Patenaude climbed the hill to the rear of the camp and reported that he had seen nothing but mountains and forest to the south. Some of the mountains had snow on their tops, but the appearance of a gradual diminution in height gave some hope of eventual open ground.

Patenaude not only returned with the news of the route ahead, but also with a black bear cub which he had shot. Once the first meal of bear meat (the first fresh meat since the mountain sheep of Jasper House) had been consumed, most of the party felt better with even the Métis exclaiming that *'Nous arriverons bientôt.'* Mr O'B, on the other hand remained convinced that they were all to meet 'a miserable end'.

The next few days proved to be a challenge to their new-found enthusiasm. Frequently soaked by heavy rainfall, slashed and pierced by thorns (probably spikeweed) and with moccasins constantly being patched with leather from the saddlebags, the party slowly made its way south along the west bank of the Northern Thompson River. Usually led by Patenaude, followed by his wife, the rest tailed behind. If the horses lost sight of each other, they broke away and went searching in the undergrowth. Time and time again, the party had to halt as searches for lost horses led to chaos. The animals frequently broke down and stood forlornly looking at the ground as a trapped hoof had to be cut free from gaps in the fallen timber. Occasionally, entire tree trunks had to be cut through to release a horse too feeble to scramble over the obstacle. Numerous streams and small rivers had to be crossed. As usual, Mr O'B treated each one as if he was crossing the English Channel in a bad storm. However, a wholly unexpected incident occurred that changed everything. Coming across a wide, deep, stream, Patenaude was the first to cross. This encouraged most of the others to follow immediately. The only figure drawing back from the bank was Mr O'B but, as soon as Cheadle's horse, Bucephalus, was about to plunge into the waters with his master on his back, the Irishman raced up to the horse and grabbed his tail as he jumped. Apparently unconcerned, the horse continued across the river towing Mr O'B in his rear. So successful was this method of getting Mr O'B across, it became the standard means of transporting him from one river bank to the opposite side.

The only food available for the animals was the fern-like 'horsetail', with occasional edible leaves. Sustenance for the party was soon rationed to two meals a day, usually a small portion of rubbaboo, supported by the occasional partridge. In one instance, Patenaude's dog, Papillon, made a significant contribution by bringing in a dead skunk. At other times, if they and the horses were lucky, they would stumble across a patch of wild raspberries or plump bilberries. When stopping to camp for the night, Mr O'B invariably disappeared with his well-thumbed copy of Paley's *Evidences of Christianity*, only to re-appear once the horses had been unpacked and the tents erected. He would then say in wearied tones, 'Now, my Lord; now, Doctor. I don't think our route was well chosen. We may have done 15 or 20 miles, but that's not at all satisfactory.' No one listening to him had the energy or will to point out that they had probably done no more than 3 or 4 miles.

During the journey from Slaughter Camp, a large, snow-topped mountain could frequently be seen to the east. Milton decided that it should be named Mount Cheadle. A little later, another mountain could be seen to the west, which was given the name Mount St Anne after the hospitality they had received two months earlier at the lake of that name. A marked distraction occurred on Saturday 8 August, (twenty days after they had left Tête Jaune Cache) when Patenaude came across the corpse of an Indian. Sat with its knees bent, its arms around its knees, and with its upper body leaning forward, the corpse displayed one distinctive feature – the Indian had lost his head. At the side of the body lay the Indian's possessions, consisting of an axe, a knife, and a 'fire bag' containing a flint, steel, and tinder. A large American cooking vessel sat beside two birch bark baskets, one with fish-hooks and fishnet inside, the other containing well-sprouted wild onions. The trace of a fire was at his feet, along with assorted ribs and splintered bones from a horse's skull. After a fruitless search for the Indian's missing head, they returned to the body and removed the axe out of 'necessity' and the steel and fishing equipment as 'mementoes'. For most, the incident remained a puzzle for which they could provide no answer. Patenaude, however, was convinced that the death, and the missing head, somehow involved Americans – probably gold prospectors on their way to the goldfields. His instinct was to blame the Americans for anything involving attacks on the Indians. Cheadle, on the other hand, thought that the death was simply a result of 'illness and starvation'.

The sombre mood of the evening was not lightened by Milton's insistence that one of the horses should be shot to provide food. Hunger played a part in the demand, but the meal that night, at which they dined off a pine marten, tasted so revolting that 'Mr O'B had not the satisfaction of retaining what it had cost him so great an effort to swallow.' Cheadle and Patenaude both stated that they were not hungry enough to risk killing one of the horses too early. Milton, however, stood his ground, and so it was agreed that Petit Noir (or Blackie, as Cheadle referred to him) would be shot in the morning. There then broke out a debate over who was to perform the execution. Cheadle and Patenaude both insisted that Milton should do the deed, as it was his idea. Milton, on the other hand, thought differently and all retired without settling the matter. The following morning the debate rekindled, with Milton still refusing to shoot the animal After a lengthy discussion, Patenaude suddenly leapt to his feet, picked up his rifle, and dispatched the unfortunate horse with a clean shot behind the ear. It did not take long before pack horse steaks were being cooked as the party cut the meat up into thin slices for 'jerking' (smoking over an open fire). All declared that the meat was very enjoyable, except for Milton who complained that it 'tasted strongly of stable'.

Patenaude stayed awake all night to keep the fire going, and, by noon the next day, they had 30–40lb of smoke-dried meat ('perhaps enough for a week'). However, much to their disappointment, having hoped for some open ground, the progress through the riverside forest over the next few days proved to be as difficult as it had ever been – possibly worse. Suddenly, without warning, Patenaude flew into a rage declaring that they had taken the wrong route. Why, he wanted to know, 'if the two Englishmen were "bourgeois" … had they not come with better horses and a larger party?' Milton and Cheadle (the former, probably smarting at being called middle class), showed the Métis the map the old Indian woman had drawn for them at Tête Jaune Cache. Despite being 'imperfect' the sketch showed the river hemmed in between hills that ran alongside both banks – just the situation they were then in. The information restored Patenaude to a better humour and he returned to his invaluable role, hacking through the undergrowth to clear the trail, and pursuing the occasional target to add to the pot. Despite the river narrowing into a long, wild, churning, stretch of rapids (named by Milton 'Murchison's Rapids' in honour of Sir Roderick Murchison, geologist, and one of the founders of the Royal Geographical Society), Cheadle had some luck with a fishing line and hooks, obtaining a small, but welcome, return of a few trout from the river. These were mainly devoured by Milton who, although the instigator of Blackie's sacrifice, claimed that the dried meat was inedible. Papillon also joined in, chasing a porcupine up a tree and staying on guard until Patenaude arrived and shot the animal. Cheadle thought the bonus meat tasted like a strongly flavoured sucking pig, and Milton regarded the fat as being 'equal to that of a turtle'.

There was, however, no escaping the fact that everyone was getting weaker, a position clearly evident when on the morning of Friday 14 August, they came up against a low mountain that descended almost vertically to the river's edge. The horses had to be led up the steep slope to the point where they could pass along the mountain side before they came down an equally steep descent returning to the river. Cheadle took charge of one of the pack horses and, after a tiring struggle, succeeded in rejoining the river. He then decided to go back to see if anyone else needed help. Just as he was about to reach the highest point of the climb, he met Mr O'B on his way down. The Irishman had been given the responsibility of bringing Bucephalus, Cheadle's horse, across the mountain side, but Mr O'B was on his own. When asked where the horse was, Mr O'B replied: 'He's gone, killed, tumbled over a precipice. He slipped and fell over – and must be smashed to pieces.' Cheadle, aghast at the thought of his awkward, but loyal, horse lying dead at the foot of some deep gully, spun Mr O'B around and marched him back up the slope demanding to see where the fall had happened. Sure enough, slip marks on the mossy rocks showed both the site and the cause of the incident. The broken branches beneath showed the route of the rapid descent. Cheadle peered over the edge, and was astonished to see, approximately a hundred feet down the almost perpendicular slope, Bucephalus astride the horizontal trunk of a fallen tree. With his legs dangling just short of the ground, he looked a sorry sight, and Cheadle 'gave him up as killed'. Taking a highly alarmed Mr O'B with him, Cheadle scrambled down the slope and reached the suspended horse. Much to his delight, on closer examination, the horse 'appeared quite comfortable in his novel position'. Removing the packs carried by the horse, the two men rolled the animal off the tree trunk onto the leaf-cushioned ground beneath. Bucephalus immediately regained his feet and appeared entirely uninjured. After catching his breath, Cheadle handed the reins to Mr O'B and led them both up the slope again, while carrying the packs on his back. At the top, the packs were re-secured to the horse's harness, and Cheadle took the reins to lead him forward. They had not gone very far when Cheadle turned back to look for Mr O'B who was finding the climb very difficult. As he did so, Bucephalus took a further step – and promptly disappeared over the edge. Fearing the worst, Cheadle looked over the cliff and was overjoyed with what he saw. Bucephalus had dropped no more than 10 feet and was resting with his back against a pair of trees. Yet again, the baggage had to be rescued, the horse put back on his feet, and hauled up the slope.

Safely back at the base of the mountain, the party rested briefly before continuing along the river bank, the waters racing through the narrowing gap. Eventually, with the river now little more than 50 yards wide, the water plunged past high rocks and fell in a steep cascade that frothed violently as it roared along, echoing against the mountain sides. There was no possibility of rafts or canoes surviving such a powerful cataract and, assuming that they had survived, with the rapids far too long to portage their large rafts along the bank, the Overlanders would have had to abandon their craft somewhere up river. Patenaude named the place La Porte d'Enfer (Hell's Gate, now Porte d'Enfer Canyon, or Little Hell's Gate), and Cheadle was reminded, yet again, of walking with his sister by the river near Bolton Abbey.

Almost 2 miles to the south-east of the rapids, a long ridge ended in a blunt bluff facing to the south. It was decided that this feature should be named 'Messiter Summit' in honour of their one-time companion, Charles Alston Messiter. That evening, Cheadle noticed that Milton seemed somewhat downcast and in low spirits, while Patenaude was limping from a cut on his foot. To cheer everyone up, he took out the old woman's map and explained that, according to the sketch, the fort at Kamloops was at the end of the range of hills they were now passing through. Their destination could not be much further, and their difficulties would soon be at an end. This possibility cheered everyone up, and they celebrated by making a rubbaboo of a brace of partridges (which Patenaude and his son 'nobbled' out of a tree by throwing sticks at them), dried horse meat and berries.

The next day, the rapids still boiled noisily past, the mountains still rose vertically from the river bank, Cheadle failed to catch any fish, and Patenaude's injured foot prevented him from playing an active part. Instead, Mrs Assiniboine took up the axe and became the party's pathfinder, hacking her way through the underbrush, and wading through black, stagnant ponds. That evening, as they ate the last of the dried meat, knowing that the only food they had was a single fish from the previous day, it began to rain. There was, however, good cause for hope. During the day, they had come across several tree stumps that showed evidence of work using an axe. Apart from the dead Indian, it was the first indication of human activity they had seen since they had left Slaughter Camp. In the morning, the rain continued to fall so heavily that there was little point in leaving the site until it eased off. Cheadle went to check his fishing lines and was rewarded by a single, small trout. On his return, he was surprised to see Mrs Assiniboine cutting up dried horsemeat. It transpired that the woman had hidden a portion of the meat away in case of an emergency. She had also saved the flour bag and had scraped the sodden dust from every corner and fold, all of which helped produce a welcome rubbaboo. It then turned out that one of the two remaining fish showed unmistakable signs of decay so a second – two fish – breakfast was produced rather than see the food wasted.

As soon as the party left the campsite, the heavy rain returned and everyone was soaked. The gloom this brought about was deepened when a horse fell while crossing a small river. All Mr O'B's scanty property was soaked, as was Milton's bedding. Mr O'B was feeling particularly depressed as his constant reading material, Paley's *Evidences of Christianity*, had caused him to question his faith. He was firmly of the opinion that his faith kept him sane, and now that he had some doubts, he was equally convinced that he would go mad in a very short time. Consequently, he began to be seen muttering to himself with a sullen air of dejection. To the surprise of all, Patenaude joined in the gloom, becoming dispirited and, on one occasion, sitting down and refusing to move.

The answer to both Mr O'B's and Patenaude's problems turned out to be simple – shoot another horse. This time it was Patenaude's Petit Rouge who made the ultimate sacrifice (after an agreed compensation had been settled).

Milton then produced another idea that would solve their problems – build a raft and take to the river. The idea was instantly rejected by everyone else. Rapids had already been encountered on the river, and no one wanted to take the risk of meeting with others while afloat on a flimsy raft. The viscount instantly resorted to his argumentative stance, and attempted to provoke Cheadle in particular. The vicar's son, however, retreated into daydreaming about tobacco, clay pipes, and beer. Milton's manner worsened over the next two days beneath heavy rain, thunderstorms, and long stretches of soft mud. On the first fine morning they had enjoyed for some days, he was riding with Cheadle and Mr O'B when they were met by The Boy on foot. Milton asked The Boy a question to which he replied in a garbled manner. Milton asked the question again, but The Boy continued walking past without answering.

At this, Milton exploded with rage and began to harangue the young Indian. With quiet deliberation, The Boy turned, took his rifle from its cover, and raised it in Milton's direction. Cheadle leapt from his horse, grabbed the gun, and 'blew the boy up soundly'. Then he turned on Milton, shouting at him for being 'apathetic, holding back, utterly reckless of the value of time, not appreciating the awkwardness of our situation, and always quarrelling about small things of no consequence'. That night, the fresh meat ran out.

In the morning, they dined on abundant fruit, and were delighted to come across a barely decipherable message notice left on a tree. After studying it closely, the words seemed to say 'This trale goos to thy steame land' (the fifth word may have been 'dream'). Cheadle was convinced it had been written by 'Yankees' making their way to the Cariboo goldfields. The effect of this contact with other human activity seemed to have a marked effect upon Milton – although his recent encounter with the gun-bearing Boy might have also left its mark. Cheadle was astonished when the viscount woke him up before daybreak, and was moved to record the incident with a sardonic 'Bravo!' A journey of 18 miles brought them out of the shadow of the low mountains and on to a small prairie where the surviving horses feasted on grass, the like of which they had not eaten since they left Fort Edmonton. Now certain that they were approaching the fort, their expectations were strengthened by a rustling in the undergrowth just ahead of them which, seconds later, produced an elderly Shuswap followed by his wife with a small child on her back. On the verge of alarm, the Indian was swamped by strangers patting him on his back, shaking his hand, and generally appearing to be in a state of ecstasy at meeting him. The family were, of course, the first humans they had met since leaving Tête Jaune Cache more than a month earlier. The name Kamloops seemed to mean something to the Indian who, in sign language, suggested that they might arrive at the fort that night. The next morning, however, saw them eating the last of the dried horsemeat for breakfast, followed by some wild cherries as they left the camp.

At midday they heard Mr O'B shouting to gain their attention. He turned up holding the hand of a Shuswap, with another, much younger, following on behind. As he approached, Mr O'B bawled loudly, 'Look here, my Lord! Look here, Doctor! I've been the means of saving us, after all.' After the usual greetings, the older Indian (who Milton and Cheadle named after Shakespeare's 'Caliban' for his somewhat battered features) indicated that they should follow him. They agreed, and he took them a short distance to where two women and several children sat around a fire cooking red berries 'of a kind of lily'. Portions of the pot's contents – 'as sweet as any jam in the world' – were shared out. As they enjoyed their unexpected meal, the Indian family they had met on the previous day arrived with the news that they had some potatoes. Soon a minor market trade grew out of nothing, with rabbits, berries, and potatoes being exchanged for shirts, needles, buffalo robes, and a pair of Cheadle's trousers. Best of all – but hugely expensive – was half an inch of rope tobacco, traded for a shirt. While the dealing was continuing, they learned that the fort at Kamloops was well stocked with goods with the Indians using several familiar English names. Tobacco, tea, salmon and whisky were all available, as was plenty of 'muck-a-muck' – food. The Indians also answered their question about the distance to Kamloops by mimicking a fast walk, and then pretending to go to sleep four times – four days at a good pace. When they arose the following day, they discovered that several of the Indians had already left in the direction of Kamloops, but the younger Indian and his wife remained to point out the trail before taking to the river in their canoe. Their instructions were that they should meet up with the Indians at the west bank of the Thompson River, where they would be ferried across to an easier path on the other side. After an easy ride, during which Cheadle gorged himself on the wayside 'lily' berries, they reached a tributary of the Thompson (Clearwater River), and found Caliban waiting to take them across in his canoe. They then camped for the night on its southern bank.

The following day, continuing on to the Thomson, they came across a pitiful sight. Two dead Indians – presumed to be husband and wife – had been laid out by the side of the path. The bodies were covered with blankets and were surrounded by their domestic possessions. They may have died from the smallpox, which was widespread in the area (the younger Indian's wife showed, by the marks on her face, that she had survived the pestilence), but

Cheadle was of the opinion that they had died from starvation. Several more such bodies were found over the next few days, leading Cheadle to revise his original opinion – the corpses showed all the signs of smallpox.

Again, they found the Indians waiting for them on the west bank of the Thompson River, complete with a pot of berries on the boil. Milton was not over keen on the fruit, and took only a small sample. Cheadle on the other hand 'ate greedily'. Almost inevitably, before they set off to cross over further down river, Cheadle was struck by a bout of vomiting and stomach ache that prevented him from leaving with the others. Unable to walk, the journey in the wake of the rest of the party proved to be very difficult with Bucephalus slipping on moss-covered fallen timber, or threatening to tumble down rock-strewn cliffs, as was his wont. While struggling to control his horse as they came down the steep side of a mountain to meet up with the rest, Cheadle heard shouting between Patenaude and Mr O'B but, in no condition to do anything about it, he carried on along the trail. Shortly afterwards, Patenaude arrived in search of a missing horse and Cheadle asked him about the Irishman. The Métis told him that he had demanded Mr O'B lead two horses along the final part of the trail, but he had refused. Patenaude, in no mood for verbal persuasion, threw a punch at Mr O'B, who promptly fled – and had not been seen since. That night Cheadle, and Patenaude set up camp with Cheadle unable to continue further. At least one of them was also concerned that Mr O'B, with his talent for becoming lost, might be in danger.

It was with some surprise that, the following morning, on arrival at the river bank where the Indians and Milton were waiting, Mr O'B was moping around looking 'very glum'. Milton explained that their lost companion had arrived at the camp in the middle of the night, and woke him up to explain that Patenaude had attacked him with an axe. It was, the story continued, thanks only to Mr O'B's 'presence of mind' in running away, that he had escaped a murderous assault. Cheadle examined the Irishman, and found a slight swelling on the right-hand side of the back of his head. Whatever had caused the swelling, it had been so lightly applied that the skin had not even discoloured. Nevertheless, Mr O'B declared loudly that he would seek justice on arrival at Fort

Kamloops and demand 'irons and imprisonment' for his attacker. Cheadle spoke to Patenaude who swore that he had used only his fist, and then only once. He did admit, however, that when Mr O'B still refused to help, he had picked up the axe – whereupon, Mr O'B fled. After sternly telling Patenaude that he should not strike any of the party with his fist, Cheadle ridiculed Mr O'B to his face until he withdrew the threat of bringing in the Kamloops authority. With matters 'nearly square' once again, the crossing to the east bank was made safely, and – in an effort to show some sympathy towards Patenaude – a prominent rocky hill rising directly from the west bank of the river, was named Assiniboine Bluff.

In the meantime, Milton, discovering that the Indian women were to be taken down river by canoe, gave the young Indian a waterproof cart-cover as his fare to join them. At this point, Caliban departed from them, having exchanged a bucketful of potatoes for Milton's saddle and Mr O'B's 'MB' waistcoat (a clergyman's waistcoat with 'MB' standing for 'Mark of the Beast'). Cheadle, still feeling 'seedy', and unable to eat the few potatoes that were available, joined the others as they made their way along a trail following the eastern bank of the Thompson. Much of the journey was now over open prairie with a scattering of low, pine-covered hills. As they progressed along the bank, it was with some interest that they watched two men on horses, closely followed by foals, ride up to them. It seemed as if the strangers were Mexicans as their harnesses were decorated by jingling bells, they sat on decorated Mexican saddles, and wore wide trousers and broad-brimmed, 'wide-awake hats' (said to have been so named as they were made without 'naps'). They also had brass-mounted pistols in their broad belts. Despite their unexpected appearance (both in dress and arrival) the two men turned out to be Shuswap Indians, who readily supplied the party with a drink of coffee and a plug of rope tobacco before joining them along the trail. After about 5 miles they found the canoe party with Milton sheltering beneath a reed mat after his cruise downriver. As they were now in range of Fort Kamloops and the opportunity of social interaction, the Indians had decided to bathe and put on clean clothes. One woman looked especially 'smart' to Cheadle, dressed in green and white, with her hair combed to fall around her face, and her cheeks and lips reddened. In exchange for a meal of potatoes and sweet coffee, he gave her a silk handkerchief which she tied in her hair. He also bought some potatoes from an old woman for a pair of socks, and two ducks in exchange for an old waistcoat and some shot.

Clearly in a hurry, the young Indian brought the party together and urged them to start immediately. He wanted to reach a place on the river where salmon could be caught. With no horse, but fitter than the rest, Mr O'B was sent on ahead, as the remainder hurriedly packed their baggage. The party arrived at the site just before dusk, and found two, perhaps three, Indian families already in occupation. It did not take long to become acquainted. Soon flour was traded for a bit of buffalo skin, and fish hooks for fish. When put with Cheadle's ducks, a couple of partridges he had shot, and ample potatoes, a fine feast was under way. To add to the event, a Métis who could speak both French and English joined them. He told them that Fort Kamloops was no more than about 17 miles from where they sat, that the 'Yankee War' was still being fought – and that the Southerners were getting 'the best of it' ('Hurrah! Hurrah!').

After a sound night's sleep, the party and their guide left beneath a hot sun. Cheadle, walking when he could as Bucephalus was very weak, was joined by Mr O'B, smoking a pipe of tobacco he had obtained from Milton. The young Indian guide rode up and told them that he could not go any further, but pointed out a range of hills in the near distance where they would find the fort. Patenaude agreed to give him his gun as a reward for his work on their behalf. After the Indian had gone, Patenaude explained that the young Shuswap had broken a rigid Indian custom that if a man died childless, his brother would marry the widow. Their guide, however, had run off with one such widow. In consequence, he was at risk of suffering from the vengeance of the offended family – and they lived around Kamloops. With Cheadle transferring to Patenaude's horse, it was arranged that the two Englishmen should press on ahead to try to reach the fort before the night set in. They set off with as fast a trot as they could manage when riding horses that were severely undernourished. Mr O'B had already set off on foot – in an effort not to be left with Patenaude – and when they passed him, he cried out, 'Don't leave me, my Lord! Do stop for me, Doctor!

Please let me come with you!' But, in the near distance, they could see the lights of a house and, with Mr O'B sprinting along in their wake, reached at the building. It appeared that they had arrived in the middle of some sort of celebration. Men and women were sat eating and drinking around a tarpaulin on the ground, while pots and pans simmered on a nearby fire. An old man rose to his feet to welcome them, saying (in a mixture of languages) that his name was 'Captain St Paul' ('Of whom we must have heard'), and that they could join them for a dollar each. With no hesitation, they joined in the feast of bacon, cabbage, cakes, and tea. Just minutes later, a breathless Mr O'B arrived, settled the price of admission with the old man, and was tucking in like a trencherman. Finally, Patenaude, Mrs Assiniboine and their son rode onto the property and joined the festivities.

Accommodation for the party was found within the house for the rest of the night. As they mingled with the people already at the house, they were all bombarded with questions about their reason for being there; questions, in the main, arising from their bedraggled appearance. Were they miners, explorers, just looking for work? The best answer that Milton and Cheadle could find was that they were 'a mere party of pleasure'.

It was not long before another group arrived – this time from the fort, and it was time for the 'Half-breed's Ball' to begin. As the fiddles started, Captain St Paul brought across a young man in his mid-twenties he wanted to introduce to Milton and Cheadle. Known simply as 'Mr Martin', Cheadle considered him to be 'full of chaff and oaths, a complete sailor in manner', which, considering he was the descendent of several Royal Naval admirals (including, at least, one First Sea Lord), was not surprising. He had served in the Royal Navy as a midshipman during the Crimean War, then set off on a life of adventure, which had included gold mining and a period of vagrancy before coming to Fort Kamloops as deputy to Joseph McKay, the fort's chief trader. He was, therefore, not prone to judging by appearances as he was introduced to the gaunt, bedraggled and unwashed strangers. Instead, Mr Martin had no hesitation in inviting the new arrivals to call on him at the fort on the morrow – before leaving to join in the stamping, whirling, dance of the Métis and their women.

After a night of intermittent sleep, frequently disturbed by the revellers, Milton and Cheadle awoke, eager for a substantial breakfast, only to find that they had to wait until almost midday before anyone emerged to provide food. Even then, their enjoyment was spoiled by their being joined by the host who insisted on telling them how important he was, with – according to St Paul – even the governor addressing him as 'Monsieur Captain St Paul'. A Métis, believed to be of French and Iroquois descent, St Paul's original name had been Jean-Baptiste Lolo. He had become involved with the fur trade as an interpreter, eventually working for the Hudson's Bay Company from 1822. During a long career with the company, he had shown himself to be a valuable contributor to the retention of good relationships between the Indians and his employers. So important had he become in this aspect of his work, that when he provoked a chief trader and received a flogging in reply, the threat of a breakdown in relations with the Indians led to him being given the title 'Chief' in compensation. When it was realised that he attached great importance to titles, he was, over time, rewarded with 'Monsieur', and then 'Captain'. To add a final touch of haughty disdain, he adopted the name 'St Paul' from the missionary parish in which he lived. Mr O'B, recognising a competitor in the pomposity field, took great pains to avoid him.

Leaving their horses on St Paul's property to recover, Milton, Cheadle and the rest of the party, at the cost of 'two old, stinking, buffalo-robe saddle-cloths', were taken down river by canoe. At the confluence of the North and South Thompson rivers, the waterway turns sharply to the west beneath low hills. There, on the north bank, beneath a large, rounded, hill (later named Mount St Paul after their recent host), sat the newly erected Fort Kamloops.

10

Farewell to Mr O'B – Royal Engineers on the Cariboo Road

The party's arrival at Fort Kamloops was greeted by one of the fort's clerks, Mr Burgess ('a civil, gentlemanly youth'). In view of their appearance, he arranged a visit to the fort's store, which procured new trousers and shirts, along with towels and soap. After a plunge into the Thompson and 'a regular scrub-down', the new clothing was put on, and they headed off for dinner. Before they sat down to eat, Martin arrived with a Mr Bingham, a world traveller who now worked for the Hudson's Bay Company. Introductions over, as they were about to start their meal, the door opened and in sauntered Mr O'B. Unexpected, and uninvited, the Irishman sat down at the table and began to devour large portions of mutton chops, potatoes, galettes with fresh butter, and rice pudding. Like the others, Milton and Cheadle ignored the interruption and listened eagerly to the news. The Prince of Wales had married, Mexico had been invaded by the French, and the Northern forces had captured the fortified Mississippi city of Vicksburg. The local news informed them that at least 300 Indians had died of the smallpox the previous winter, and two clerks, responsible for transporting money from the goldfields, were shot at by two men – one, an Englishman, the other, an American. One clerk was killed, the other fled with the money in his saddlebags. A reward of $6,000 was offered for the capture of the would-be robbers. Such a crime was unusual, as the Governor of Vancouver Island and British Columbia, James Douglas, in an effort to avoid the lawlessness of the California Gold Rush, had reacted strongly to any criminal activity in the area. Of particular interest to Milton and Cheadle was the story of the different Overlander groups. Those who had gone downriver on the Fraser as it headed north-west to Fort George (modern Prince George) before curving south to Quesnel and the road to the goldfields, started off well. But, in time, they encountered rapids on the river and four men lost their lives. The remainder pressed on and, after great trials and determination, eventually reached their goal. The southern party's experiences were similar to that suggested by Patenaude. After reaching the North Thompson, they found it impossible to make any progress to the west. The cattle they brought with them were all killed at Slaughter Camp and their horses set loose. Large rafts were constructed and drifted down the Thompson – only to be wrecked and overturned at the Murchison Rapids and at La Porte d'Enfer, where two men died. Again, however, courage and determination kept the remainder going until they reached Kamloops. Of all the Overlanders, few, if any, showed the astonishing courage of the only woman in the entire party, Catherine Schubert, who gave birth to a daughter the day after she arrived at the fort.

A smaller party, consisting of three brothers and two other men, arrived at Tête Jaune Cache after the other Overlanders had departed, and decided to take the Fraser route. Buying two canoes from the Indians, they later lashed the two craft together in the belief that such an arrangement would see them safely through the rapids. A month later, two of the brothers staggered into Fort George asking for help to rescue the remaining three men who were unable to move through frostbite and exposure – their canoes had overturned in the rapids. A party of Indians were sent out to try to rescue the men, only to return with the news that two of the stranded men had killed the third, and resorted to cannibalism. When the Indians approached, the two survivors drew their guns, and the Indians had fled. Months later, a pile of bones and frozen bodies were found. The worst news, however, for Milton and Cheadle, was that the trail to the Cariboo goldfields from Kamloops took twelve days to cover, and by the time they would be ready to leave, snow would have made the route impassable. The news left them with two problems that needed to be dealt with as soon as possible.

The first question was – should they press on, and by what route? They could have remained at Kamloops over the winter and set off after the thaw. Milton was quite prepared to spend another year in the Colony of British Columbia but Cheadle, eager to continue his medical training, preferred an earlier return to England. In fact, the idea (particularly in the mind of Milton) of a route to transport gold eastwards across British North America, rather than sending it via the United States of America, could be considered during a visit to the goldfields whether snow was on the ground or not. That agreed, there still remained the question of a route. The answer probably came from one of the staff or other visitors at the fort (Martin knew the area from his gold mining experiences). It was suggested that the party travel down the Thompson River until it joined the Fraser. That river would take them to the newly built city, New Westminster, near the Fraser's estuary. The settlement had been built in 1858 as a response to the pressure of American gold miners, which, it was feared, would lead to a full-blown invasion by the USA. On the north bank of the river, the site was moderately defensible, and also provided an administrative and trade centre for the colony. Of greater interest to Milton and Cheadle, however, was the fact that a trail via rivers, lakes and portages had been created as far as Quesnel. From there it was just a few days overland, eastwards, to the goldfields.

With the route agreed, it was also decided to make a modest extension of their route by visiting Victoria, the capital of the Colony of Vancouver Island. Not only could they collect the mail they had arranged to be forwarded to Victoria, but they could take Patenaude, Mrs Assiniboine, and The Boy on a visit to their first large city before they returned to their home east of the Rocky Mountains.

With their immediate future travels settled, there just remained the second problem – Mr O'B. The eccentric Irishman had succeeded in irritating all those with whom he came into contact. Mr Martin complained of his walking in on meals, and helping himself without so much as a word of greeting or thanks. Martin also disliked Mr O'B's long discourses on influential people he knew, clearly delivered in the hope of some connection with the listener that he could use to solicit food, goods, transport, and accommodation. On the last day of August, the deputy chief trader decided the matter by giving Mr O'B twenty-four hours to leave, after giving him the information that transport and accommodation were easily found between Kamloops and Vancouver Island. Cheadle was immediately approached with a plea for minor items of clothing, tea, sugar, bread, and money. Milton was asked for a letter of introduction to replace the one Mr O'B had obtained from Archdean Cochrane at Portage La Prairie as part of the desperate cleric's attempt to get rid of him. A similar desperation moved Milton to provide a letter, along with tobacco and matches. Martin contributed with bacon and cake. Just before leaving, Mr O'B approached Cheadle once again to ask for money. When rebuffed, Mr O'B launched into a tirade saying that he had done all he could while behaving in a polite manner. He then blamed Patenaude for the loss of his horse, and suggested that Cheadle and Milton, somehow, had a hand in the animal's disappearance. Cheadle walked off in disgust as Mr O'B set off on his journey after assuring his former companions that he 'bore no ill-will, and would forgive and forget all his sufferings on the journey'.

Mr O'B's long wished-for departure did not herald a period of peace and quiet. The morning after Mr O'B's departure, Milton and Cheadle were at breakfast with Martin and Bingham, when Martin began a belligerent attack upon the Fort's absent chief trader, Joseph McKay, calling him, among other things, 'a damned half-breed'. Bingham – McKay's uncle – responded in kind and, within seconds, the verbal assaults had descended into a bar-room brawl with food and broken crockery flying throughout the cabin. The two Englishmen looked on with horror and disgust before resorting to a close study of the contents of their plates. When Bingham stamped off in outrage, Milton and Cheadle quietly finished their breakfast.

As if a breakfast interrupted by a ridiculous and embarrassing affray was not enough, later that day, a tall, bearded American rode into the fort. His name was Jerome Harper and, for almost three years, he had been herding cattle from California to the Cariboo goldfields – and becoming very rich in the process. Hearing about the presence of Milton and Cheadle, he tracked them down and without introduction began to harangue them very loudly about the British not having recognised the breakaway Southern States as soon as the war had broken out. A Virginian by birth, and with a family who had been deprived of their estates, Harper bellowed that no one in the North was fit to govern people such as those to the South, and the Southerners were all intellectuals compared to their northern neighbours. Furthermore, Harper forcibly assured Milton and Cheadle that General Robert E. Lee was a better commander than both Napoleon and Wellington, and that, by not recognising the government of Jefferson ('Jeff') Davis, the British were 'truckling (being obsequious and servile) to Lincoln'. Milton and Cheadle (the latter, at least, sympathetic to the Southern cause) listened politely to the tirade until a pause for breath allowed them to respond. They pointed out (while omitting mention of arms sales to the North) that Great Britain was the largest customer for the South's cotton, that British blockade runners were supplying goods to the South, and that warships were being built for the South in British dockyards. Furthermore, after two Southern diplomats were forcibly removed from a British ship in mid-ocean, troops were poured into British North America, and the threat of war against the United States led to President Lincoln releasing the imprisoned diplomats and allowing them to leave the United States on a Royal Naval warship. Therefore, they concluded, the South (and Harper) should be grateful for such British support. After a few seconds of thoughtful consideration, Harper continued his rant, which lasted until midnight ('wearying everyone').

Much to Milton and Cheadle's relief, Harper left the fort the following morning to be replaced, later during the day, by the welcome arrival of the chief trader, Joseph McKay. Cheadle described their new acquaintance as an 'undersized man in cowhide coat and breeches, jackboots and large peaked cap; like an overgrown jockey'. He also had facial features 'remarkably like Fanny Essex' (a Victorian female impersonator). Nevertheless, McKay proved to be full of information and to be of great practical assistance. He told them that, as a result of the attack on the clerks transporting the gold from the goldfields, security had been improved with the result that the last delivery had amounted to more than 4.5 tons of gold, worth a third of a million pounds. Unfortunately, however, he identified the gold-coloured crystals given to Milton at Tête Jaune Cache as iron pyrites – good for gun flints, and even as an indicator of local gold sources – but generally valueless. To offset any disappointment over the iron pyrites, McKay gave both Milton and Cheadle specimens of opals, which had been discovered close to Kamloops Lake, a broadening of the Thompson downriver of the town. Because cattle drivers, such as the recently departed Harper, were buying land on which they could graze their cattle, the price of land was soaring. McKay had recently bought land at Victoria at £1 an acre, only to sell it a short time later at £24 an acre. As they had almost no money between them, McKay provided a cheque that could be used to obtain cash at either New Westminster or Victoria. Instead of buying horses for the journey to the gold mining town of Yale, where the animals would have to be sold for a loss when they arrived, McKay allowed them to borrow enough horses for all the party, including Patenaude's family. Furthermore, he offered to escort them as far west as the settlement at Yale. Cheadle modified his initial opinion of McKay to 'very kind indeed' and 'a good fellow'. With the chief trader engaged on several administrative tasks, the final few days at Fort Kamloops was spent inspecting horses, hunting pheasants, and preparing for their departure. They left on Tuesday 8 September, and after a long fight with their pack horse which – despite an agreement between Milton and Cheadle to reduce their baggage to a single pair of saddlebags – refused to carry its share of the load.

After a day travelling along the hilly southern shore of Kamloops Lake and camping near its western end, they crossed the Thompson River the next morning and continued to follow the river's northern bank until it began to trend to the south west. At this point, McKay left them to attend to some company business. He advised them to find the camp of a company of Royal Engineers, who were at work constructing parts of the road from Yale to the Cariboo. After that, they should continue until they reached the small settlement at Cook's Ferry and wait for him to rejoin them.

Parting company with the river, the party reached the Yale to Cariboo trail (at modern Cache Creek) where the Patenaude family looked in astonishment at the broad highway – the first they had ever seen. The Boy, in particular, was much taken with the sight of other travellers on the road and repeatedly shouted (according to

Milton), '*Aiwarkaken! Mina quatuck*', meaning (again, according to Milton), 'By Jove! there's another fellow.' Two ranches and the Ashcroft Manor Roadhouse owned by former Cambridge University men, brothers Clement and Henry Cornwall, were disappointingly by-passed as the owners were absent. The two brothers had arrived from England the previous year with the intention of gold mining but, seeing the condition of many of the miners, decided to farm horses and cattle, open a roadhouse, and offer legal representation. Their enterprise had already made them very wealthy.

The trail had led them past numerous rounded hills, many sparsely clothed with trees, and with the appearance of a biblical wilderness familiar to visitors to the Middle East. The desert-like landscape, with its tumbleweed and sagebrush, would continue all the way south-west to Lytton where the Thompson River was embraced by the mighty Fraser. At the Cornwall's ranches, the road made contact once again with the Thompson, now running beneath high, wide and level terraces known as 'benches'. These features on both sides of the river had been noted as far back as the North Thompson, and they would continue on the Fraser until just to the north of Yale. It seems probable that the benches were created by huge volumes of water being released during a period of melting glaciers. The benches are the remains of lakes or river beds left behind as the subsequent narrower watercourse eroded the riverbed beneath, taking the water level down. Two or more benches existing in parallel on either side of the river suggest that the river has seen ice dams on more than one occasion. These features could range from just a few feet wide, to a depth of several miles, with some carrying entire communities on their surface.

Although considerably improved by the Royal Engineers and other contractors, the trail continually verged on the hazardous, and was, in parts, downright dangerous. Frequently suspended above the river on a timber scaffolding, without fencing, and with a drop of several hundred feet, Cheadle noted that he 'should be sorry to drive on a dark night'. On the other hand, where the trail had yet to be improved, the hazards could be even greater. Milton recorded a trail 'a few inches in width' zigzagging up a mountainside with the river 'hundreds of feet immediately below'. Much of the road-levelling work was done by gangs of Chinese labourers. The sight of these previously unknown people with their different facial features, pigtails; long, trailing, moustaches and conical hats reduced the Patenaude family to an uncontrollable shaking with mirth.

A few miles short of Cook's Ferry, a large camp could be seen. Assuming it to be the base of the Royal Engineers McKay had recommended, they rode in only to find – to their considerable disappointment – that it was a contractor's camp. However, as the cooks were just completing a large meal for about 25 men who were about to return to their base, it seemed impolite to refuse to join them in the meal. Another guest was a failed prospector on his way south. He told them that during his time gold prospecting, he was shown a copy of a letter from the colonial secretary to the governor, asking if anyone had heard about Milton and Cheadle crossing the Rocky Mountains. To Cheadle, trying to sleep on a 'very rough bed among the rocks', it prompted a depressing thought – 'I am afraid there is much anxiety about us in the two homes in England.'

They arrived at Cook's Ferry at noon the following day. It proved to be an unprepossessing place with many failed miners, some limping from the long walk south, shuffling their way home with their only comfort an old and dirty blanket carried on their backs. Harry Guillod, a Londoner returning to his family, wrote to his mother saying that he was

…in the remnants of my clothes and without a cent in my pocket. I had to leave my watch in deposit for my Steamboat fare, and as I left Cariboo without a change of clothes, here I am without a shirt to my back; what remains being only a collar and the tattered front; in a dilapidated coat and with one boot between two feet, and all things considered in a pretty respectable plight to present myself at Church; in fact having rather a wild appearance for beside my rags my hair has not been cut since I left England in May.

The tiny settlement had grown as a result of a rope ferry being constructed in 1861 by Mortimer Cook, an American from Mansfield, Ohio, to take gold miners across the Thompson. When

Milton and Cheadle arrived, apart from a few domestic dwellings, the site consisted of a blacksmith's forge, a store, and a roadhouse (owned by Cook). Cheadle found the site 'a wretched place', made even worse by there being no sign of McKay. After booking into the roadhouse, an invitation to dine from a Chinese man had to be refused on the grounds that they had no money. Eventually, beef and flour had to be obtained 'on tick'.

The next day seemed never-ending as McKay continued to be absent, but just as the sun was setting, a man of 'gentlemanly manners' rode in and encountered Cheadle. The stranger proved to be an Inverness-born Scotsman, Donald Fraser, who, until the previous year, had a seat on the council of Vancouver Island, and was a good friend of the governor. At first, he took Cheadle to be one of the Cariboo Road contractors, but when he was corrected, he told Cheadle that McKay was at the Royal Engineer's camp, and could be expected in the morning. Milton, Cheadle and The Boy were awoken in their tent the following morning by torrential rain, which threatened to flood their flimsy shelter. At first, they retreated to a hay barn, then decided to have a breakfast at the roadhouse. Once again living on 'tick' until McKay could arrive with cash to help them out, they enjoyed beef steaks and potatoes with hot rolls and butter at the cost of $1 per person. The meal was cooked by another Scotsman, John Ferguson who, when required, could entertain visitors by playing the fiddle. They were joined at the meal by Fraser who loaned an unkempt Milton a coat and a pair of trousers. The clothing could be returned on reaching Victoria's Hotel de France where Fraser kept permanent quarters. Later that day, McKay arrived. After settling their accounts ($49 – 'Not bad for two days!' as Cheadle's noted, probably with a hollow laugh), the chief trader plied them with brandy while telling them that he had to wait an extra day to check his trains of pack animals, which would arrive on the morrow. Another arrival was Mortimer Cook, the founder of Cook's Ferry. Cheadle found him to be the 'usual Yankee, but quieter'. The American's quietness may have been the result of an activity being carried out just a few hundred yards down river. A former Royal Engineer, Thomas Spence, now operating as a private contractor, was starting the construction of a bridge across the river. Within a year,

Cook's ferry was redundant, and Cook returned to Ohio to marry before moving on to Kansas, where he built a bridge of his own.

Leaving the Patenaude family to escort the baggage being carried in a wagon, Milton, Cheadle, and McKay were joined on the journey to Yale by Lieutenant Henry Palmer of the Royal Engineers. The British Columbia Detachment of the Engineers had been disbanded two months earlier, and Palmer had been left behind to supervise the administrative aspects of the return to England. (Of a detachment total of 153 officers and men, 130 chose to stay in British Columbia.) He was also on his way to marry the 15-year-old daughter of the Archdeacon of British Columbia before returning home. It was almost certainly this personal attachment that gave Governor James Douglas a welcome opportunity to open a new front against the Engineers commanding officer, Colonel Moody – whose independence of mind caused the governor great irritation. On 1 September, Douglas wrote to the following letter to Moody:

Dear Col. Moody.

I notice that Lieutenant Palmer is still here where I believe he has been for the last ten days or more.

There is nothing I desire less than to interfere in any way with matters affecting the details of the duties of your particular Department; but as this is the second if not third occasion of Lieut. Palmer's prolonged absence from an important public work which he was elected to superintend, and which it appears to me, if his presence there is necessary at all, cannot be thus forsaken without serious detriment to the public service. I cannot refrain from calling your attention to the matter, for apart from the expenses attendant upon these constant journeyings backwards and forwards and setting aside the question of injury to the work it exposes the Government to unpleasant reflection.

I trust you will not feel hurt at my thus quietly bringing the subject before you, but amidst the many things which I know you have in your mind at the present moment this particular matter may not have occurred to you with same force that it does to others.

I have, etc..........
James Douglas

Nevertheless, Palmer had proved to be a competent surveyor and on one of his surveying expeditions had encountered Captain John Palliser, who was leading an expedition westwards across the southern prairies and Rocky Mountains of British North America. Palliser was concerned that the already existing Hudson's Bay Company's trail between Fort Langley and Lake Osoyoos ventured south of the 49th Parallel – the recently established border with the USA. After carefully testing and measuring the situation, Palmer was able to assure Palliser that the trail did not breach the boundary. He was, furthermore, almost certain to have regaled his companions on the journey to Yale with his favourite story. On another of his expeditions, Palmer fell foul of the local Indians by catching salmon without the permission of the Salmon God – and the penalty was death. When the engineer realised that the Indians had only one Salmon God, he sternly replied that he had *two* Salmon Gods – one was the Great God in the sky, the other was the earthly Goddess who lived in a palace in London. If anything should happen to him, the salmon would stop coming upriver. Faced with such an appalling prospect, the Indians retired – only to return with two Indian maidens and a request that he marry them both and become one of the tribal chiefs. Palmer managed to sidestep the offer by declaring that if he married without the permission of his two Gods, they would, once again, stop the salmon. The ploy worked, thus saving him from 'the dual dangers of death and matrimony'. In truth, the thought of having to have two wives had left him wondering if 'he did not prefer that the Indians carried out the purpose of their first visit'. Lieutenant Palmer married the Archdeacon's daughter at Holy Trinity Church, New Westminster, and sailed for England on board HMS *Camelion* on 11 November.

The small settlement at Lytton – named after the colonial secretary and novelist, Sir Edward Bulwer-Lytton – was built on the site of an earlier Indian village. The settlement had taken root as a result of the gold finds on the banks of two rivers that had led to the 1858 gold rush. Occupying a wide bench above the confluence of the Fraser and the Thompson, an onlooker on the heights could not fail to notice how the distinctive waters of the two rivers were reluctant to merge. The muddy-brown, silt-carrying waters of the Fraser, and the clear, almost sediment-free waters of the Thompson, shared the canyons below Lytton until rapids forced their blending into the dominant, and longer, 'Fraser River'.

Milton and Cheadle were soon introduced to the Stipendiary Magistrate and Assistant Gold Commissioner for the District – Captain Henry Ball (late of Her Majesty's 11th and 55th Regiments of Foot). Ball had arrived unannounced from England and knocked on the governor's door clutching a letter of introduction from none other than Sir Edward Bulwer-Lytton himself. The governor, James Douglas, immediately appointed Ball to the post at Lytton. With a loveless marriage, Ball was most happy being out of town fly fishing (he had a habit of wearing fishing flies in his hat), or touring his district on his horse, Happy Jack. Cheadle thought him to be 'a very jolly fellow indeed'. The jollity expressed by Ball, however, may not have been entirely spontaneous. On 4 July, Earl Fitzwilliam had written to Douglas requesting that he give any help needed by Milton as he passed through Victoria. The letter arrived on 14 August, and Douglas replied immediately (punctuation as in the original):

My Lord,
  I have just received your letter of the 4th July by the Mail of this morning and I hasten to assure your Lordship, as it may relieve your natural anxiety on account of Lord Milton that I will have great pleasure in affording him every assistance in my power, during his stay in this Colony I may also state that I will take an early opportunity of recommending him to the care of the Magistrates through whose Districts he may probably travel in British Columbia on his way to this place.

I remain,
James Douglas

After a night's rest, the party set off for Yale, about 100 miles downriver. Until the completion of the new road, the trail had been little but a rough, hazardous pointer for all who were eager to reach the gold along the river's banks. The huge mountain bluffs that reached down to the river could only be passed by climbing their sides and passing along wooden stages hundreds of feet high, supported by ropes made from tree bark or deerskin. The deaths of men and pack animals were commonplace. The new road, started by the Royal Engineers, but still incomplete, had been created by the use of dynamite to blast a way around the bluffs, and wound its way up and down the lower contours of the hills and around the gulches.

Some 30 miles below Lytton, at Jackass Mountain (named after a mule that fell to its death), they encountered the steepest slope on the entire Cariboo Road. A weary 'tacking' (zigzag climb) up the sides of the western slopes led the supply mule trains to the ridge top, and down again on the other side. At one time, camels were tried on the mountain in the belief that they would find the slope less arduous. Their feet, however, suffered badly on the grey granite and they were abandoned in the surrounding country – with at least one surviving until the twentieth century. When stagecoaches were introduced to the road, one passenger deeply alarmed during the passage of an unguarded 500-foot drop above the river, nervously asked the driver what would happen if they went over the edge. His reply became legendary: 'Lady, that all depends upon what sort of life you've been leading.'

The party spent a night at Boston Bar at the roadhouse run by 'Boston Bar Alex', an establishment noted for its 'good food and sufficient sleeping accommodation'. The tiny settlement had received its name from the local Lillooet Indians – the large number of Americans passing through, or stopping to 'pan' for gold, being assumed to have come from that town. The Americans, with their different view of the Indians compared to the British administration, were often the cause of clashes. In 1858, however, it was reputed to be a French miner violently mistreating an Indian woman that led to the headless bodies of miners found floating in the Fraser River at Yale. An immediate panic broke out among the miners and 3,000 of them gathered for protection while some of the Americans organised themselves into three 'regiments', which set out northwards in retaliation. It did not go well. Two of the regiments travelled up the east bank of the river, as the third travelled on the opposite side. After minor vandalism of native property and crops, they camped

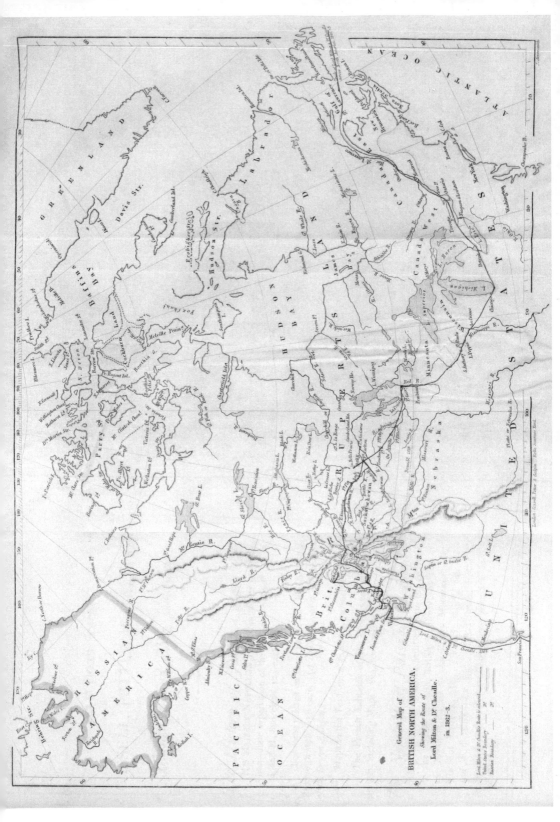

Milton and Cheadle's map.

The church at Bingley where Cheadle's father was the Rector.

Left: The Assinboine River where it was crossed by Milton and Cheadle just before they arrived at Fort Ellice on Thursday, 4 September 1862.

Below: La Belle Prairie. Milton and Cheadle considered it to be 'a lovely little spot... surrounded by low wooded hills'.

Above: The lake at La Belle Prairie – the site of the winter camp.

Right: The Rocky Mountains.

The Athabascan Valley.

Crossing point at the Athabasca River.

The Miette River joins the Athabasca.

The view from the camp at the head of Buffalo Dung (Yellowhead) Lake, reached on Thursday, 9 July 1863.

Mount Fitzwilliam.

Right: Mount Bingley.

Below: The Fraser River: At this point the Fraser is 30 miles from its source and more than 800 miles from the Pacific.

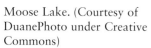
Moose Lake. (Courtesy of DuanePhoto under Creative Commons)

Robson Peak, now Mount Robson, from the shore. (Courtesy of Jeff Pang)

Mount Robson, the highest point in the Canadian rockies. (Courtesy of Jeff Pang)

The Albreda River, upper centre, joins the North Thompson River.

The North Thompson, looking eastward.

Above: The junction of the Thompson and the Fraser rivers, at Lytton.

Below: The Fraser River showing the terraces or 'benches'.

Hell's Gate, or *Porte d'Enfer*, on the Fraser River.

Lady Franklin's Rock.

Seton Lake.

The northern slope of
Pavilion Mountain; compare
this photograph to the
modern one below.

Below: Looking over the edge
of the Pavilion Mountain
trail. The lower end of the
trail can just be seen at
bottom centre.

The northern edge of 'The Chasm'.

Left: The view south down 'The Chasm'.

Above: A modern reconstruction of Barkerville, built on the same site as the original.

Left: The Courthouse at Richfield, used by Judge Begbie.

Barkerville in the 1860s; the path to Richfield can be seen at the bottom, on the left.

The walk between Richfield and Barkerville as it is now; William's Creek is to the right.

Above left: Williams Creek, with its gold-rich banks.

Left: The Cameron Claim on William's Creek.

Below: The site of the Cameron Claim as it is now.

The Fraser River at Hope, between Yale and New Westminster.

'English Camp', the Royal Marines' base on San Juan Island.

San Francisco in the 1860s, 'the Paris of the West'; booming in between the cholera epidemics of the 1850s and the devastation of the earthquake and subsequent fire in 1906.

An Adah Isaacs Menken postcard, advertising her appearance in Byron's *Mazeppa*.

The graves of Walter Butler Cheadle, right, and his second wife, Emily, in Ocklynge Cemetery, Eastbourne.

for the night. As the Americans on the western bank slept, a rifle was discharged accidentally. This resulted in carnage as the Americans – many of whom had taken part in gunfights during the Californian gold rush – blindly opened fire on each other with such effect that, when the firing died down, it's said only three men were left alive. With their militant ardour extinguished, the Americans pressed on to meet the Indians and agree a peace treaty.

By December 1858, and with the end of hostilities against the Indians, the Americans began a conflict between themselves. Many had worked in the Californian goldfields and were members of different gangs of miners committed to defending their claims and other interests – frequently with violent, and fatal, results. Yale, at the southern end of the Fraser Canyon, was in the grip of one of the Californian gangs, while Hill's Bar, an almost-exhausted gold panning site just a few miles downriver from Yale, was in the hands of another gang with a loathing of their neighbours. The conflict started over a dancehall brawl at Yale, which resulted in a Yale man being put into the town's already overcrowded jail for his own protection. At this, the leader of the Hill's Bar men, Ned McGowan, a former Pennsylvanian lawyer and politician turned Californian judge who was known for his less-than-respectable associates, had the Hill's Bar Justice of the Peace, George Perrier, a Frenchman, send a constable to demand that the Yale man be sent to Hill's Bar.

The Yale Justice of the Peace, Captain Peter Brunton Whaddell, seems to have had all the qualities of a pantomime comic villain. Born in Madras to an Indian Army officer, he spent a short time in the British Army in the early 1840s before returning to India as a postmaster. He then turned up in Melbourne, Australia, where he worked as a 'Captain' of a goldfield security patrol. He sailed to San Francisco in 1856, deserting his wife and child while running off with another man's wife. While on the west coast, Waddell worked as a saloon keeper in a mining camp before making his way to Vancouver Island, where he persuaded Governor Douglas to appoint him as Justice of the Peace at Yale. On taking up his post, he adopted the daily dress of a British Army uniform as worn during the Crimean war, complete with sword and an imposing military shako. Full of manly self-assurance – and with the support of the Yale Americans – Whaddell arrested the Hill's Bar constable and incarcerated him in the local jail. Such a decision by the Yale Justice of the Peace suited McGowan's purpose admirably. Armed with a warrant, he took a nine-man bodyguard upriver by canoe to Yale, marched ashore, arrested Whaddell and broke all the prisoners out of the jail. He then paraded the hapless Justice of the Peace through the town before returning to his canoes and proceeding downriver with the victim of the original assault, the constable, and the magistrate. When they arrived, Whaddell was taken before the Hill's Bar Justice of the Peace who fined him $50 for contempt of court (the money to be spent on a lavish celebration of the Hill's Bar men's victory) and given a canoe ride back to Yale.

When word of the incident (in a letter written by Whaddell) reached Governor Douglas, he had no doubt what was at the bottom of all the activity taking place on the Fraser. He was convinced that the large number of Americans in the entire Fraser and Cariboo area (between 25,000 and 30,000), represented a threat of invasion from British Columbia's southern neighbour. It was only a couple of years since the Hudson's Bay Company's 'New Caledonia' had been renamed as 'British Columbia' and there remained much to do to secure the colony from active American interest. The Governor had luck on his side. An advanced party of Royal Engineers had arrived at Victoria, under the leadership of the detachment commander Colonel Richard Moody. The colonel had no experience of the battlefield (he had spent the Crimean War on the Island of Malta) but, clearly, had enough courage, initiative, and enterprise to lead disciplined men when the situation demanded. Although the Royal Engineers were short of men, seamen and Royal Marines were available from HMS *Plumper*, a survey vessel involved in a boundary dispute between the British and the Americans. The ship could also provide a 9-pounder gun field gun, and a crew to man it. The arrival of Moody's force shattered any dreams of conquest among the American agitators. The fact that the British could provide an armed force within a week of the disorders breaking out came as a shock. Combined with the declining returns from the river banks and bars of the Fraser, the response was enough to persuade many of the American miners to return home. Soon, with the end of 'Ned McGowan's War', the number had fallen to less than 10,000. McGowan left British Columbia to cause trouble elsewhere. He departed with $500 from the sale of his claim, and $5,000-worth of gold dust. Moody sacked both the Justices of the Peace before returning to plan the construction of the new capital of British Columbia at New Westminster.

In mid-September, 1863, Milton and Cheadle experienced no alarms from such insurrections. They both considered the journey from Boston Bar to Yale to be 'probably the most wonderful in the world' (Milton), and 'a beautiful ride' (Cheadle). Furthermore, the beauty of the trail was considerably enhanced by the work done on the Cariboo Road. Yet to be completed, the road improvements had blasted through granite to provide a firmer, wider, and frequently timber-supported surface for the traveller. At the Nicaragua Slide (a site where part of the mountain had fallen into the river) the horses were sent up the old zigzag as Milton and Cheadle walked along the new, still uncompleted, section that curved around the front of the slide 700 feet above the river. Some 20 miles from Yale, their immediate destination, they came across a sudden narrowing of the river where the grey granite walls of the canyon intruded far into the waters. The site of an ancient Indian salmon fishery, the accelerated waters exhausted the salmon, making them easier to catch. In 1808, impressed by the violent water roaring through the narrow gap, the eponymous explorer, Simon Fraser, referred to the site as 'the gates of Hell' (the modern Hell's Gate). Cheadle, however, was very irritated by the version of the name then in use – *La Porte d'Enfer* – considering the spectacle to be 'not so fine, however, as the one we named like it on the North Branch of the Thompson'. He would, nevertheless, have been impressed when, 13 miles south of La Porte d'Enfer, the party was able to walk across the river on a brand-new bridge. Finally completed only a week or so before their arrival, the Alexandra Bridge was the first suspension bridge in western British North America. Named in honour of the Princess of Wales, the bridge provided an important link on the Cariboo Road.

The landscape and civil engineering achievements along the road between Boston Bar and Yale were, however, not the only features of note to attract the attention of those passing along it. Many Chinese gold-seekers were to be seen panning on the bars and banks of the river, as Indians were passed on the road competing with the mule trains by carrying heavy weights supported by a leather strap worn across their foreheads. Milton noted one woman carrying a 50-lb sack of flour, surmounted by a box of candles, the whole providing a perch for a small child. Numerous Indians were to be seen fishing for salmon. The fish were filleted and the heads taken off before drying. Any dried fish remaining at the start of the next fishing season could be stored away for anything up to a further three years. The heads were boiled separately. The ample oil produced was then stored in prepared fish-skin containers, later to be used for cooking and medicinal purposes. The method of catching the salmon had evolved over countless years. A small wooden platform was constructed on a projecting rock above a quiet eddy on the downstream side. There, the salmon rested from its constant struggle upstream, only to be caught in the landing net of the patient fisherman suspended above.

Less than a mile before their arrival at Yale, the river turned sharply to the west before the final stretch ended in a narrowing of the waters between two tall cliffs. It was not only the narrowing that increased the flow. In the main stream – slightly to the left of the river's centre – nature had deposited a huge rock, bristling with pine trees. Once beyond these mighty obstacles, the river opened out, escaping from its confinement within the Fraser Canyon.

Two years earlier, Yale had been visited by Jane, Lady Franklin, the wife of the famous explorer who had disappeared with hardly a trace during his attempt to discover the Northwest Passage across the top of North America. The settlement, being the head of the Fraser navigation, was reached by paddle-steamer before Lady Franklin's party transferred to a large canoe, which would transport her up the Fraser Canyon as far as the narrows at La Porte d'Enfer. The canoe was paddled by twelve Indians, all wearing red woollen shirts and with brightly coloured ribbons in their hair. As they approached the boiling rapids of their destination, a large banner was unfurled over the waters bearing the words 'Lady Franklin Pass'. This local initiative, however, did not find favour or support among the dignitaries at Victoria. Nor did the alternative suggestion that the massive rock at the end of the canyon should be named Lady Franklin's Rock receive any attention. In the latter case, however, any official objections were ignored, and the name stuck. Some said the name was suggested by the 'inhabitants of Yale', others by the Royal Engineers (the lady had been entertained for dinner by Colonel Moody just a few days earlier). Lady Franklin, who was not consulted on the matter at any stage, showed her appreciation by buying each of the Indian paddlers 'a gay cotton handkerchief', and treating them to a meal of 'bread, well smeared with treacle'.

As Milton and Cheadle rode past Lady Franklin's Rock, they saw Yale itself. Situated on a flat area on the northern bank, the settlement consisted of a single street running parallel to the river. Mountains rose as a backcloth to the town, while the foreshore – scoured for its gold – lay a forlorn width of mud, apart from the occasional Indian or Chinese who scraped away in the hope of finding the odd nugget. By now, the bulk of the Americans had given up and gone home, and there was plenty of room at the Colonial Hotel for Milton and Cheadle. They entertained McKay and his wife, Helen, that night, and were delighted to be joined by Donald Fraser, who was waiting for the next paddle-steamer. Their greatest delight, however, came in the form of a stranger introduced by McKay. He was a Scotsman, Roderick Finlayson, who was the senior Hudson's Bay Company official in the west of British North America. Even more impressive was the fact that he had received a letter of credit from none other than the 6th Earl Fitzwilliam. The money transfer – addressed to Milton – was worth £400, the equivalent of ten years of full-time work for the average British workman, and equivalent to fourteen years for the average agricultural worker. As a result, champagne flowed freely (much to the delight of any nearby miners) with the additional entertainment of an American visitor who not only believed he was Admiral Lord Nelson but for some reason known only to himself, gorged on cucumbers to confirm his identity.

With most of the party suffering 'tremendous headaches' the next morning, Milton, Cheadle, Lieutenant Palmer, and the Patenaude family boarded the stern paddle wheeler *Reliance*. Her captain and owner was Captain William Irving, a Scotsman who moved to the United States before moving up to the Fraser to set up in business ferrying passengers and freight between New Westminster and Yale. Fending off strong competition (at times with the assistance of exploding ferry boilers), Captain Irving had earned the title 'King of the Fraser River'.

The voyage down the widening river took the passengers past the small town of Hope, which Cheadle considered to be 'most beautifully situated' on a flat area with magnificent mountains behind. Sadly, however, the discovery of gold in the Cariboo led to the local searches for gold being abandoned and the town had 'gone in' – become destitute and desolate. Next, they passed Fort Langley, an old Hudson's Bay Company site that had been expected to be the capital of British Columbia. However, when Colonel Moody arrived with his Royal Engineers, he quickly pointed out the problems with the defence of the site in the event of an American invasion. As a result, Moody transferred his attention to New Westminster. On approaching the site of the newly proposed capital, it was soon evident that New Westminster had problems of its own. Built on the north bank of the Fraser with a steep south-facing slope, the site was clearly vulnerable to artillery fire from the south bank – where the British Government had refused permission for a defensive military base. It was also vulnerable to any attack from the north mounted by an enemy entering Burrard Inlet. To counter this, Moody had a road built to a new harbour (Port Moody), and created a military reserve on the south bank of the inlet's narrow entrance (Stanley Park). Another road was constructed to the nearest ice-free port to ensure winter supplies could get through. Mounting costs, the redeployment of the Royal Engineers on other road-building tasks, and the delay caused by the building of the nearby engineers barracks (Sapperton), were all blamed for holding up the completion of the project. On the site itself, the biggest practical problem was the density of the trees that had to be cleared. Thousands of tree stumps studded the terrain – each costing an average of $3 to remove. The greatest irritant, however, were perpetual clouds of savage mosquitoes.

After a night in the town's Colonial Hotel, during which time Milton had one of his 'attacks', the party boarded the steamship *Enterprise;* a San Francisco 'side-wheeler', the vessel was 147 feet long, with a beam of 27½ feet. At full power, her 19 feet diameter paddlewheels could rotate at 27 revolutions a minute. By the time the *Enterprise* had reached the Gulf of Georgia, separating Vancouver Island from the mainland, Cheadle's hope of a quiet voyage had all but vanished. With tales of their adventures now widely spread, 'everyone' wanted to buy them a drink. Milton was 'very seedy' and suffering from repeated 'symptoms'. Donald Fraser introduced him to Billy Ballou, a 'regular Yankee', and thus 'a loud-talking rowdy, nasal twang excessive'. Ballou had a well-earned reputation in the goldfields for supplying goods to the miners at a reasonable price, and for delivering mail and newspapers. Known for his dependability, he was frequently referred to as 'the man who never failed to deliver'. At the arrival of serious competition, Ballou had sold up and was returning to California. There was, however, the threat of worse to come. While ambling around the ship, Cheadle only just managed to avoid none other than Mr O'B. Milton, it appears, was not so lucky, and recorded their former companion as 'wonderfully altered'... 'more corpulent' ... and that he had 'quite regained his spirits'. The latter achievement was evident in the return of his 'loquacity, which had flagged so notably during our journey through the forest'.

When he could escape to take in the scenery, Cheadle took to the upper deck where the snowy slopes of Mount Baker could be seen glistening miles off the port bow. Also to port, the rigidly straight strip of cleared land denoting the 49th Parallel stretched to the east through the forests, clearly marking the border between British North America and the United States of America. Then there was the island of San Juan ('or "San Wawn" as the Yankees call it'). The shooting of a pig by a failed gold miner had led to Royal Marines and American soldiers being landed on the island but, instead of facing each other from trenches – while the politicians adopted threatening postures – the troops came together at parties, balls (the ladies coming over from Victoria), horse racing, and sports days. As the *Enterprise* steamed past, many of the American troops had been sent to take part in the Civil War (on both sides). Among those who left was Captain George Pickett, who later achieved notoriety at the Battle of Gettysburg as the result of the infamous 'Pickett's Charge', but the Royal Marines continued to see that those remaining were well catered for. No one dreamt of walking over and capturing the American lines – to do so, would not be fair play.

The *Enterprise* arrived at Victoria just as the sun set. A small party waited to greet Donald Fraser and, from this group, he selected a young man to take Milton and Cheadle to the Hotel de France. On their arrival, the proprietor took one look at their buckskin shirts, tattered trousers, generally unkempt appearance and absence of baggage before deciding that he had no vacancies. Both Milton and Cheadle turned on their heels and started for the entrance. Their guide, however, pointed out to the owner exactly who it was that he was dismissing. A waiter was immediately dispatched to bring the – now – distinguished guests back. They refused the offer of accommodation but sat down in the hotel's Coffee Room to consider alternative arrangements. Over drinks, the guide brought over two young men he introduced as James Judson Young, the private secretary to the governor, and Thomas Elwyn, an Irishman who had served in the Crimean War and who was responsible for the safe transmission of gold from the mines. Elwyn had rooms in the St George Hotel and knew that others were available. Before long, accommodation had been obtained, Milton, still feeling unwell, retired to bed, while Young and Elwyn escorted Cheadle to a nearby tailors where he purchased clothing more suited to refined parts of Victoria. On their return to the hotel, Cheadle, wearied after an eventful day, retired to the bar for a final drink. There, he was accosted by a waiter who told him that a slightly built gentleman with an Old Testament prophet-style beard would like to meet him. The stranger turned out to be Colonel Richard Clement Moody, the Commanding Officer of the Royal Engineers. Cheadle considered him to be 'a gentlemanly old bird' who 'treated' him to 'a full and complete history of the Colony, resources, etc, lasting about 1½ hours'.

The following morning, with Milton fitted out in a new suit, protocol demanded that the visiting dignitaries paid a call upon the governor. Their timing proved to be extremely fortunate as Governor Douglas was able to inform them that a letter from the secretary to colonies had arrived that morning advising him that he was to be 'raised to the second rank of the Order of the Bath, as a recognition of [his] public services'. They were invited to join the governor and Donald Fraser for a celebration lunch; they were very pleased to do so. Although frequently blunt in his approach, few could object to the governor's elevation to a knighthood. He had chosen the site for the building of Fort Victoria, overseen its construction, and ruled it with an iron hand when 30,000 – mainly American – miners descended on the settlement as the gold rush got under way. Cheadle thought him to be 'a fine old fellow with a magnificent presence, but rather affected drawling air'.

The next few days were dedicated to showing the Patenaude family around Victoria. The Hudson's Bay Company had provided them with accommodation, and many people had called upon them out of interest in their adventures. The 'Englishmen's Indians' were given clothing more suitable for wearing in town before being taken around Victoria in a carriage driven by Cheadle, with Milton sitting beside him. They were taken on board HMS *Sutlej*, named after a river of the subcontinent, a three-masted, 50-gun 'Fourth Rate' that had been converted into a 'screw' frigate with the introduction of a 500 horsepower engine. Six of her old cannon were replaced by an equal number of 40-pounders, and an additional 100-pounder gun was provided in support.

Most astonishing of all for the Patenaudes, was a trip to the theatre to see an American ensemble known as 'The Marsh Troup of Juvenile Comedians'. The show consisted of girls of about seventeen years old dressed as girls of twelve, 'which did not go very well with their womanly development'. To complete their stay on the island, the party encountered, once again, Mr O'B. He had been adopted as a worthy cause by the city's clergymen and, as a result, had rediscovered his religion to the extent that he could shake hands as a symbol of forgiveness towards Patenaude. Before they could leave Victoria, it was arranged that the party (without Mr O'B) should have their photograph taken. With this aim in mind, Milton and Cheadle had kept their buckskin shirts. All dressed as they had been clothed during their travels. Cheadle wore his tweed hat favoured among gentlemen during country pursuits, Milton – looking rather 'seedy' – wore his headband and carried a clay pipe, while The Boy wore his cap with the patent leather peak. Patenaude and Mrs Assiniboine wore the clothing that had seen them through the Rocky Mountains and all the way to Victoria. All seem to be looking at a mark over the photographer's right shoulder, with the exception of The Boy who appears to be suspicious of the cameraman.

The party left Vancouver Island on board the *Otter* as the *Enterprise*, taking the governor and his party to New Westminster, suffered a broken shaft driving the side wheels. The ship only narrowly avoided running onto rocks. Intending to travel lightly, Milton and Cheadle restricted themselves to a spare pair of socks, a toothbrush, and a flannel shirt rolled up into their blankets. Their feet and legs were encased in large jack boots, having been 'recommended for the mines', with all their remaining baggage being put into storage at the St George Hotel. Having failed to reach the Cariboo goldfield by the various routes from Tête Jaune Cache, it still remained the prime objective of their travels.

They were joined on the ship by Charles Good, an Oxford-educated clerk to the Under Colonial Secretary, who had absconded with one of the governor's daughters. The pair had crossed the border into the USA, married, and returned in the hope that the governor would forgive their youthful indiscretion. He refused to see them, so Good marched into the governor's office in the expectation that he could persuade Douglas to accept the situation. Instead, the governor knocked him to the floor with a single blow. In time, however, everyone was reconciled and Good was accepted into the colony's public service.

On their arrival at New Westminster, arrangements were made for the Patenaude family to remain on board overnight as the remainder transferred to the Colonial Hotel. As they were having supper, Young arrived with an invitation from the governor to join him for breakfast at 8.30 the following day. With the invitation accepted, Milton and Cheadle first called upon the Patenaudes and supervised their transfer to the *Reliance,* placing them in the reliable care of the captain, William Irving. They also gave the captain a note for the Hudson's Bay officer in charge at Yale requesting that he 'look after' the family. Patenaude's plan was to spend the winter employed as a shepherd at Kamloops, before crossing the Rocky Mountains by the Kootanie Pass. There was a strong warmth of feeling in their departure, as they had made a significant contribution to the successful journey undertaken by Milton and Cheadle. Despite the irritation at Mr O'B's manner and feebleness, and the occasional bombastic outburst from Milton, they had remained loyal to the enterprise.

In addition to Milton and Cheadle, Young and Good attended the breakfast, with Arthur Bushby, a London-born amateur musician who was serving as British Columbia's Registrar of Deeds. Three years earlier, he had been one of the founders of the Victoria Philharmonic Society and, in 1862, had married one of the governor's daughters.

Douglas, a 'Scotch West Indian' as he had been known during his time with the Hudson's Bay Company, took great delight in regaling his English guests with his version of the events that had taken place on San Juan Island. In a – rather fanciful – monologue, he explained how the 'Pig War' began when a 'Yankee officer' with just twenty men had landed on the island and 'kept off' several Royal Naval ships. When the American general, Winfield Scott, arrived on the scene, the governor demanded that the Americans left the island immediately – a demand to which Scott promptly agreed. In fact, Captain George Pickett (not a 'Yankee', but an ardent Confederate) had landed with sixty-five troops armed with three brass howitzers. HMS *Tribune,* armed with 31 heavy guns, had arrived off-shore with orders from the governor to remove the Americans, by force if necessary. Her captain, Geoffrey Phipps Hornby (the son of a Lord of the Admiralty and brother-in-law of a former Prime Minister), went ashore to speak to Pickett. Despite being massively out-gunned, and in a position devoid of shelter, the American refused to budge. Consequently, faced with the prospect of slaughtering the invaders just to please the governor while, almost certainly, instigating a war between the USA and Great Britain, Phipps Hornby returned to Victoria and informed Douglas of his decision not to act. When the furious governor demanded that he return immediately and open fire, the captain politely, firmly, and finally, reminded Douglas that a Royal Naval captain's orders came from the Admiralty – not from a civil servant. As for the visit of General Winfield Scott (who was neither a friend of Pickett, nor a supporter of his actions), Douglas had done no more that make an amicable agreement that an equal number of Royal Marines should be landed on the island to match the Americans.

Milton and Cheadle's intention had been to board the sternwheeler, *Hope*, that day and make the journey between New Westminster and Port Douglas (usually shortened to 'Douglas') at the head of Lake Harrison. However, the vessel was not expected to arrive until later in the afternoon, or even on the following day. With time on their hands, they decided to walk to the nearby Royal Engineers camp and call upon Colonel Moody. He, in turn, invited them to an auction of land in New Westminster. Having listened to the colonel's flattering description of the sites as excellent opportunities for investment, they decided to attend the sale. On their way, they called in at the governor's office and collected an official letter from Bushby requesting the gold commissioners along their route to give them any assistance they could, especially if their funds became depleted.

At the sale, Milton 'carried away by the excitement' purchased seven lots ranging from between 3 and 9 acres, the price of the lots varying between £20 to £32 each. Cheadle made a bid for one lot – only to be outbid ('by mistake') by Milton. Immediately after the sale, they went to have a look at the newly purchased properties with Captain William Spalding, the District Magistrate who, by opening the first New Westminster post office in his own house, had earned the appointment as the town's first Postmaster General. Disappointingly, Milton's land was indistinguishable from the rest of the closely compacted forest and did not bear too close an inspection. Returning to their hotel, they found a calling card from British Columbia's Attorney General, Henry Pering Pellew Crease.

Breakfast the next day was eaten in company with Good, who then took them to the local assay office, where they witnessed gold dust being melted and moulded into gold bars. At the office, they were introduced to Crease, whom Cheadle – noticing the similarity between himself and the attorney general – considered to be 'a good-looking bearded fellow like someone I know'. Another former Cambridge man, Crease got on well with the visitors. He was making steady progress up the British Columbia legal and political ladder, and was well-known for the English garden he and his wife had created at their New Westminster home. The contact with Henry Crease had no immediate value for Milton and Cheadle, but it was always useful to be able to mention his name to any obstructive magistrate that might be encountered en route.

Now it was finally time to leave for the goldfields.

11

Lake Steamers, the Goldfields, and Whist with the Royal Marines

When gold was discovered near an old Hudson's Bay Company fort close to the Columbia River in Washington Territory, the Governor of Vancouver Island, James Douglas, decided that the find – 20 miles south of the 49th Parallel – was close enough to inform the colonial secretary. In a letter dated 16 April 1856, and addressed to Henry Labouchère, a minor diplomat at the British Embassy in Washington, he suggested that the discovery of gold at Fort Colville might indicate that there was gold to be found north of the border. This opened up the possibility of a tax on any gold uncovered, and a tax could only be enforced if a military force was made available to him. After a wait of four months, he received a lukewarm reply from Labouchère stating that, 'Her Majesty's Government do not at present look for a revenue from this distant quarter of the British dominions, so neither are they prepared to incur any expense on account of it.' The following year, the possibility of gold being discovered north of the USA border began to take on a more menacing aspect. In July, Douglas wrote to Labouchère saying,

> There is much reason to fear that serious affrays may take place between the natives and the motley adventurers who will be attracted by the reputed wealth of the country from the United States possessions in Oregon, and may probably attempt to

overpower the opposition of the natives by force of arms, and thus endanger the peace of the country.

Five months later, having received no support or advice from the government in London, or the Embassy in Washington, Douglas decided to act. On his own authority, he began the appointment of a law officer to protect the Indians along the Thompson and the Fraser rivers, and to generally keep the peace, and issued an associated proclamation forbidding

> ...all persons to dig or disturb the soil in search of gold until authorised on that behalf by Her Majesty's Government.

The governor had taken this action because word of rich finds was spreading and

> ...causing much excitement among the population of the United States territories of Washington and Oregon, and I have no doubt that a great number of people from those territories will be attracted thither with the return of the fine weather in spring.
> In that case, difficulties between the natives and whites will be of frequent occurrence, and unless measures of prevention are taken, the country will soon be the scene of lawless misrule.

Douglas was certainly right about the attraction to those across the border. On the morning of Sunday 25 April 1858, the *Commodore*, a wooden, side-wheeled paddle-steamer, arrived at Victoria carrying 450 miners. Within a few weeks, more than 20,000 Americans had come ashore. However, in a letter to Labouchère dated 8 May 1858, it seemed the governor's concerns had come to nothing. Certainly, the influx of American gold-seekers had grown enormously but, although they far outnumbered the authorities in Victoria and along the banks of the Thompson and the Fraser, they did not appear to be 'the very dregs of society' that Douglas had expected. In fact, although exposed

> ...to many temptations to excess in the way of drink, yet quiet and order prevailed, and there was not a single committal for rioting, drunkenness, or other offences during their stay here.

This civic orderliness had led to a result that Douglas had not foreseen:

> The merchants and other business classes of Victoria are rejoicing in the advent of so large a body of the people in the colony, and are strongly in favour of making this port a stopping point between San Francisco and the gold mines, converting the latter, as it were, into a feeder and dependency of this colony.
>
> ...Victoria would thus become a depot and centre of trade for the gold districts, and the natural consequence would be an immediate increase in the wealth and population of the colony.

Furthermore, steamships would connect Victoria with the highest navigable point on the Fraser. Not only would the miners benefit, but there was every chance that the area would become a centre for British manufactured goods and trade. There was, however, one possible flaw in the predicted rosy future. With the almost overwhelming flood of Americans and other foreigners into the region, there was the danger that

> ...if the country be thrown open to indiscriminate immigration, the interests of the empire may suffer from the introduction of a foreign population, whose sympathies may be decidedly anti-British.

Many of the Indians were in favour of obstructing, even forcibly rejecting, the 'Bostons' (their word for Americans), but many others recognised that the Americans paid more for their labour than 'King George's men' and were quite willing to be hired as guides and canoe paddlers. The natives were not the only ones to take advantage of the large numbers of miners arriving from south of the border. Between June and December, 1858, in excess of half a million dollars' worth of gold was recovered from the banks of the Fraser and Thompson, and a noticeable expansion of the mining was taking place northward up the Fraser. A miner's license costing 10s a month, payable in advance, was introduced in late December 1858. Within one month, the licence had increased to 21s. Building lots at Victoria at the beginning of the gold rush could be bought for $50, within months they had increased to $1,000, while six adjoining lots in the city were sold for an astonishing $10,000.

The 1858 advance up the Fraser had brought the miners to the mouth of the Quesnel River, a tributary of the Fraser that curved southeast before meeting the Cariboo River, which continued eastwards and then north-eastwards before broadening out into Cariboo Lake. Some miners chose to continue up the Fraser until they reached Fort George (modern day Prince George) where gold was found in modest quantities. Others made their way up the Quesnel and Cariboo rivers, both of which provided their share of gold, but a broad, rapid, stream (Keithley Creek) flowing into the lake, proved to be even more profitable. When searches were made to the north of Cariboo Lake, further creeks were discovered lacing their way down and between the mountains. Many were carrying gold along their beds and banks, but William Dietz ('Dutch Bill' – although actually a Prussian seaman) and a small group of fellow miners decided to press on northwards and followed the flow of a stream to a point about 20 miles north of Cariboo Lake. Here they decided to try the creek to see if it contained any of the precious metal. The banks revealed just a modest amount and other streams such as the Harvey, the Antler, the Snowshoe, and the Lightning proved to be more rewarding. For those, however, who stuck with William's Creek, there was to be a stunning surprise.

With his partner away collecting supplies, one miner decided to dig deeper and broke through to a layer of gold-bearing gravel. By the time his partner returned after being away for forty-eight hours, over 3lb of gold had been recovered. Once word got out about the find, hundreds of miners made their way to the Cariboo area and, before long, every creek was lined with new claims as mining was taken to depths of 60 feet and more. By the end of 1861, one mine produced almost 26lb of gold in a single day, while another produced 190lb in six weeks without having to dig more than 4 feet. Altogether, the value of British Columbian gold produced in 1861 amounted to more than $2.5 million.

This amount of gold created an unusual situation, in which there was more gold in the colonies of British Columbia and Vancouver Island than there was currency. Consequently, successful miners were having difficulty in converting their gold into cash. Gold dust and nuggets were being used to buy stores and supplies at wildly varying rates of exchange.

In 1858, Governor Douglas had sent 50lb of gold dust to the mint at San Francisco to raise funds – and, inadvertently, started the gold rush of Californian miners. The Americans immediately opened an assay office at Victoria. Once the gold had been assayed, the customer was paid, and Wells Fargo sent the gold by ship to the San Francisco mint, where it was made into ingots or United States' gold coinage. An assay office was authorised by Douglas at New Westminster in 1860, to which was later added a mint. Neither enterprise prospered, and the British Government ordered the manufacture of gold coins, and the production of paper money to be closed down. Even an experimental production of $20 and $10 gold coins produced by the San Franciscan mint, and authorised by Douglas, was quickly stopped by the Government in London.

Another problem was caused by the American miners ignoring any British Columbian or Vancouver Island laws and simply taking their gold across the border into the USA, or taking it to San Francisco by ship. The scale on which this was happening can be judged by a report in the *New York Times* dated 11 September 1862:

> Three passengers, who arrived yesterday from British Columbia per steamer *Brother Jonathan*, deposited in the San Francisco Mint 12,000 ounces of gold-dust, worth $200,000. This treasure was not on the steamer's manifest, but was concealed by the owners in their baggage to save freight-money.

Inevitably, San Francisco's economy was booming at the expense of the colonies. It was this straightforward fact that prompted Milton and Cheadle to have as their key underlying motivation the possibility of an east-bound route to the Atlantic. Ideally, it would be a trans-British North America railway line reaching as far as a port on the northern shore of the St Lawrence River – well away from the border with the USA. Although neither man was a civil engineer, they had shown that the prairies over which they had travelled would present little difficulty in the establishment of a railway line, and that the Rocky Mountains had at least one pass that would serve for such a link and – again – be well clear of the American border. All that remained was to visit the gold fields to see the lie of the land.

The start of their journey did not seem very promising. Having paid $2 each for an overnight bunk on board the stern-wheeler *Hope*, they were kept awake by the vessel's 'wooding' as a gang of men hauled nets full of 4-foot long baulks of timber on board to fuel the ship as far as Port Douglas. When they eventually steamed off, just before sun-up, a large hay barge was lashed alongside, slowing their progress. After approximately 44 miles, they reached the confluence of the Fraser and the Harrison rivers. The latter, named after a deputy governor of the Hudson's Bay Company, had banks lined by low hills, its ample shallows foaming as vast shoals of salmon drove their way northwards while providing sustenance for the many Indian spearfishermen. As the river met Douglas Lake (now Harrison Lake), they passed a spot where, a few years before, a group of miners were paddling their way north when their canoe overturned. Expecting to receive a freezing swim, they were somewhat surprised to find the waters almost warm enough for a relaxing bath. They had discovered the warm water springs (Harrison Hot Springs) considered sacred by the Chehalis Indians.

With no such incident affecting them, Milton and Cheadle relaxed on the voyage, enjoying the pine forests, backed by snow-topped mountains. By 5pm, the *Hope* entered the short river at the north-east corner of the lake, passing through into Harrison Lake (now Little Harrison Lake). At the northern end of the lake lay the small settlement of Port Douglas, where they booked into MacDonald's Hotel.

MacDonald was a widely travelled adventurer who lived mainly on his wits. He had worked for the Hudson's Bay Company, served as a bank clerk, and taught English in Japan. In late 1863, in addition to providing accommodation, he also ran a pack animal business up to the Fraser, and a ferry across the same river. There they dined on a 'wretched' meal of pork and liver, surrounded by drunken miners busily gambling away their hard-earned gains. There were few women, but a 'preponderating', number of Americans. Cheadle decided that Port Douglas was a 'vile hole', which had cost both him and Milton £10 each for passage in the *Hope*, including bed and three meals. Clearly, the inflationary economics of the goldfields were beginning to be felt. The following morning offered little in the way of cheer. The stagecoach due to take them across the 29 miles to Little Lake Lillooet, would not be leaving for another two days. Probably remembering their brief acquaintance with Henry Crease, the British Columbia Attorney-General, before their departure from New Westminster, they decided to call upon the local magistrate and assistant gold commissioner, John Gaggin. He proved to be a 'regular jolly Irishman' and 'a whale for a drink' who, after plying them with copious amounts of beer, agreed to lend Milton (descended from Irish aristocrats) a horse, and charged Cheadle (neither Irish, nor an aristocrat) $10 for the hire of a mule.

The next day, after some delay caused by the continuous supply of beer, Milton and Cheadle – accompanied by Gaggin – left Port Douglas to meet the Lake Lillooet ferry. The passage was, at best, leisurely, as the magistrate insisted on calling at every 'wayside house' to have a drink. Lunch was taken at the 10-mile house (a wayside hostelry) and it was decided to spend the night at the 16-mile house. Milton, already feeling the effects of too much alcohol, retired while Gaggin and Cheadle enjoyed 'two jugs of mulled claret' before sleeping 'like tops'. The ferry across Little Lillooet Lake was due to depart at midday, and Cheadle – whose mule was beginning to limp – was keen to press on to reach the lake in time. Milton and Gaggin, however, were equally keen to taste the bottled stout available at the wayside houses. Using his lame mule as an excuse, Cheadle rode on alone, stopping only to examine the hot water springs ('T'sek Hot Springs), which announced themselves by the smell of sulphur. He discovered that the water, flowing out of the rocks, was 'hot enough to boil an egg'. Arriving at the 29-mile house an hour before the ferry was due to leave, Cheadle had a meal and waited for Milton to reach him. Unfortunately, Gaggin had met some friends along the way, and celebrated the meeting with several bottles of stout. Consequently, much to Cheadle's annoyance, the ferry left without them. There was, however, at least one benefit from the delay. Cheadle managed to borrow a horse to replace his ailing mule.

After a night at the 29-mile house ('very nice clean beds'), and in company with Gaggin, they boarded a small steamer that took them to the top of the lake. A short portage using their horses took them to the bottom of Great Lillooet Lake (now Lillooet Lake) where they boarded the *Prince of Wales* and, with Gaggin continually steamed, steamed up the lake overlooked by snow-covered, rock-strewn mountains. On arrival at Pemberton ('a miserable rocky place'), they said farewell to Gaggin ('a kind adieu') before riding to Anderson Lake where they were invited to dine with a Virginian named Ketteral. A great supporter of the Confederacy's cause in the civil war, even his youngest daughter – just a small child – announced that she was 'for Jeff Davis', and wanted to 'fight the Yankees'. Cheadle found their host to be 'the most gallant American we have ever met, very quiet and does not "blow"'.

At 6.30am the next day, they set out across Anderson Lake in the stern-wheeler *Marzelle*. The lake had initially been surveyed for the Hudson's Bay Company by Alexander Anderson, who named it after himself. The top of the lake was connected by a fast-flowing river to Seton Lake, named by Anderson after his soldier cousin who was lost in the 'women and children first' sinking of HMS *Birkenhead* in 1852. Anderson named the river 'Birkenhead Strait' (modern-day Seton Portage). The mountain-dominated Seton Lake was crossed in 90 minutes on board the stern-wheeler *Champion*, leaving only the 4-mile ride to Lillooet.

As the reverse direction over the lakes had been taken by Mr O'B on his journey down to Victoria from Kamloops, it had come as no surprise to Milton and Cheadle that his name continued to be heard in many conversations with those with whom he had come into contact. Everyone seemed deeply impressed by his knowledge of family connections, where the families came from, and the latest news from that part of the world. Many, thanks to their natural hospitality, lavished food and accommodation on the Latin-quoting, Shakespeare-trumpeting stranger who had suddenly appeared in their midst. He also made a lasting impression due to his ability to drink enormous amounts of whisky, frequently being found smoking his pipe as the lone survivor of a drinking bout.

On their arrival at the top of Seton Lake, Cheadle returned his borrowed horse to its owner, who rode into Lillooet accompanied by Milton. Cheadle, preferring some exercise, walked the 4 miles into the settlement and joined Milton as he booked into the Stage Hotel.

Originally an Indian village named Cayoosh, situated on a broad bench of the Fraser and surrounded by imposing mountains, Lillooet consisted of a single wide street and had been developed as a supply depot for the Cariboo goldfields. Ranching had been established to supply beef to the miners, and stores had been opened to provide other foods, clothing, and mining equipment. The wide street had been created to allow ox-trains hauling goods wagons to turn around in a single manoeuvre. Lillooet was also the site of the '0-mile' marker from which all the road houses on the original route to the Cariboo goldfields were named and measured. There they met 'Judge' Elliot, the local magistrate who had encountered Milton on his visit to New York, prior to his journey with Cheadle. Elliot invited them to his house for dinner, where they met the Belfast-born Dr David Walker. He had served as the surgeon and naturalist in the screw-yacht *Fox* under the command of Captain Leopold McClintock in the search for evidence from the 1845 Franklin Northwest Passage Expedition. Sponsored by Jane, Lady Franklin, the *Fox* spent two years in the Arctic and uncovered the tragic loss of the expedition's two ships off King William Island with all the 129 men who had sailed in them. Cheadle considered Walker to be a 'very jolly fellow indeed' despite his warning them that, thanks to the snow and slush, they would be lucky to reach the Cariboo 'with horses, if at all'.

On their return to their hotel, they found the bar area packed with miners heading to Victoria for the winter. The place resounded with strange new phrases such as 'Bully for you', 'You bet your bottom dollar' or 'You bet your gumboots', as mines were 'caved in', and men 'played out'. As they had a drink, a miner staggered to the bar in a state of distress. Short of breath and coughing, it was soon evident to Cheadle that the man was suffering from a heart condition caused by an imbalance of bodily fluids. Supplying him with medication, Cheadle sent the grateful man to bed rather than allowing him to numb his symptoms with alcohol. When they retired to their room, Milton and Cheadle had not been asleep for long when the door bust open and a drunken miner lurched into the room. Despite the man insisting that the room had originally had three beds, one of which was his, Cheadle rapidly made sure the unwelcome visitor 'made tracks'. Then, at first light, the door burst open once again as another man bellowed into the room the unwelcome (and unwanted) information that the stage for Seton Lake was about to leave. Struggling for an undisturbed half-hour of sleep, Cheadle woke up with a start as the bottom half of his bunk collapsed, and he was forced to lay out his mattress on the floor and try to sleep there. Unfortunately, however, having rated the hotel's services at a higher level than they truly were, Cheadle had left his boots outside the door 'in the vain hope of their being cleaned a little'. Such an expectation led only to loud comments from passing miners such as: 'Who's that damned fool – putting on the frills, is he?' Nevertheless, the new day brought the news that the miner treated by Cheadle the previous night was both 'better' and 'very thankful'.

The middle part of the day was spent at Elliot's house where they were joined by the local rector, the Reverend R. C. Lundin Brown. A Church of England priest, Brown had been chosen by the Bishop of British Columbia to go to Lillooet because of his youth and energy. Not only was he sent there to spread the Word of God, but also because of his strong belief that mixed-marriages were against the will of God. Both he and the bishop believed Indian women were pagans who would only qualify for marriage to white men if they became Christians – specifically Christians within the Church of England fold. While such an ambition would take time to come to fruition, Brown wrote to the London Female Emigration Society for help. He had calculated that there were 600,000 more women than men in Great Britain. It would, he reasoned, help such women, the many single gold miners at work in the Cariboo goldfields, and his work for God, if 'a plan of emigration be set on foot'. *The Times* helped the cause by announcing that: 'The miner is not very particular – plain, fat, and 50 even would not be objected to.' Thus, with the support of such luminaries as Charles Dickens and Bishop Samuel ('Soapy Sam') Wilberforce, three 'bride ships' set sail with 'select bundles of crinoline' on board. The first reached San Francisco where the women were allowed ashore to stretch their legs – none of them were ever seen again, settling for the charms of the American men they encountered. The second and third ships, however, reached Victoria as hundreds of men thronged the landing wharf. Before long, most of (possibly all) the women were married and adding to the growing population of good Christians.

That evening, Milton and Cheadle were invited to the sheriff's home where, in company with Doctor Walker and other guests, they sang 'glees' such as Samuel Webbe's popular *Glorious Apollo*, and Burns' O *Wert thou in the Cauld Blast*, the final verse of which reminded Cheadle of some unspecified sentimentality back home:

> Or were I in the wildest waste,
> Sae black and bare, sae black and bare,
> The desert were a paradise,
> If thou wert there, if thou wert there;
> Or were I Monarch o' the globe,
> Wi' thee to reign, wi' thee to reign,
> The brightest jewel in my Crown
> Wad be my Queen, wad be my Queen.

Following several reports of snow in the Cariboo region, it was decided that the horses should be left behind and the stage taken as far as Soda Creek, from where a steamboat would take them further north. They left mid-morning on Sunday 11 October. The stage turned out to be a five-horse light wagon, which was also carrying almost a ton of freight. They were joined by just one other passenger whose horse had drowned during a ferry crossing. The driver, Johnny, was an American and, like all Americans (according to Milton), 'a most unquiet spirit, always engaged in talking to us or the horses, chewing, spitting, smoking and drinking'. The latter activity was especially popular with Johnny. Any stops where alcohol could be purchased were taken full advantage of, despite the driver assuring all who would listen that he was 'a total abstainer' – except when he was not. The first night on the road was spent at the 15-mile road house, 'a wretched place' where their companion slept on the bar, Milton curled up beneath the counter, and Cheadle shared the floor with five other miners.

Back on the trail the following morning, the first big event was overhauling a small group of horsemen led by a tall, upright (almost military), moustachioed figure. He turned out to be the highly respected Judge Begbie, who had come out to Victoria from England in 1858. At that time, the governor was looking for someone to oversee the law in British Columbia and Vancouver Island, with the aim of avoiding the lawlessness that had marked the Californian gold rush. The kind of man Douglas was hoping for was one 'who could, if necessary, truss a murderer up and hang him from the nearest tree'.

Begbie was just such a man – legally trained of course but with the physique of a boxer, he instinctively balanced his physical strength and powerful personality with a fairness that, despite his fearsome remit, often saw him coming to the aid of an untutored and undefended miner who was actually facing him in court. On the other hand, his perception of unjustness when the scales seemed weighted in the other direction annoyed him greatly. On one occasion, when a jury returned a verdict of manslaughter, an outraged Begbie thundered at the prisoner,

> Prisoner, it is not a pleasant duty to me to sentence you *only* to prison for life. You deserve to be hanged. Had the jury performed their duty, I might have the painful satisfaction of condemning you to death.

As for the jury,

> ...permit me to say that it would give me great pleasure to sentence you to be hanged each and every one of you, for bringing in a murderer guilty only of manslaughter.

Nevertheless, it was widely recognised that it was mainly due to Judge Begbie's skills that peace and quiet was the general situation throughout the gold fields.

Later that day, at a site identified by a large white flag raised to show that the nearby native village consisted of 'friendly Indians', Milton and Cheadle were forced to face another test of nerves. After losing one of their stage horses to exhaustion, Pavilion Mountain reared almost 7,000 feet up before them, with the Cariboo Road on it. The resulting track up the mountainside was so steep and winding, and with just four horses available, the passengers decided to walk up to the top. Grateful for a rest after a 'killing' climb, they rejoined the stage and were carried 3 miles along the mountain ridge until they came to the 29-mile house where they had luncheon. Any thoughts, however, that the next part of the road might provide an enjoyable, uneventful ride were soon dispelled. Shortly after their departure from the roadhouse, they met the northern slope of the mountain. Not only was the track alarmingly steep, with a succession of sharp bends, (hence its name of Rattlesnake grade), crudely supported across gaps by overhanging baulks of timber, it also had a huge, plunging precipice on either side. As if that was not enough, Johnny took the violently swaying wagon down the mountainside 'at a fearful pace'. If the rudimentary brake failed, if a wheel came off, or the shaft broke, the consequences would have been disastrous. Nevertheless, Johnny's skills brought them down safely, and they were soon enjoying the level road and the sight of a lone camel – a survivor of those who failed to live up to their mountain-climbing expectations.

The night was spent at the 47-mile house at Clinton. The settlement had been recently named after the Duke of Newcastle, Henry Pelham Clinton, who was the current colonial secretary. It was at Clinton that the lake and river route used by Milton and Cheadle met the new Cariboo Road from Yale. From that point onwards, the routes merged.

As they journeyed on the next day, they came across a sight that almost matched all the Alpinesque scenery they had passed through. At the end of the Ice Age (8,000 BC) the melt-water, loaded with scouring silt, had cut its way through many layers of volcanic lava that covered the area, creating a huge chasm with sheer walls. The spectacular feature was 5 miles long, ⅓ of a mile wide, and 1,000 feet deep. Known as the Chasm (sometimes Painted Chasm) the different layers of lava were of various shades of red, purple, yellow and brown, all fringed with ponderosa pines. The vertical walls of the chasm appeared to Cheadle 'as if cut with a knife', and they were home to the sure-footed bighorn sheep. Continuing from the Chasm, they met several pack trains of mules and large groups of despondent miners walking to the south.

They also heard that the wealthiest of the miners, John Cameron (owner of the fabulous Cameron Claim on Williams Creek), was on his way south with 630lb of gold but, unknown to the miners spreading the news, Cameron's wife was on her death bed, and he was already planning to take her body to Canada West via San Francisco, Panama, and New York. When the bullock wagon carrying the gold eventually passed them on its way south, it was guarded by twenty armed miners on foot.

Luncheon was taken at the 70-mile house where Cheadle was shocked to be charged $1.25 for a pint of porter. He was also dismayed by the condition of the stage horses, all were 'wretchedly thin' and one was lame. Even worse, news reached them that the exchange horses at the 84-mile house were unavailable ('lost'). Their concern for the horses was real but, somehow, the animals kept going over the next two days and brought the stage into the scattering of wooden buildings that was Soda Creek. They arrived on Cheadle's birthday – which he forgot – and stayed at a roadhouse run by an American who annoyed Cheadle by constantly referring to doctors as 'Docs', and ship's captains as 'Caps'. Equally annoying were the miners who left the steamer when it arrived in the early afternoon: 'The swearing was something fearful'.

The *Enterprise* (not to be confused with the Victoria to New Westminster sternwheeler of the same name) was a vessel that truly reflected her name. Completed earlier in the year, she was built of local timber, her boiler, engine, and shaft having been brought up from Port Douglas by mule train. Those who could not afford the full price of a ticket could work their passage by helping to load the boiler's supply of wood. Coming from the other end of the social scale, Milton and Cheadle were given the captain's cabin and a non-stop supply of free drinks as Captain J. W. Doane proudly introduced them to all and sundry.

The voyage took two days to complete against strong currents and dense fog. Light rain was falling when the steamer came alongside the wharf at Quesnel, a small community named after the river that joined the Fraser at that point. Once ashore, they set off towards 4-mile house on the road to their destination, Williams Creek – a walk of about 50 miles. They had not gone far when they encountered Captain Doane, already 'half seas over' who insisted that they join him for champagne at every bar they could find. Eventually, they managed to escape and spent the night at the roadhouse.

The next day, Monday 19 October , was a miserable affair. The trail had been crudely hacked through the woods leaving only stumps and mud littered with dead horses and personal belongings thrown away by retreating miners. Plodding on, carrying a 30lb pack, they joined a group of random strangers heading in the same direction, crossed the Cottonwood River and stopped at a roadhouse 2 miles further on. Cheadle, wearing his stout leather boots, was suffering from sore feet after the trudge of 20 miles, while Milton, who had opted for moccasins, 'got through famously'. His mood was not improved by their accommodation. Sleep was very difficult when sharing a room with eighteen other men, all with just one blanket each, cracks in the walls and floors letting in the chill wind. Milton and another guest talked loudly in their sleep and one miner woke up regularly with cramp, which had him hopping about while swearing loudly. In the morning, a search among the abandoned stores outside the roadhouse revealed two pairs of gumboots, one of which fitted each man. The rubber footwear, designed and introduced less than ten years earlier, proved to be a great improvement for both, especially as the rain was turning to snow and 3 inches already lay upon the ground.

The second big event of the day was meeting a strong wagon led by twelve armed men on horseback, accompanied by more armed men marching beside and to the rear of the wagon. This was the gold escort, responsible for getting the gold safely to Victoria. In fact, it was a rare sighting for, between 1861 and 1863, the escort was only used five times. With no official guarantee that the gold would get through, the miners generally preferred their own systems of transport. Among the group of strangers who walked alongside Milton and Cheadle was a tall 'Yankee' from Maine named Robert Putnam, who entertained them by shooting partridges and martens out of the trees. Using only his revolver, his accuracy was 'astonishing'. After stopping at Halfway House (modern Pinegrove) where an outraged Cheadle had to pay 50 cents for a single cup of coffee, they reached the mining works of the Company of Welsh Adventurers. The entirely Welsh enterprise was made up of former lead miners, who had brought out Bibles in the Welsh language and held prayer meetings every night. Any prayers for a rest had clearly been answered as the mine was at a standstill due to the waterwheel, used to pump water from the mine, breaking under the weight of ice. At Beaver Pass House they enjoyed a 'capital' lunch of 'beefsteak pie & onions & pancakes!' The substantial meal fortified them for the final march towards their immediate destination, William's Creek. The 'long weary walk winding along hill sides' through deepening snow took them around Bald Mountain until, with dusk descending, they reached the mining town of Richfield (given its name by Lieutenant Palmer, the same Royal Engineer officer who annoyed the governor by his elopement). At their feet gurgled the broad stream that was the goal of unnumbered miners. The discovery of gold on its banks cost William Dietz the price of the 'the first basket of champagne' to arrive in the area. He later died in poverty at Victoria. Dietz, nevertheless, did better than at least one of his fellow miners. A Scotsman named John Rose, who had been one of the first into the Cariboo, was found dead in the depths of a forest. Hanging from a nearby tree was his tin cup with the words 'Dying from starvation' scratched into its side.

Advised by their pistol-shooting American companion, Putnam, that better accommodation would be found further down the creek, they set off along the trail bordering its western bank. The journey, through a narrow canyon barely a mile and a quarter long, was fraught. Without lights, and depending upon Putnam's guidance, they stumbled and fell repeatedly as they crunched through snow-covered mud crossed by ditches, hampered by tree stumps, planks of wood and mining equipment. Their gumboots, which had served them well so far, now proved to have a lack of grip and frequently sent them sprawling headlong into the freezing slush. In the end, however, the struggle to maintain their balance turned out to be worth the effort. At the end of the canyon lay the town of Barkerville, named after an English canal worker who struck gold on the site. There, lights and the sound of fiddles, pianos and laughter indicated a lively nightlife as they continued walking. Just before the edge of the community, they came to Camerontown, the site of the immensely productive Cameron Claim. After a warming drink at Putnam's cabin, they went to Cusheon's boarding house owned by John and Margaret Cusheon who, in addition to offering accommodation, were also noted gold prospectors. There, according to Cheadle, they received 'a good supper & plenty of blankets'. Milton, however, thought sleeping on a blanket on the loft floor, and being pestered by lice, was 'vile'. As for the food, the viscount considered that the beefsteak, bread, and dried apples, was 'wretchedly cooked and frightfully expensive'.

The following morning, too stiff and sore for an early start, they rested until after midday, when John Cusheon took them to the Cameron Company hut. John Cameron was at Victoria, where he was involved in the beginning of a macabre scandal. On his wife's death, a funeral was held in Barkerville, before he accompanied the body, encased in an alcohol-filled metal coffin, down to Victoria. By the time, he had arrived, a rumour had grown that his wife had not died, but had been sold to an Indian chief. This led to a demand at the graveside that the coffin should be opened. Cameron refused, and the interment took place. Shortly afterwards, the body was disinterred, and Cameron took it, via Panama and the east coast of America, to the northern shore of the St Lawrence River. Nine years later, with the rumour undiminished, Cameron agreed that the body should – again – be disinterred. The body, preserved in the alcohol, proved to be that of his former wife, and was reburied – with a fourth funeral service.

The secretary of the Cameron Company was James Steele ('very kind and intelligent'). After supplying Milton and Cheadle with a steadying drink of brandy and water, Steel allowed them to be lowered down the 38-foot mineshaft. At the bottom, several dark, damp tunnels branched off into the gold-bearing gravel, which was scooped up and sent to the surface in buckets and wooden kegs. On their return, they were each invited to 'wash out' a pan of gravel, which produced a combined 1⅓ ounces of gold, valued at $21. Steele showed them a bag containing gold worth $1,000 and explained that the claim was averaging gold finds of $29,000 a week.

The early part of the next day was spent in walking back to Richfield through the canyon that had proved so hazardous at night. As they made their way past the succession of claims, they could now clearly see the array of mining equipment used for the extraction of gold. The simple principle of gold recovery was based around the fact that gold is much heavier than sand, pebbles, or gravel. Water was the general means of washing the unwanted minerals away, while the gold sank to the bottom awaiting recovery. The basic pan was used to collect a sample of the river bed, isolated bar, or bank. Water was added, swirled around, and released over the lip of the pan, taking the sand, etc., with it, and leaving the gold behind. Rockers or cradles were box-like arrangements with holes in the bottom. When the box was rocked, the gold was washed through the bottom holes onto a canvas apron beneath. Where water was not easily at hand, small aqueducts called flumes were used to bring water down from a high point. They were often co-ordinated with sluices (sometimes known as dump-boxes or Long Toms). The rocker-like boxes used the gravity-powered water to wash through the gravel. As at the Cameron Claim, shafts had to be dug to reach gold deep below ground. Men were lowered and raised and gold-bearing gravel lifted to the surface by means of a windlass. Where the tunnels beneath the ground became flooded, a Cornish wheel, such as was used by the Welsh miners, was driven by water falling from a flume operating a simple reciprocating pump. The surrounding landscape would have told Milton and Cheadle that most of the equipment, and the entirety of the building works – including of course the shafts and tunnels – would have to have been constructed locally. Consequently, the surrounding hills, which nature had clothed thickly in pines, had been reduced to vast, muddy fields of stumps.

The reason Milton and Cheadle were visiting Richfield was to call upon William Cox, an Irishman who was the local magistrate and gold commissioner for Cariboo. Cheadle described him as a 'fat, tall, thick set fellow with a very short coat ... very German, but not in manner', and 'gentlemanly and jolly.' He had a quirky sense of humour. On one occasion, when a challenge arose over the ownership of a claim, he settled the dispute by ordering that the two men should race on foot to the site of the claim – whoever won, received title to the site.

In the middle of their conversation, the door opened and in walked a heavily built man who was introduced as the local constable, Captain Napoleon FitzStubbs ('What a name!'). FitzStubbs, a former army officer, had come out from England with a sense of adventure. While on the crossing, he had fallen in with another former army officer, the very wealthy Charles Edward Barrett Leonard, who had brought out his personal yacht, *Templar*. On arrival at Nootka Sound, on the west coast of Vancouver Island, Barrett Leonard and FitzStubbs put the yacht into the water and became the first persons to circumnavigate the island, resulting in a nearby small island being named as Leonard's Island. They then made their way to New Westminster where Barrett Leonard set off on his own, and FitzStubbs accepted employment as a constable at William's Creek. The discussion that followed caused Milton and Cheadle to be late returning to Cusheon's house, to find that other guests had eaten their lunch. However, they were taken in by their host's mother-in-law and her daughter, who lived next door, and given a meal. The 'very nice' refreshment was followed by an invitation from James Steele to spend some time with one of the miners. They were pleased to spend an educational evening sharing a pipe of tobacco with someone who knew the other end of the business from the gold commissioner.

On the following morning, they were shown around other claims by FitzStubbs. At the Caledonian Claim they went down the mine but their guide refused to accompany them on the grounds that he was on duty, and could not be seen in a dirty coat. Milton brought up a pan of gravel, which was washed and produced almost an ounce of gold. The miner's hut provided lunch, a pipe, and a chat, where one of the miners said to Cheadle:

Well, doctor. I've the greatest respect for both the professions of law & medicine, but it's a curious fact that in this creek last year we had neither lawyers nor doctors, & we lived without litigation & free from illness. This year there has been a large influx of both lawyers & doctors, & there has been nothing but lawsuits & deaths in the place!

The lunch break was followed by a visit to the Raby Claim, owned by a Cornishman. Raby, although not the first to try it, had done very well by sinking his shaft at a spot where the stream had flowed thousands of years previously. At that time, some great force of nature had caused the stream to alter its course, leaving a 'streak' of 'pay dirt' buried several feet below the ground. The evidence for this was demonstrated by Raby when they descended into the mine to see where a large rock – originally in the ancient stream – had provided a 'pocket' on the downstream side where the water's flow had deposited its gold. The mine owner, using an empty preserved meat tin capable of holding about a quarter of a gallon, scooped up the black sand at the base of the rock and brought it to the surface. Milton washed the sample and produced about an ounce of gold. When the same material was washed through one of the sluices, a day's work could be expected to produce £1,000 of gold – and Raby's claim extended for 1,000 feet along the creek.

Much of the next couple of days were spent allowing the local civic and mining leaders to indulge in their desire to display their prize specimens. These were large nuggets of gold, and Cheadle quickly became bored with the game – 'I am already beginning to hate the name.' However, that did not stop him, or Milton, from accepting gifts of 'several nice nuggets'. After a day of praising other people's nuggets, they had dinner with Gold Commissioner Cox, who introduced them to Doctor Walter Black, the chief surgeon at the newly opened Barkerville Hospital. He had spent time working at the Australian goldfields, knew his way around the techniques of mining, and offered to take them to the nearby Lowhee Creek mines, about 3 miles from William's Creek. The dinner proved to be a 'jolly evening', finished off by a walk back to Barkerville through the snow, lit by a bright moon.

The four mines at Lowhee Creek were situated beside a small stream flowing through a narrower canyon than William's Creek. Each of the mines had done well and showed excellent prospects. Even the gold was of higher quality than their near neighbours'. William's Creek was assayed at .830, whereas Lowhee Creek was .920. Milton purchased $37-worth of gold, while Cheadle settled for $10-worth. While visiting the mines, Cheadle noted that the pump-driving wheels were often frozen. This caused a halt in the mine working (as had been seen earlier at the Welsh mine), and affected production. On raising the matter, he learned that steam engines were on their way by sledge in an attempt to solve the problem.

On their return to Barkerville, they met 'Mr Dixie', an escaped slave from Tennessee who had opened up a barber's shop in the town. On discovering the identity of Milton, he said he 'should die happy if I could shave a real live lord'. The viscount agreed, and Mr Dixie was 'to operate on Milton tomorrow'.

The following day opened with a visit to the community's bowling alley where both John Cusheon and Cheadle beat Milton. A visit to the Raby Claim saw Milton purchasing 2oz of gold, while Cheadle – no longer hating specimens – obtained $10 worth. While they were there, a shift and a half's gravel and sand was put through the sluice, and enough gold to fill the quart preserved meat tin to the brim was recovered – with a total value of $4,000.

A visit to Mr Dixie saw them looking presentable, as they had been invited to see the new hospital. There had been doctors on William's Creek for some time, but the need for a hospital was generally agreed throughout the community. The Government refused any aid, so the miners held a fundraising ball. Little more than a log cabin, the hospital consisted of a doctor's room, a single ward, and a kitchen. Water for washing and cleaning had to be brought in jugs from the creek. Collected from their lodgings by Doctor Black's assistant, Cheadle and Milton arrived at the building expecting a short inspection of the facilities. Instead, as they entered, a shout went up accompanied by the banging on a table top and the clapping of hands. Having heard that the visitors were to leave in a day or so, a party had been organised. A table had been laid out on the ward, with the only patient – who was suffering from a swelling of the body due to excess fluids – screened off by a large green baize cloth. In addition to Black, there was his assistant, Brown; another doctor, Thomas Bell (wearing a tail coat); Courtney, a visitor from the east; Blenkinsop, formerly a Hudson's Bay Company trader; Cocker, the local bank manager (wearing a frock coat); and Farren, a 'boisterous' Irish sailor who had done well at the Caledonian Claim. The dinner was prepared and cooked by a 'fair, fat, and forty' Scotswoman named Janet Morris, who was better known as 'Scotch Jenny'. Famed for her caring nature, she was immensely popular throughout Richfield, Barkerville, and Camerontown, particularly for her work among ill or injured miners. When the food was brought in, she was greeted with loud acclaim and invited to join the table – which she did.

The menu of soup, roast beef, boiled mutton, and plum pudding, all washed down with champagne was a great success until – much to Cheadle's annoyance, who was half way through the plum pudding – Dr Bell caught the eye of Dr Black and was given a nod in response. Despite the toast to the Queen having yet to be given, Bell, whose father was a Northamptonshire tenant of Milton's father, banged the table, stood up, and launched into a 'maudlin', rambling, speech, which Cheadle recalled beginning:

Gentlemen, Dr Black invited me here to meet a noble scion of the noblest house in England. I don't exaggerate when I say so. I can't exaggerate. I feel grateful to Dr Black, deeply grateful for asking me here to meet the noble scion of one of the noblest houses England ever produced. It is a proud day for all of us & for this creek; it is the commencement of a new era. Etc., Etc.

Cheadle felt the speech to be 'quite nauseous', with a succession of toasts to the Fitzwilliam family and the repeated choruses of *For He's a Jolly Good Fellow*. At last Dr Black stepped in and proposed an equally fulsome toast 'To Queen and Country', followed by the singing of the national anthem. Then it was Cheadle's turn. Dr Bell rose unsteadily and toasted the visiting doctor, again followed by more *For He's a Jolly Good Fellow*. Just as Bell was about to rise and offer further toasts, Scotch Jenny stood up and suggested that the party move into the kitchen, probably to allow the single patient, swelling quietly behind his baize sheet, to get some sleep. Once everyone was settled comfortably in their new surroundings, the sole lady in the party presented Milton with a $25 nugget, which he was to give to his mother. After another 'gushing' speech, this time by Dr Black, Milton was presented with a ring made from $50 of gold taken from the Creek's 'Never Sweat' mine. Scotch Jenny and Farren then each presented Cheadle with a nugget – two 'specimens' that he gratefully accepted. Bell then tried to propose more toasts, but was drowned out by Blenkinsop singing *Annie Laurie*. When the song had finished, Bell tried once again but this time he was defeated by the entire party singing *Auld Lang Syne*. Bell fell asleep, only to wake up with a start and, in an effort to leave the kitchen, repeatedly charged the chimney breast under the impression that it was a door. Taken to a bed in the doctor's room by Brown, Dr Black managed to fall from the couch onto a pile of medical stores with a huge crash, and hit his head on the stove. He thereupon retired for the rest of the night. For the remainder, the early morning saw them playing card games as Scotch Jenny sang the saddest of eighteenth-century songs, *Auld Robin Gray*, about a woman whose young lover dies at sea and she marries a gentle old man for security:

> I derena think o' Jamie, for that wad be a sin;
> But I will do my best a gudewife aye to be,
> For auld Robin Gray he is kind to me.

When the party eventually broke up, the temperature outside was 5°F (-15°C), and Milton and Cheadle returned to their lodgings weighed down with gold, and 'both quite sober'. Later that morning, Milton went down one of the Caledonian Claim's shafts while Cheadle, 'sick of going down in buckets', walked to Richfield to have a pipe with the gold commissioner, William Cox, and to ask for a loan of $500, which was immediately agreed.

The following day, being the last complete day of their stay in Barkerville, was spent in saying their farewells to their new-found friends. Dr Black, apparently no worse for his excesses at the party, took them to Scotch Jenny's house, then on through deep snow to Cox's home to collect the loan he was providing. Scotch Jenny – of whom it was said that she 'dressed like a man, drank like a man and died like a man' – married the following year, but died in 1865 when she rolled her carriage over a steep drop. The day ended with drinks of whisky punch at the Caledonian Claim, and a gift of a bottle of Hudson's Bay Company rum from John Cusheon.

The return walk to Quesnel was completed in three days despite heavy snow and repeated stops to look at mining claims. Amongst those visited was the Company of Welsh Adventurers. Twenty-eight Welshmen – sponsored by Manchester businessmen – worked hard at the claim but, though determined, they had not had a lot of luck. A possible source of silver had been found, and new sites were being investigated as the 'Last Chance' shaft was being dug. The journey down the Fraser from Quesnel presented Milton and Cheadle with an unexpected problem. The *Enterprise* had developed engine problems and had been hauled up the bank for repairs. A call upon Captain Doane led to an immediate supply of cocktails, followed by a champagne lunch. Eventually escaping from their 'very jolly' host, they purchased two tickets at $10 each from 'Captain' McBride, who owned a boat, which he had built from scratch, that would take them over the 56 miles to Soda Creek. Solidly built, double-ended, and powered by six oars, the craft had originally been built to make a journey from the Fraser River to Lake McLeod and the Peace River through the Rocky Mountains.

On a cold, snowy day, Milton and Cheadle joined 38 other passengers to be crammed into the boat (McBride claimed he had taken 50 passengers the previous year all the way down to Yale). Their only immediate sustenance were several bottles of whisky, quickly downed in the first few miles. The greatest concern of the captain and his passengers was that the river was at one of its low-water stages. This was evident from the succession of 'riffles' on the surface. At a point about 35 miles south of Quesnel, a very active riffle appeared in the centre of the stream. McBride, manning the tiller, was unsure which side to pass down but, urged on by several passengers who told him that the steamer always went to a certain side, followed their advice and promptly ran aground. The only remedy was for some of the passengers to go over the side into the freezing waters to lighten the boat. Both Milton and Cheadle looked down at their feet 'in the most cowardly manner' as half a dozen men rolled over the gunwale – only to find that the water reached no further than their knees. When the boat still refused to move, more volunteers climbed onto the shoulders of the first men in the water and were carried ashore. One rather small man took on his shoulder a very large American. Inevitably, both toppled full- length into the water, much to the loud amusement and applause of the onlookers. The second discharge of passengers released the boat which, with all back on board, continued on its way. It had not gone far, however, when McBride suggested that, as it was getting dark, they should head for the bank and stay there until first light the next morning. Democratically, he took a vote on the matter and found that most of the passengers agreed with him, the main concern being the concealed shallow stretches all along the remaining 10 miles before Soda Creek. By sheer luck, they found themselves at a wood supply dump used by the *Enterprise* as a fuel reserve. At first, probably through damp matches and tinder, no one could get a fire started until Milton managed to coax a spark into life. The giant log pile was raided, and soon several blazing fires were heating water for tea to accompany the bread and bacon supplied by McBride. After building shelters from pine boughs, using pine leaves as a mattress and sleeping with their feet to the fire, all had 'a very comfortable night'.

Soda Creek was reached without incident the next morning. Rather than suffer the portages of the lake route that had brought them up to the Cariboo goldfields, they decided to take the two-horse Barnard's Express stage wagon down the Cariboo Road to Yale. As the stage had been delayed, they left their baggage at the 'BX' office and walked the 3 miles to the head of William's Lake to take a look at one of the few successful farms in the area (Their interest stemmed from the fact that upon achieving the earldom, Milton would inherit a huge acreage of English farmland). The delay continued ('Heigh ho; rather wearisome') as Cheadle tended to the injuries suffered by the local people.

They learned that Burgess, the kindly clerk at Fort Kamloops who had arranged their replacement clothing and toiletries, had been killed when a boat he was bringing to the fort with stores exploded. The probable cause seemed to have been the stowage of matches next to kegs of gunpowder. News also came in that a party coming down the Fraser from Quesnel in canoes had been swamped at the first riffle, and seven men, with a large quantity of gold, had been lost.

When the stage did eventually arrive (complete with a broken shaft, crudely lashed together), it had a drop-off before it could continue to Yale, its final destination. An official letter had to be delivered to the local constable on a nearby ranch. When the stage returned, the driver told the story that when he arrived with the letter, the constable, George Gompertz (who had been made a constable at New Westminster the same day as Richfield's constable, Napoleon FitzStubbs), was so drunk that he could not read the letter. Equally drunk were his Indian girlfriend, and seven

Indian prisoners, three of whom had been sentenced to death. Cheadle was not impressed – 'Nice state of things, eh!'

Much the same could have been said of the weather when they set off at last in company with the third passenger, Captain Harrison, a widely travelled Englishman now involved in the hunt for gold. A fierce wind raged, and hailstones rattled on the flimsy canvas of the stage. Trees brought down by the wind in forests on both sides of the road sounded to Cheadle 'like cannonading'. Where the road was iced over, the passengers were required to disembark and push the wagon, or lift up the horses when they slipped. To help his steersmanship in such conditions, the driver drank an entire bottle of whisky while telling the passengers that when carrying gold (they had $8,000 of gold on board as they travelled), he always expected to be attacked and have his body thrown into the Chasm they had encountered on their way up. They arrived, however, at the 59-mile house, situated on the lip of the Chasm, without incident and with heavy snow falling. The roadhouse had stables with fifty stalls for the BX Company horses. As the stabled horses were vulnerable to attack by wolves, when howling was heard near to the building, a man rose from the bar, picked up his rifle, went out into the night and shot the nearest intruder.

On their arrival at the Ashcroft Manor Roadhouse, having been delayed by a broken suspension spring, the Chinese cook had already gone to bed and was distinctly unhappy over demands that he provide food. After some bad-tempered exchanges, he agreed to supply beefsteaks, only to return to his surly attitude when Harrison provoked him further by demanding toast. Eventually, the food was supplied. Henry, the youngest of the Cornwall brothers (both of whom had been absent when they passed through from Fort Kamloops) invited them to visit his nearby house. The Cambridge man, who had completed his degree in 1859, had moved to British Columbia with his older brother in 1862 and after a brief and unsuccessful attempt at gold mining, introduced cereal farming to the area. However, so poor had been the results that they were now considering a change to cattle farming in the hope that the grass available was of sufficient quantity and suitable quality.

Setting off the next morning for Cook's Ferry, they went 4 or 5 miles on part of the road built by the Royal Engineers when

Lieutenant Palmer probably had his mind on his bride-to-be. Intended to be 12 feet wide, small rock slides had reduced the width to half that distance, tricky for a wagon that had no brakes, a broken shaft lashed together with rope, one of the springs broken, the leather driving traces falling apart, three passengers, baggage, and 170lb of gold. Furthermore, the edge of the road, suspended over the 700-foot drop to the Fraser, showed signs of collapsing. Cheadle considered it to be 'an awful place'. After luncheon at Cook's Ferry, they drove at an alarming pace over the continuing Cariboo Road to Lytton and then on to Boston Bar ('a miserable hole'). Rattling past the roaring waters of La Porte d'Enfer, darkness had already fallen when they clattered over the Alexandria Bridge suspended across the Fraser. Just a couple of hundred yards past the bridge, the shaft was wrenched apart and the wagon rolled into the rear of the horses. By sheer luck, the wagon was on level ground and soon lost its momentum. In fact, overall, luck was on their side. Another wagon belonging to the BX had hauled up by the roadside close to the southern end of the bridge. Their driver, leaving his passengers to guard the gold, walked back to seek help. By the time he returned with the other wagon, the passengers had kept themselves warm by building a large fire. The two drivers then unhitched the pair of horses from the north-bound wagon and hitched them in front of the two horses of the southbound stage. Refreshing themselves with a shared bottle of whisky, the two men then set of at a brisk pace with the traces incorrectly attached, leaving the fresh lead horses to navigate around the sharp bends and over the steep climbs and descents. In the beginning, both Milton and Cheadle were 'in a funk' as the creaking wagon – on the verge of disintegration – hurtled along the road in the dark but, after a while, recognising that the horses were behaving magnificently, they both managed a fitful doze. At 10.30pm, two hours after they had left the bridge, they reached Yale, with the extra driver taking the opportunity to visit a bar before returning to the bridge with his horses.

The next morning, they visited the Hudson's Bay Company offices and borrowed $30 from Ovid Allard, the company's officer-in-charge at Yale who had been so successful at his work that Mount Allard, south-south-east of Yale, had been named in his honour. Using some of the loan, they bought two tickets for a journey to New Westminster on board the *Reliance*. After an uneventful voyage, they arrived at the city in the late afternoon, and were entertained by the district magistrate, Captain William Spalding, who raged at Colonel Moody's choice of site for New Westminster as a defensible position against possible attack from the United States. When calmed down by his wife, Spalding spent the rest of the evening rambling on about his time in India ('very long, wearisome, yarns about tigers and serpents').

Later that night, they went on board the Hudson's Bay Company sternwheeler, *Enterprise*, due to leave for Victoria in the morning. With the last of the money they had between them, they went to purchase their tickets to find that the company refused to let them pay, considering them to be distinguished guests and friends of the governor. Once in the Gulf of Georgia, a rough sea caused Cheadle to 'retire & assume recumbent position to quieten sundry qualms'. But by the time they steamed past San Juan Island – with the Royal Marines still peacefully engaged in their long boundary war with the United States Army – the waters had calmed down enough for the doctor to prepare to step ashore on Vancouver Island. Having booked into the St George's Hotel (where they were 'rapturously welcomed'), a bath was followed by a visit to the theatre to see *Camille*, a stage version of Alexandre Dumas' *La Dame aux Camélias*. The title role was played by Julia Dean Hayne, an American Southerner who had made a fortune playing to miners in California who paid in gold dust and nuggets to see her perform. She was also in the throes of divorcing her abusive husband – a situation perhaps relevant to Cheadle's opinion of her performance as 'much overdone'. When the play was finished, Cheadle returned to the hotel and an early night, while Milton visited The Fashion, an elegant gentleman's dining club.

The next few days were spent in seeing the local sights and socialising. The governor invited them to dinner where they met Judge Begbie who, without meeting them, had crossed their path on the Cariboo Road, just north of Lillooet. Cheadle, in particular, was particularly impressed with the judge's demeanour. He described him as, 'a fine tall fellow of 6 feet, well made & powerful, magnificent head, hair scanty & nearly white, with nearly black moustache & beard, full of wit. I was much taken with him'. Another guest was Captain John Martley, an Irishman who was a former officer of the 9th Regiment of Foot, and had fought in the Crimea. Hearing that the British Columbian authorities were offering grants of land to former British officers, he sold his commission and arrived in Victoria with his family and a servant in 1861. The land he obtained was on Pavilion Mountain where he proved to be a successful rancher who had nearby Mount Martley named in his honour.

They attended the St Andrew's Society dinner, a 'very mild affair', which required the hire of evening dress. There they met Lieutenant The Honourable Horace Lascelles RN, a younger son of the 3rd Earl of Harewood, brother of the 4th Earl, and the captain of the 12-gun brig HMS *Forward*. Although not quite in Milton's class, Lascelles was very rich, and not afraid to use his money in any way he saw fit. Such an example happened after the *Forward* came under small arms fire from an Indian village and one of his seamen was killed. He retaliated by destroying much of the village, but ceased firing rather than cause more pointless deaths. A local newspaper proprietor accused him of 'running away', so Lascelles invited him on board his ship. When the man arrived, Lascelles threw him overboard, an act resulting in court action being taken against him. On being found guilty, Lascelles was fined and ordered to pay costs. He did so immediately, dismissively handing over the money as small change. After the Society dinner, Cheadle played whist with Judge Begbie, as Milton and Lascelles set off to have a night on the town.

The following evening, Milton had an attack of his malady, which caused Cheadle some concern as there had been no warning symptoms as usually happened. Most of the following day saw Milton's 'seedy' condition preventing any activities, a situation that prevailed over the next few days. Eventually, Milton's health improved enough that they could accept an invitation from the leading Chinese citizen of Victoria, Kwong Lee. Speaking excellent English ('free from any Yankee twang and slang'), their host taught them the rudiments of the tea leaf. Black tea came from the older part of the plant, while green tea not only came from the younger shoots, but was also coloured to meet European and American taste with Prussian Blue, a chemical formulation widely used in medicine.

Following an invitation from Lascelles, Milton and Cheadle boarded HMS *Forward* at 9am on Monday 9 December. Although they sailed on time, they were soon back in harbour after a rapidly increasing wind sent the spray over the decks, ('We were all glad to be let off.'). They tried again the next day, this time with success. Their first port of call was at 'English Camp' on the north-west corner of San Juan Island. There they were greeted by Captain George Bazalgette, the commanding officer of the Royal Marines based on the island. Cheadle thought him to be 'a merry fellow'. Just 12 miles away, lay the 'American Camp'. So extraordinary was the situation that Bazalgette apologised for not having spare horses so that he could take his guests over to meet the Americans. Both sides consisted of fighting men, both sides were fully armed, and both sides showed a commendable lack of interest in shooting at each other. That night, however, Lascelles decided to liven things up. Taken back to his ship, he organised a couple of broadsides from his cannons, backed up by 24lb rockets that howled unnervingly through the cold night air. Those on shore returned the 'salute' by letting loose with their rifles and pistols. Offered beds ashore, Milton and Cheadle accepted and finished the night with a pipe and a large glass of 'grog'.

In company with Captain Bazalgette, they sailed the following morning to Nanaimo, on the coast of Vancouver Island, 50 miles north-west of San Juan Island. Their destination was clustered on the lower slopes of Mount Benson (named after a Hudson's Bay Company surgeon), which dominated the western skyline. In 1863, its chief value was in its coal mines, linked to the nearby town harbour. Calls were made on Captain Nicoll, the manager of the coal company, and the Justice of the Peace, Captain Franklyn. Lascelles was keen to see an outcrop of coal that he intended to mine, and an entire day was spent in searching for the site. Despite having a local guide, and being accompanied by Dr Benson, no one could find it. Nevertheless, a few months later, the Harewood Company started its mining operation. The evening was spent at Franklyn's home where his eldest daughter entertained them by playing on 'a horribly tuneless piano'. They sailed the following morning, a forelock-touching honour having been bestowed upon Milton. No fewer than three streets – Fitzwilliam, Wentworth, and Milton – were named after him and his family. Lascelles had to manage with just 'Harewood Road'. The *Forward* sailed in a snow storm, and when Lascelles left the bridge to take luncheon, it was not long before a crestfallen Officer-of-the-Watch sent a message down to say that he was lost. Although both Lascelles and Bazalgette knew the islands of the Gulf of Georgia intimately, it was nearly three hours before a beacon was spotted off Saltspring Island and a safe harbour found for the night.

The next day was spent on San Juan Island playing skittles and whist with the Royal Marines, ending in a musical evening where the junior officers made up a concert party, playing guitar, tambourine, and 'bones'. After three boring days at Victoria, during which the deepening snow preventing much activity while they waited for the steamer to arrive, Lascelles invited them to join him in his theatre box to see *Fazio – A Tragedy*, a play about an alchemist, followed by a shortened version of *The Taming of the Shrew*. Again, the leading lady in both was Julia Dean Hayne. The Shakespearean work amused them, but the former play – which was derided by the playwright himself, and produced without his permission ('done without even the common courtesy of giving me notice of their intention') – went without comment, probably because of such lines as that declaimed to the alchemist by his wife, Bianca:

> Oh, then, let that black furnace burst! dash down
> Those ugly and mis-shapen jars and vials.
> Nay, nay, most sage Philosopher, tonight,
> At least to-night, be only thy Bianca's.
> *(She clings to him).*

Relief came on the morning of Saturday 19 December. The sound of a gun booming from the harbour announced to the city that the steamer had, at last, arrived. Having seen their baggage safely on board the side-wheeler, SS *Pacific,* and politely refusing a suggestion by the governor that they should stay on the island for Christmas, they embarked on a round of farewells as their vessel would not finish coaling until after midnight. The final port of call was at Lascelles' home, reached by one of *Forward*'s boats from Duntze Head, the western point of the naval dockyard. There they were met by Lascelles' pet silver fox and his Japanese golden pheasant before an evening of pleasant conversation and champagne. There were two other guests, Captain Bazalgette, who would be returning to San Juan Island in the *Forward* the following day, and Doctor Wallace, the senior surgeon at the dockyard hospital. All went well until it was time to leave for the *Pacific*. They walked down to the beach near to the Fisgard Lighthouse, and loudly hailed the *Forward* – having been assured by Lascelles that at least one boatswain's mate would be on the upper deck keeping a lookout. However, no one answered. With growing concern that they could miss their ship, they continued shouting until someone approached from their rear. It was Doctor Wallace who had come down to meet his own boat, which would take him back to the hospital. When their predicament was explained, he immediately offered them the use of his own boat, which arrived shortly after. With everyone on board the boat, they set off for the *Pacific* but, halfway across, it became evident that the craft had a significant leak. By the time they came alongside their ship, the boat was on the verge of being swamped, and they only narrowly escaped a cold plunge.

Safely inside their state room, they met the third occupant who was to share their accommodation. He was Captain George Elliott, an officer in the United States Army – whom Cheadle considered to be 'a very intelligent, gentlemanly fellow'. An engineer, Elliott was on his way to help construct a fort on Point Adams at the mouth of the Columbia River (later, Fort Stevens).

An American Lady, San Francisco, the American Widow – and Home

The 1,000-mile voyage to San Francisco was not to be plain sailing. Bad weather drove the ship to take shelter in Neah Bay before they had even reached the open Pacific Ocean. When the conditions improved, they steamed off, only to have a boiler pipe split, requiring a return to the anchorage. After two days repairing the damage, they set off again into choppy weather that caused Cheadle to stay on his bunk all day. Milton, however, 'got up, ate & chatted & ate again as is his wont'. As if that was not bad enough, the doctor was asked to look after a man suffering from dysentery ('will die'). In such a mood, Cheadle had to spend Christmas Day at sea when he had hoped to be ashore in San Francisco. A dance was put on in the evening with the music being provided by one of the crew with a guitar. Milton danced a quadrille with a 17-year-old newly wedded bride who had just married 'a surly looking Yankee'. She was 'very well to look at, but the moment she opened her mouth, oh! it is all over; a sharp, shrewish, voice, nasal twang, & quick manner.' Another woman, whom Cheadle described sarcastically as an 'American Lady', amused herself by 'chalking' the back of passing gentlemen's jackets – 'even with strangers'. Consequently, the 'fun of the dance' was totally lost on the doctor.

On the following morning, the *Pacific* steamed past the fort on Alcatraz Island to arrive at San Francisco at eight o'clock. Within a very short time of their arrival, a carriage had taken them to the Union Club where they spent the day luxuriating in the comfort of the club's lounges, where they found George Walkem, a lawyer they had met in Victoria, who offered to act as their guide to San Francisco and its people. After supper they played billiards until the early hours of the morning, resulting in their missing Holy Communion through their failure to get out of bed in time. Much of the rest of the day was spent on the 'street railways' with Walkem, touring the city, and being introduced to William Booker, the British Consul. With so much to see, both in the city itself, and in the surrounding area, they decided that they would miss the next Panama steamer and spend a few days exploring – an idea that expanded into the best part of a month.

On Booker's advice, and accompanied by Walkem, they took a steamer up the San Joaquin River to Stockton, and then a stagecoach directly east to Columbia, passing many abandoned goldmines. That night was spent in a boarding house run by a man from Gloucestershire, who had served with the British Army in Australia – where he deserted. Cheadle considered him to be 'a very civil, decent fellow'. On his advice, they took a buggy north to the town of Murphys, then east to the start of the Sierra Nevada where they arrived at the somewhat unimaginatively named Big Trees Grove. When Jane, Lady Franklin visited the place in 1861, she was invited to dedicate some of the trees. She chose the two tallest she could find, and named one after the American explorer, Dr Elisha Kent Kane, who had been involved with the Arctic search for her husband, and the second after her lost husband himself, Captain Sir John Franklin.

There were sugar pines; Douglas firs; and especially the astonishing giant sequoias, taller than St Paul's cathedral; stumps with ballrooms built on them; one stripped of part of its bark that had been displayed at the 1851 Great Exhibition in London; and fallen trees hollowed-out so that a man on horseback could ride through them; Cheadle thought they were 'the most astonishing sight [he] ever saw'.

Back at Columbia in time for the New Year's Eve celebrations, they had to endure listening to their host's 16-year-old daughter ('a regular Yankee gal') play the piano and sing ('very forward and chaffed us tremendously'). When a band came around to play the New Year in, Milton joined in the singing, and Cheadle retired early.

On their return to San Francisco, they were invited by Captain Elliott, their former cabin-mate, to call on him. He introduced them to Dr Ringgold, whose sister had both Milton and Cheadle 'smitten'. Another young lady, a friend of the sister, had a similar effect, leading Cheadle to observe that American women could 'beat English ladies in conversational powers, so much more general information'. An observation, however, possibly prompted more by a 'glorious smile & complexion & little twang' than by enlightening discourse.

Ringgold's mother was of advanced years and could remember the funeral of George Washington. She also proudly claimed that she could 'walk 5 miles a day in her prime'. Cheadle, rather ungallantly, let her know that his sisters 'could do 20 miles a day'. That evening, they decided to visit Maguire's Opera House where the notorious Miss Adah Isaacs Menken was performing in a version of Lord Byron's poem *Mazeppa*. The plot concerned the young lover of a wealthy woman who was punished for his infidelity by being bound to a horse and sent off into the wilderness to die. It was, however, not the fate of the lover that drew the crowds, but the sight of Miss Menken tied to the back of a real horse wearing little but a few wispy items of underwear as she trotted up and down the stage. For those who could not get tickets, Miss Menken made available a wide variety of photographic postcards of herself dressed in the minimum of clothing – and making a fortune in the process. Cheadle was not convinced of the show's artistic merit, calling it 'a miserable piece only to show her figure in scant costume'.

After a day of relaxing to get over the shock of Miss Menken, they set off by rail, south to Santa Clara, from where they went by stagecoach to San Jose. Spending the night at Crandell's Hotel on Market Street, they left in the morning driving a two-horse buggy to the New Almaden Works close to a 'quicksilver' (mercury) mine. There they watched as the crushed cinnabar ore was 'roasted' until the mercury vapour was released. Once cooled and condensed, the resultant mercury was stored in cast iron jars before being used to extract gold and silver from the ores. In the afternoon, they went down the mines wearing 'villainous old coat & hats', their way lit by a candle stuck in the end of a stick. On their return to San Jose, they discovered some genuine Burton draught English ale, which they drank with gusto. This over-indulgence led to a juvenile pillow fight, which only ended when Cheadle confiscated Milton's pillows 'to keep him quiet'.

Tickets were purchased for two berths on board the side-wheeler SS *Constitution*, due to sail for Panama in five days' time. Cheadle was keen to be under way, but Milton, settling in to the comforts of California, made it quite clear that he would have no objection to staying a little longer. The hand of Fate decided the outcome – the *Constitution* broke her wheelshaft. Her replacement, the aging *Orizba*, despite being advertised as 'splendid and popular', failed to find any recommendations among the local population. Thus, forcibly guided by destiny, Milton and Cheadle resorted to a slow life of billiards and glasses of 'Buch and Brecks' – a cocktail named in honour of James Buchanan and John Breckenridge, the President and Vice-President in office before Abraham Lincoln entered the White House. They also attended a Chinese opera with an orchestra consisting of 'a two-stringed fiddle of curious shape, a kettle drum, castanets, & a metal drum something like an iron pot, with a pipe which made a noise like bagpipes'. When Cheadle was told by an American that he had attended an opera about the complete history of China, which had lasted six weeks, the doctor 'left early'.

One probable reason for Milton's reluctance to depart from San Francisco was that both he and Cheadle had been invited to a grand ball given in honour of the marriage of a Miss Walkenshaw to Joseph, one of the fabulously wealthy Barron family who had made their money selling the New Almaden Works to the American Government. The ball was being given by the equally wealthy, 6 foot 7 inch Isaac Friedlander, a grain merchant. He had been born in Germany but raised in South Carolina, and had become the 'Wheat King' of California. Consequently, the event was to be run on 'Old South' lines – elegant, sophisticated and stylish. This stipulation caused Cheadle some difficulty. Milton, with his slight frame, had no problem borrowing a suit of 'tails', but Cheadle was a different matter. After a long search, Booker, the consul, managed to find a suit and promised to send it over to the Union Club. Cheadle then found that his laundry had been stolen and, even worse, Booker's suit arrived without trousers. At this, he decided to give up and miss the ball, but Booker rallied round and produced a pair of trouser that were perfect in every way, apart from a large rip in the rear. A hurried dash to a tailor saw the defect remedied and he and Milton arrived at the Friedlander's home at 10pm.

The early part of the ball was a rather muted affair until the older fogies withdrew to play cards. Milton proceeded to cut a dashing figure on the dance floor, and Cheadle enjoyed himself, taking part in several quadrilles and lancers with 'a very pretty set of girls' who, nevertheless, had 'the usual failing of the women of this continent, rather too flat chested and without that lovely roundness of form & limb so characteristic of our girls at home'. The dresses worn by the women were 'on the whole in very good taste, of silk or muslin, expensive, & the jewellery costly'. He was not impressed, however, by two women who had applied face powder – 'effect not pleasing'. As for the behaviour of the young men, he was equally impressed that they did not behave as badly as 'many of our haw-haw-ing fellows.' After a champagne supper, they left at 3am 'half in love with several beauties'.

Over the next few days, as Milton rode out with the local dignitaries and ladies, Cheadle stayed at the Union Club feeling bad. He blamed his 'languor & fever & headache' on not being allowed to smoke his pipe in the club, and stopped smoking cigars in the hope of an improvement. After four days, Cheadle, still 'too seedy to enjoy the glorious weather', visited the Mare Island US Navy Yard to see the visiting Russian fleet. Admiral Popov had brought four steam corvettes and two sail supply ships across the Pacific ready to fall upon British and French colonies if those countries supported Poland in her year-old uprising against the Russians. Groups of Russian seamen were allowed ashore under the command of midshipmen. Cheadle found the former 'powerful looking fellows, but dull, heavy & sullen looking', while a midshipman with whom he talked was 'very civil'. In response to the fleet's visit, the Polish population of San Francisco held a requiem Mass at the city's Cathedral of the Immaculate Conception (now, Old Saint Mary's Church) on the anniversary of the uprising, followed by a grand dinner. No Russians were invited.

After a further two days of suffering aches and pains, Cheadle began to shiver uncontrollably. This convinced him that he was suffering from a form of ague. Buying a bottle of quinine, he 'stodged it off completely with a dose that almost made my head blow off'. Suddenly, he was cured: 'Quite magical'. Both he and Milton celebrated the cure by each buying a locally made, pure silver 'watchguard' – usually known in England as an 'Albert' watch chain.

At last, on 23 January, accompanied by Booker, Walkem and others, Milton and Cheadle boarded the side-wheeler SS *Golden City*. Milton looked despondent, and Cheadle admitted to being 'dismally enough inclined', both being 'sorry to part with such pleasant friends'. However, the ship itself made a considerable impression on them both with its huge, exposed engine beam rocking backwards and forwards, driven by the pistons below deck; and the vast saloon in which the thirty passengers being carried could easily get lost. Particularly notable was the fact that the ship was carrying more than $1.5 million's-worth of gold, on its way to New York.

Less impressive was that male passengers were expected to join the ship's 'fire brigade', the ship's 'orders' that insisted that lights had to extinguished by 10pm, and that cabins had to be tidied and vacated by 11am so that Captain Pearson could carry out his daily inspection. Almost inevitably, just two days later, a small mutiny broke out. A boy steward entered the cabin the morning after Milton and Cheadle had spent a long night drinking whisky punch. When he requested that they rise from their bunks and leave the cabin, both 'positively refused'. When pleading failed, the boy resorted to threats, informing them that a Mrs Wilson had also refused to rise when requested. This had resulted in a stewardess being called and the lady being forcibly – if decorously – removed from her cabin. Eventually, the steward gave up and went to fetch the ship's purser. He, however, being older and wiser –and probably not quite sure how to handle a recalcitrant viscount – sent the boy back with tea and toast, followed by breakfast.

Two days later, the ship was off Cape Lucas at the mouth of the Gulf of California, when a frisson of excitement went through the whole vessel. A three-masted screw ship appeared over the horizon, and a passenger – a nine-year-old boy – claimed that it was the British-built Confederate raider *Alabama*. When asked how he knew that it was the much-feared vessel, the boy said that he had been on board a ship that had been stopped by the *Alabama*. As it was known that the raider was in the Pacific, and that the cargo of gold (which had been reported in the San Francisco press) would be a tempting target, every telescope on board was pointed at the newcomer. However, their young nautical expert, on the approach of the vessel, changed his mind and told everyone that she was 'not like her'.

With a sharp rise in temperature, everyone changed into lighter clothing. Both Milton and Cheadle donned light linen suits, Cheadle in a straw hat, and Milton – ridiculed by Cheadle – wearing a tropical 'pith' helmet, such as was 'much used on this coast'. It was not long after they had sailed that a 'Society Addicted to Whisky Punch' had been formed with Milton as its President. Within its ranks, an elite was formed known as 'The Owl Club' consisting of those members who slept throughout the day as a result of the Society's activities. The president of the 'Owls' was – Milton. After five days at sea, the ship hauled into Manzanillo, the main port for the Mexican State of Colima. Supplies and cargo were taken on board including 150 bales of cotton (to compensate for the loss of the cotton trade with the Southern States). The rolling of water barrels across the upper deck kept everyone awake, forcing them to consider the rumours that French warships (involved in the continuing Franco-Mexican War) were cruising outside the harbour – a rumour that proved to have no more substance than the *Alabama* alarm.

Milton and Cheadle were about to be subjected to a much greater alarm when the ship sailed. Their only neighbour, across the passageway from their stateroom, was a man who, despite the high temperature, perpetually wrapped himself in a thick blanket. Believing that his food would not be digested unless he ate it while wearing a hat, all his meals were taken in his cabin. To underline his sense of imminent personal disaster, he had arrived on board with his own coffin. Next door to the hypochondriac's cabin, and directly opposite to Milton and Cheadle's stateroom, a previously empty cabin was commandeered by Mrs Wetzner, a woman from the Province of Canada (now the Provinces of Ontario and Quebec). Known for her rumbustious attitude, and raucous laughter, she was referred to as 'The Widow' – itself a shortened version of the American term 'grass widow', a label attached to women whose husbands had found better things to do than be in their company. Cheadle was keen to safeguard his moral security against a woman to whom he had not even been introduced: 'Has she a design upon us?'

The entry into Acapulco provided another burst of excitement. As they entered the harbour, a French frigate fired a blank warning shot. The *Golden City* rattled to a halt and a polite French officer came on board. He explained that the French were about to take the town, and hoped that their invasion would be carried out in a peaceful manner. However, if the townspeople fired a single shot in opposition, the place would be shelled. In an attempt to reduce the chances of an accidental outbreak of hostilities, it was the boarding officer's duty to check the weapons being carried on board. Once the formalities were completed, Milton and Cheadle went ashore with the captain and found the place notable mainly for its flowers, fruits, pelicans, and iguanas. The local people, the women in light dresses, and the men slumbering beneath 'huge-brimmed' sombreros, showed little concern at the French ships blockading the harbour, or the looming threat of invasion. The Mexican authorities had promised the French that the few cannons that guarded a local, ruined, fort would be unmounted, but rumours were in the wind that they would 'probably' be used to fire on the invaders. Nevertheless, a signalling gun, carelessly fired by the *Golden City,* requesting Captain Pearson's immediate return on board, failed to stir up any action. The French fleet, however, was on its way, and, almost within minutes of the captain's return, the paddle steamer was, once again, at sea.

A small number of additional passengers had been picked up at Acapulco, and even Cheadle found his thoughts diverted by the wife of a Mexican who had just come on board. Unusually, among his notes, he penned the following detailed description of the woman:

> The lady is the best specimen of Spanish beauty I have seen, beautiful olive complexion, very transparent but too uniform in colour; eyes very black & languishing, beautifully pencilled eyebrows & long looping lashes; delicate little nose & tiny mouth, with the reddest lips I have ever seen; oval face & delicate ears, figure pretty, rather too embonpoint in bust; graceful walk peculiar to Spanish women.

The Mexican lady, however, was not available for social activities, so Milton and Cheadle had to make do with the young Miss Van Sickle from near Chicago, 'good-natured & as innocent as a baby', who, finally, contrived an introduction to The Widow. After a gentle game of whist, they 'induced' the two ladies to accompany them to the captain's cabin where they ended the evening drinking champagne.

The same group meeting up once again, the following evening began with iced claret on the warm upper deck before going down to dinner with the captain. Cheadle set the tone of the evening by getting into an argument with their host over the visit to England of Henry Ward Beecher, a Congregationalist Minister, brother of the writer of *Uncle Tom's Cabin*. Beecher was an ardent anti-slavery activist who had gone to England to give a number of lectures on the evils of slavery, and Captain Pearson applauded his activities. Cheadle thought that a bellowing American preacher could do more harm than good to the British anti-slavery campaign. When the heated debate had calmed down, The Widow launched an attack on the 'absurdity of an Immaculate & Supernatural Conception'. She based her argument on the premise that, if she were to have a child, no one would assume that the conception had been immaculate or supernatural. Why, therefore, should anyone assume that a birth over nineteen centuries earlier *was* either immaculate or supernatural? Miss Van Sickle fled in embarrassment, leaving the remainder 'all disgusted with the strong-minded Widow'.

Two days later, The Widow returned and asked Milton if he would escort her around the ship to arouse the envy of another passenger, the Peruvian Consul, with whom she was eager to become involved. She had already sent the Peruvian romantic verses and 'accidently' met him in quiet corners of the ship. Milton refused, but The Widow did not give up that easily and pestered him about the matter in front of other members of The Owls, frequently employing 'double entendres' at which everyone instantly shuffled in discomfiture and closely studied the bottom of their whisky glass. Eventually, The Widow gave up and was later found in close company with 'a most obstinate Yankee' named Kennedy. His reputation for obstinacy came from his insistence that snow could never exist on tropical mountains.

Almost within sight of Panama Bay, it was decided to hold a final meeting of the Society Addicted to Whisky Punch and its side chapter, The Owls. Both Miss Van Sickle and The Widow were invited. The activities began with a game of 'Eating Philopenas', in which nuts were broken open, and if a double kernel was found, the finder presented one to a lady and demanded a small forfeit. However, as all the extra kernels were offered to Miss Van Sickle, leaving The Widow on the verge of explosive outrage, it was decided that they would play 'Consequences' instead. Each player would write the next word in a hidden sentence, or series of sentences. Then, to great hilarity, the result was revealed. It was at this point The Widow was exposed in taking her revenge when so many 'objectionable' words appeared in her handwriting that a large number of papers had to be destroyed to save the gentlemen from embarrassment.

The anchorage off Panama City was reached at half-past midnight, and the shore gong sounded at 2am. The landing wharf was close to the railway station and, by first light, the train pulled out bearing Milton, Cheadle and Miss Van Sickle, ready to be fortified with a hamper of sandwiches, champagne and whisky, obtained from the ship's purser. The distance by rail between Panama City and Aspinwall (modern Colón) on the Caribbean Sea was about 50 miles. It only crossed one river (the Chagres), but the journey, with its wide loops and sharp bends, took three hours to complete. Cheadle was enthralled by the 'wonders of tropical vegetation', the vibrant colours of the abundant flowers with their stark contrast to the black, grey, and silver of the winter Cariboo. Aspinwall, on the other hand was 'a miserable place', made even more depressing at having to wait for their ship to fire her signal gun before they could board. With Miss Van Sickle in tow, they went to a hotel to finish off the remainder of their hamper before walking the streets in search of curios – none could be found.

The SS *Ariel* was a side-wheel steamer that had seen service on the Transatlantic run, but, in 1861, the Union Government's War Department had chartered her for use in ferrying United States Marines to the Pacific via the Panama Isthmus railway. She still, however, carried civilian passengers on the voyage. Among the passengers when she was on her way to Aspinwall in December 1863 was the nine-year-old boy who had caused the excitement off Cape Lucas when he thought the *Alabama* was about to close with them. He had good cause. On 7 December, the Confederate ship had come up with the *Ariel* off Cuba and fired warning shots. With the paddle steamer stopped, the *Alabama* sent a boarding party across, disarmed the 126 Marines being carried, and took the captain back to the raider as hostage. The ship's safe was opened and $9,500 removed. The captain was then returned to his ship having signed a bond of $260,000, to be paid six months after the Confederacy was recognised by the United States.

With the *Alabama* roaming the Pacific, the passage to New York seemed reasonably safe; but once the ship had left the harbour, it became clear that there was to be little in the way of conviviality on board. Not only were the cabins tiny in comparison to the *Golden City*, and the food 'only passable', the weather afflicted many of the passengers, including Milton, with seasickness. Furthermore, some of the Unionist Americans on board were very anti-British as a result of the *Alabama*'s activities. One Northerner complained loudly to Cheadle that England was clearly aiding the South in its 'infernal, wicked, devilish rebellion'. The doctor replied that 'Englishmen do not care how the war goes' and, anyway, it was no different to 'the American Revolution'. After that exchange, the two men were 'very polite to one another'. Trouble, however, still stalked Cheadle. In the middle of a game of whist after a 'dreary day', he was 'abused by Miss Van Sickle for neglect'. He was also swamped with

American expressions such as 'didn't oughter', 'kind o', 'quit', and 'doggoned'. There was, however, one glimmer of light – 'The Widow has cut us all dead'.

New York was reached on the morning of 15 February, and the passengers were quickly removed from the ship without breakfast, or even a cup of coffee. At the same time, the captain sent formal notice of his arrival to the Collector of Customs:

DISTRICT OF NEW YORK – PORT OF NEW YORK
I, Master of the SS *Ariel*, do solemnly, sincerely and truly swear that the following List or Manifest, subscribed by me, and now delivered by me to the Collector of the Customs of the Collection District of New-York, is a full and perfect list of all the passengers taken on board of the said *Ariel* at Aspinwall from which port said *Ariel* has now arrived; and that on said list is truly designated the age, the sex, and the occupation of each of said passengers, the part of the vessel occupied by each during the passage, the country to which each belongs, and also the country of which it is intended by each to become an inhabitant; and that said List or Manifest truly sets forth the number of said passengers who have died on said voyage, and the names and ages of those who died. So help me God.

Milton and Cheadle, having been properly 'designated' on the 'said list', moved into the smart New York Hotel, after delivering Miss Van Sickle to the rather plain, brown brick-built, Astor House – a Broadway hotel favoured by both President Lincoln and the Confederate President, Jefferson Davis. That evening they went to the local music hall, followed by a supper of oysters.

The following day was spent in exploring the city as snow fell. The people were described as 'extremely quiet & subdued, very unusual among Yankees'. The reason, it seemed, could be seen in the large number of black armbands, top hats banded with black crepe, and the lack of talk of the war. Later in the day, they said their farewells to Miss Van Sickle, the 'unsophisticated, natural, good-natured, buxom lass' who was returning to Chicago, before going to see a play at the Academy of Music – 'as large as Covent Garden' – oysters again for supper.

After booking their passage across the Atlantic in the Cunard Line's *China*, a steam screw-ship with auxiliary barque-rigged masts and sails, they went skating in Central Park ('Ladies skate very well') before catching the train to Washington where they arrived the following morning. They booked into the luxurious Willard's Hotel on Pennsylvania Avenue, where Lincoln had hidden from assassins, and Julia Ward Howe had written the words of *The Battle Hymn of the Republic*. With a substantial breakfast enjoyed in the hotel's dining room ('the longest & best lighted room I ever saw'), they set off to call upon the British Minister to Washington, Lord Lyons.

Their reception at the Embassy was not as they had expected. When Viscount Milton announced his visit, they were held waiting before an official returned to say that Lord Lyons was 'too busy', and that if Milton wanted anything, 'he must write'. Cheadle noted: 'We therefore retired discomforted, Milton much put out.' The afternoon was spent visiting the Capitol where there was an animated debate in the House of Representatives on the wisdom of releasing slaves who were left to fend for themselves while starving and diseased in deplorable conditions around Washington. In the evening, they went to the theatre to see George Colman's play *The Iron Chest*. The leading actor was Edwin Booth, whose younger brother, John Wilks Booth, was to gain his own notoriety – also in a theatre.

On their return to New York, the baggage was sent on board the *China*, and they spent their last night in the city among friends at Delmonico's on Beaver Street, the first establishment in America to be accorded the title 'restaurant'. In the place where several dishes, including 'Baked Alaska' and 'Eggs Benedict', were first created, they had 'a most magnificent supper' at a dining table 'literally covered with flowers, camellias, orchids & rare exotics in epergnes'.

Milton and Cheadle's health was drunk after toasts so effusive that Cheadle considered them to be 'twaddle'. The party went on all night until carriages were summoned and the revels continued on board the *China*. At last, the bell rang ordering all those not sailing with the ship to leave. After a round of rowdy farewells, followed by much traditional handkerchief waving, the ship sailed at 9.30am and Milton and Cheadle retired to their beds until dinner that night.

The crossing proved to be a succession of days when storms and rough seas prevented much social interaction. Beyond the presence on board of the soldier, Lord Abinger, and his American bride, 'little, dark, nice figure, pretty face with marks of a very fierce temper', little was worthy of note. They arrived at Liverpool on the evening of 7 March 1864. The 'mere party of pleasure' was back in England.

Epilogue

There is little record of Milton and Cheadle's actual arrival at Liverpool. Even the dates conflict with Milton stating that it was 5 March 1864, while Cheadle's journal records it as 'Monday, 7 March'. Cheadle's last words in his account read: 'At 2.45 passed Holyhead'; Milton's version appreciates 'the pleasures of a return home in the company of old friends, who welcomed us as we disembarked from the *China*'.

Whatever the delights of their welcome home after being away for almost two years, one thing was paramount in their minds. Using Cheadle's journal as its foundation, their thirty-seven-page account – *An Expedition across the Rocky Mountains into British Columbia, by the Yellow Head or Leather Pass* – was, within a year of their arrival, read before The British Association for the Advancement of Science, and The Royal Geographical Society. After the former event, the President of the Royal Geographical Society, Sir Roderick Murchison, praised Milton and Cheadle for their crossing of British North America, and the eminent biologist Sir Joseph Dalton Hooker wrote to his friend Charles Darwin, saying that 'a young Lord Milton (a mere boy) & Livingston were the great guns.' The work was published early in the New Year with excerpts appearing in *The Quiver – An Illustrated Magazine for Sunday and General Reading*. The following year, Milton and Cheadle were elected Fellows of the Royal Geographical Society. Clearly encouraged by the success of these events, their book, *The North-west Passage by Land* was published in June 1865. It bore the stamp of Milton's self-censorship combined with self-promotion (he referred to Messiter, his fellow Etonian and contender in their petty quarrels, as 'Treemiss') the book became an instant best seller. Within two years, five new editions had been published, and further editions reached into the twenty-first century.

The book was illustrated with the sketches Cheadle had drawn on the journey. Although the word 'photographs' occurs once in the Preface of the early editions, there is no other mention of photographic activity on the entire trail. Cheadle's journal mentions only visits to a photographer in Victoria, one of which resulted in the group photograph with the Patenaude family. An engraving of that particular photograph was used in the book after being reversed and altered (Milton's pipe was removed, and trees sketched into the background).

The final sketches were done by the popular artist R. P. Leitch who worked for the *Illustrated London News*, and the engravings produced by W. J. Linton and J. Cooper. The maps were the work of the leading cartographer of the day, John Arrowsmith, who had been awarded the Royal Geographical Society's Gold Medal in 1863, and who later had a mountain named after him on Vancouver Island.

In addition to his involvement with the book, Milton commissioned the Minton China Co. to produce two sets of dessert plates, each plate gilded with pure gold using the newly patented acid etching technique, and bearing a coloured copy of one of the Linton-Cooper engravings. There were sixteen plates in each set, with one set bearing the monogram of Milton, the other, Cheadle's.

With the book's publication, it seems as if Milton and Cheadle's widely differing lifestyles kept them, in the main, apart from each other. Milton pursued a political career, being elected to Parliament as a Liberal to represent the West Riding of Yorkshire South constituency in 1865. Supporting education for all children, admission for all to universities, and the widening of the franchise, he soon gained a reputation for his sensitive temperament when he could not have his own way – sometimes with good cause. On one occasion, he asked the Chancellor of the Exchequer a question regarding Crown payments by the Hudson's Bay

Company. James Stansfeld, a Treasury Lord, rose to answer, only to be interrupted by Milton who said 'I beg your pardon. I asked the Chancellor of the Exchequer'. When Stansfeld refused to give way, Milton stormed from the chamber. He also sat on the Select Committees looking at the Railways (Guards' and Passengers' Communication) Bill, and on the Petitions and Corrupt Practices at Elections (re-committed) Bill. He was on much firmer ground when he demanded,

> I wish, therefore, to know what was going to be done by the British Government with the island of San Juan and the group of islands connected with it? I desire to receive from the Under Secretary of State an explicit assurance that no concessions would be made as to the water boundary, which so vitally affected, not only Vancouver's Island and British Columbia, but the future of Canada as a whole.

(With the eastern Provinces united in 1867 as the Dominion of Canada, British Columbia joined the Dominion in 1871.) Unfortunately, the British Government eventually gave in to American demands that the Kaiser of Germany should make the decision whether the San Juan Islands belonged to Great Britain or the USA – with the inevitable result.

Milton's – and, indeed, Cheadle's – achievements, however, did not go unrecognised. During a debate on the future of western Canada, Charles Adderley, the Secretary of State for the Colonies noted,

> In the interests of our fellow-subjects across the Atlantic, also, it was essential that this vast district should be settled. We had already a very large colony to the west of the Rocky Mountains, and no one knew better than the noble Lord opposite [Viscount Milton], who upon this subject had produced one of the most interesting and able books ever written, how essential it was to the development of the mineral wealth of British Columbia that the agricultural country lying to the east of it should have its wealth also developed, the two together forming, perhaps, one of

the finest dominions in the world, but each being supplementary to the other.

In the same debate, another MP remarked that 'there were many excellent books of travels, among which the works of Lord Milton and Dr Cheadle occupied the foremost place'.

Brushing aside the compliments, Milton, went straight to the point:

> The British Pacific colonies had no direct means of communication with one another, but derived even their food from the United States, although the interior of the country was well calculated to supply their wants. There was every year a great influx of Americans, who went to the gold mines during the fine season; and while we in this country had been pondering and wasting time, the staple commodity of the colony had been, to a great extent, worked out and depreciated. This state of things was an injustice to those who had been induced to settle there. The gold went out of the country never to return, and no labour or improvement could replace its value. This had been going on for some years, and unless active steps were taken it seemed likely to continue.

Outside his Parliamentary duties, Milton was appointed President of the Association in Aid of the Deaf and Dumb. The Association existed

> ...to provide extended religious and secular instruction among the deaf and dumb throughout the metropolis after they have quitted school; to visit, under the direction of the parochial clergyman, sick and other deaf and dumb persons at their homes; to assist those having good characters in obtaining employment; to relieve, either by gifts or loans of money, such as are deserving and necessitous; and to encourage the early training of deaf and dumb children preparatory to their admission into educational institutions.

Based upon his own experiences, and on subsequent research, Milton also wrote *A History of the San Juan Water Boundary*

Dispute Question as Affecting the Division of Territory between Great Britain and the United States, published in 1869.

In 1866, the 27-year-old Milton fell in love with Mary, daughter of the Marquess of Ormonde. The announcement of his engagement brought on the same reaction as it had five years earlier after his engagement to Dorcas, the daughter of Lord Chichester. Again, his parents let his fiancée's family know that Milton was suffering from long-standing and frequently manifested mental difficulties. This time it took a little longer, but the outcome was the same – the engagement was broken off.

Milton's response was to act immediately. Without telling anyone in his family, he asked 18-year-old Laura Maria Theresa Beauclerk, grand-daughter of the Duke of St Albans and daughter of Captain Lord Charles Beauclerk, to marry him. She agreed, and the ceremony was arranged to take place at St George's church, Hanover Square on 10 August 1867. During the ceremony, Milton placed a ring on her finger made of gold he had brought back from the Cariboo goldfields. The newlyweds then moved into 6 Hyde Park Place, Cumberland Gate.

Five years later, Milton, in declining health, resigned his seat in the House of Commons. Lady Milton had bought 130 acres of land at Callaghan in Alleghany County, Virginia, on the lower slopes of a gentle mountain overlooking a small stream (Johnson's Creek). Her younger brother, Herbert Augustus Corbett Beauclerk, lived nearby. Milton sailed with his pregnant wife and two young daughters – Lady Laura Mary ('Daisy'), and Lady Mabel Florence Harriet – in the Cunard's side-paddle wheeler, *Scotia,* to New York. They took the family doctor and a nurse with them to look after Lady Milton in her forthcoming confinement and, on their arrival in the United States, they crossed the border into Canada, probably in order that the child would be born on British soil.

There is, however, another possible reason why Milton chose the site. Part of the negotiations that brought British Columbia into the Dominion the previous year centred around the need for a railway to connect the east and west of the country – Milton's key Parliamentary interest. The possibility of such a railway had also been the prime reason why Milton had travelled westward with Cheadle. Even before Milton had thought of moving to live in the USA, the eastern end of a proposed railway it was suggested should be sited near Fort William, on the north-east shore of Lake Superior. From there, the railway would provide a link to Winnipeg. Viscount and Viscountess Milton's temporary home was a wooden farmhouse on Pointe de Meuron, close to Fort William and the Kaministikwia River, a tributary to Lake Superior (near modern Thunder Bay, and across the river from the site of a large, modern railway marshalling yard).

William Charles De Meuron Wentworth Fitzwilliam was born on 25 July 1872. The birth gave rise to a pantomime allegation – possibly started by members of his close family – that Lady Laura had been drugged by the family doctor, and a substitute baby had taken the place of her real child. The alleged substitution supposedly extinguished any risk that Milton's illness could be inherited by his, apparently authentic, male heir, and the line of succession would be secured. It all came to naught when – with commendable honesty – Milton's brother, Henry, who would have inherited the vast Fitzwilliam fortune had the rumours proved to be true, declared the child to be the legitimate son, and the accusations fell away.

When the child was ready, the family travelled to their land in Virginia and moved into an existing house on the property. According to Milton's nurse, Matilda Count (or, possibly, Matilda Kingdon), the house was 'thoroughly done up, inside and out, and beautifully carpeted and furnished, and made as pretty a Gentleman's residence as could be desired, in such a lonely solitary spot'. Then, disaster struck in the early morning of 30 December 1873, when the house caught fire and was totally destroyed. The family moved into adjoining buildings while plans were set afoot to rebuild the family home. Milton decided that the new building should be in the English neo-Gothic style, one already falling out of fashion in America. He probably arranged to have the plans drawn up in England, with the actual construction work being undertaken by local builders as the required building materials were readily to hand. During the construction, Lady Milton twice returned to England for furniture and fittings for the imposing house then being built among the tree-clad, rolling hills. The first return to England was on board the *China* where the nurse, Mathilda, almost swooned at the sermons of the celebrated American preacher, Dr Theodore Cuyler, who believed that

> Those who have sat before my pulpit will testify that I never spared my lungs or their ears in the delivery of my discourses. The preaching of the Gospel is spiritual gunnery, and many a well-loaded cartridge has failed to reach its mark from lack of powder to propel it.

His sermons were followed by the singing of *Nearer My God to Thee*.

It may be nothing more than coincidence, but the design of the new house nestling in the Allegheny Mountains was very reminiscent of the 'East Lodge' on the grounds of Milton's childhood home, Wentworth Woodhouse, and may have been built in the same style in response to fond memories from his early years. (In 2015 the property was taken over by the Wentworth Woodhouse Preservation Trust and is now open to the public.)

Once the Virginia house had been completed, Viscount and Lady Milton held a grand ball to which many of the neighbours were invited. The idyll, however, was not to last. Worn down by his ill health, Milton and the family returned to England for a visit in late 1876, during which time they crossed the English Channel to France. While staying in Rouen, (a source of 'medicinal' waters) the 37-year-old Lord William Wentworth Fitzwilliam, Viscount Milton, died of an unidentified illness.

His body was brought back to Wentworth Woodhouse before being taken out of the back doors on a rather undignified shortcut (instead of the usual route taken by the dead heirs) to the Holy Trinity Church where it was placed in the family vault. The tomb bore an inscription chosen by his brother, Henry:

> Fear not for I have redeemed thee,
> I have called thee by thy name,
> Thou art mine.
> (Isaiah XLIII)

Henry was clearly a man of honour who refused to support the family's constant disparagement of Milton's struggles in life. God had called, and Milton had answered. Nine years later, he was joined by Lady Laura, Viscountess Milton. She died, also aged 37, on 30 March 1886.

* * *

Although Cheadle was deep in the production of the papers and the book he and Milton were writing, this was not allowed to get in the way of his main aim – the pursuit of his medical career. He passed his Doctorate in Medicine in 1865 and became a Member of the Royal College of Physicians (a 'Fellow' after 1880). The following year, he found time to marry Anne Murgatroyd from Bingley, a daughter of a former Mayor of Bradford, and, in 1867, was elected Assistant Physician to St Mary's Hospital, Paddington, where he lectured on pharmacology, clinical medicine, and pathology. Cheadle moved into 2 Hyde Park Place, Cumberland Gate, with his wife and growing family. His near neighbours – just two doors down – were Viscount and Viscountess Milton.

Cheadle was appointed Dean of the Medical School in 1869, where he founded scholarships and rewarded excellence by presenting portraits of leading teachers and students to the library. He also strongly supported the School's sporting and athletic clubs. In the same year, he became Assistant Physician to the Hospital for Sick Children, Great Ormond Street, and earned an international reputation for his work among the young patients. His greatest research was in the connection between the health of children and the nutrition they were provided. In 1878, he had found himself with three patients aged between 16 months and three years old. All were suffering from rickets but, when he studied their diets, he came to the conclusion that: 'The diet was, however, more than a rickety diet – it was a scurvy diet'.

With meat being expensive, the usual food for weaning children consisted largely of potatoes and gravy, supported by commercial baby food. In the case of his patients, however, they had not been fed on potatoes, nor were they provided with fresh milk. Cheadle fed his patients with fresh milk, raw meat, and a mixture of mashed potatoes and milk, a process which provided a cure for the scurvy. In effect, Cheadle had recognised that many children were suffering from scurvy as a result of the lack of Vitamin C – a component lacking in commercial baby food, and not yet identified by science. This research resulted in the publication of his widely acclaimed work entitled *On the Principles and Exact Condition to be Observed in the Artificial Feeding of Infants: The Properties of Artificial Foods and the Diseases Which Arise from Faults of Diet in Early Life.*

In the paper, Cheadle narrowed down the cause of scurvy, noting,

> There is, however, an invariable factor, without the presence of which all other casual and irregular factors are powerless to set up the disease. This essential factor, it has been proved over and over again, is the absence of certain elements in food. If the body is deprived of these elements, [scurvy] is produced. What these elements are has not yet been absolutely settled with scientific precision, but we know positively that they exist in fresh vegetables, in lime-juice, in milk, and in less considerable degree, perhaps, in some other fresh animal foods.

It was to be another fifty years before the Nobel Prize was awarded for the 'scientific precision' that announced the discovery of vitamins – of which Vitamin C (Ascorbic Acid) proved to be the answer to scurvy.

Cheadle also provided significant progress on infantile rheumatism and cirrhosis of the liver. The term 'Cheadle's disease' was given to the wasting syndrome caused by malnutrition resulting in involuntary loss of weight and appetite, muscle wasting, fatigue, and weakness.

Despite being the son of a vicar, Cheadle was not a supporter of orthodoxy and dogma, whether theological or secular. In an article published in the May 1872 edition of *Popular Science Monthly* entitled *'The Early Superstitions of Medicine'*, he wrote,

> This profound reverence for authority, this belief in supernatural agencies, and this stagnation of true science, was the condition which prevailed at the beginning of the sixteenth century. But education gradually spread, and at this time thinkers arose,

who, dissatisfied with mere assumptions, or the baseless dicta of previous authorities, commenced working at the rudiments of the science which had hitherto rested on such imperfect foundations.

His outstanding medical protégé was Doctor Frederick Poynton, a young physician who was also captain of Somerset County cricket team between 1891 and 1896. His attitude to life may have been an attraction to his tutor when he wrote that 'hell is staying in a "Scotch" temperance hotel in Glasgow'. After scoring 305 runs in an opening partnership against Sussex, Poynton drank the great England and Sussex batsman Ranjitsinhji 'under the table' – an incident of which Cheadle would have approved greatly. Poynton wrote of Cheadle's work among children noting that: 'By nature very shy, he had a loud voice, and with patients was very human and encouraging. His experience was very extensive and he had a natural clinical gift, not realised by many. His great hand would almost obliterate a child, but that child would be shouting to him to give him a sweet.'

In 1889, Anne, the mother of Cheadle's five sons, died ('The silver Cord is loosed, The Golden bowl is broken.' Ecclesiastes 12:6). She was buried in the grounds of Bingley church where they were married, and Cheadle had a stained-glass window installed in her memory. In addition, like the practical man he was, Cheadle presented the Alice Ward at the Great Ormond Street Hospital (named after Queen Victoria's second daughter) with a baby's cot.

Not generally being a great advocate of causes beyond research and clinical medicine, Cheadle did take part in the great controversy of his time – the place of women in medical practice. Ignoring the 'wrath and indignation' of his medical colleagues at St Mary's, he became actively involved with lectures at the newly established London School of Medicine for Women. He also gave lectures on hygiene at the Nursing Institute. It may have been this latter activity that brought him first into contact with Robert Mansel, the Inspector of Queen Victoria's Jubilee Institute for Nurses, and the former Superintendent of the Metropolitan and National Nursing Association, whose daughter, Emily, Cheadle married in August 1892.

After endowing St Mary's with the Cheadle Prize and Gold Medal for the best essay on clinical medicine, Cheadle accepted an appointment as Honorary Consulting Physician at Great Ormond Street. This gave him the opportunity to open his first private practice, at his new home with Emily and his sons, 19 Portman Street, London, concentrating on childhood ailments. According to the British Medical Journal, Cheadle was 'greatly beloved by his patients, both rich and poor, and with children he was particularly charming. In social life as in professional life he was dignified, courteous, and reserved, but deeply affectionate'.

Endearing qualities, however, are no defence against tragedy. In 1884, Cheadle was invited by the British Association (founded in 1831 with a Viscount Milton, later the 5th Earl Fitzwilliam – Milton's grandfather – as President) to lecture in Canada. One of the party, Professor J. P. Sheldon of the College of Agriculture at Downton, Salisbury, travelled with Cheadle and later recorded:

Perhaps the most remarkable member of the party was Dr W B Cheadle, MD, who, twenty years ago, in the company of Viscount Milton, MP, travelled across the North-West Territory, and over the Rocky Mountains into British Columbia .... Dr Cheadle's reflections and reminiscences must have been of a singularly interesting nature as he thundered along with us in the train, over the prairies and mountains which had cost him so much pains to traverse on a previous occasion. To the attention drawn by Dr Cheadle and Lord Milton's book to the North-West Territory may in no small measure be attributed the action which was taken by the Dominion Government in opening up the close preserves of the Hudson's Bay Company, followed after a time by the confederation of the provinces of Canada into one political and commercial unit – the Dominion of Canada.

Unfortunately, it was during this visit to the land he admired so much that Cheadle contracted dysentery. The rest of his life was spent in declining health as the infecting bacteria and viruses combined with his body's own immune cells to damage the intestinal tissue. The resulting painful and debilitating intestinal cramps, internal leakage, and water and mineral loss had a marked effect on his mental and physical activity. The best defence against dysentery did not appear until Alexander Fleming – one of Cheadle's students – discovered antibiotics.

The misfortune continued with the death of his 26-year-old fourth son, Thomas Alec, in June, 1900. Less than two years later, and ten days short of her 41st birthday, his 'Devoted wife and true comrade' Emily, died.

Cheadle's health declined over the next eight years before he died, aged 74, at Portman Street, on 25 March 1910. He was buried next to his second wife in Ocklynge Cemetery, Eastbourne. His friend and protégé, Dr Frederick Poynton noted,

> He was one of the greatest physicians I ever knew, and his superb knowledge of illness was never recognised as I should have expected, partly because he was in reality a sad man who cared little for any advertisement.

Immediately after Cheadle's death, Poynton also recorded a desperately depressing incident regarding the baby's cot Cheadle had presented to the Alex Ward at Great Ormond Street Hospital in memory of his first wife:

> I remember it well in the middle of the ward. To my horror it was 'scrapped'. The very fact that it was a memorial to one of the hospital's greatest physicians, and had been in his ward, made me mentally sick to hear of its fate, and is a warning to all of the forgetfulness of even intelligent people, and of the instinct to destroy what is a little difficult to keep, though that is a charming gift, or a scrap of history.

Cheadle was not forgotten. While the 7,564-feet Mount Cheadle carried his name in the towering landscape of British Columbia, the Canadian Pacific Railway honoured Cheadle in the early 1880s by naming a small community on the line 20 miles east of Calgary, Alberta, after him. The name, however, seemed to have caused the succeeding generations some confusion as a twenty-first century 'Community Profile' recorded:

One tradition says the community was named for Walter Cheadle, who travelled across the prairies and Rocky Mountains in the 1860s. Another says it was named for William [sic] Butler Cheadle, author.

There can be no doubt that Cheadle would have been highly amused to think that he was doubly honoured for his separate, and distinctive, achievements. He would have been equally astounded that the notes he made on the trail would be transcribed and published in 1931 under the title *Cheadle's Journal of Trip Across Canada 1862–1863*. Republished forty years later, the notes are clearly the basis for the combined Milton-Cheadle publication, *The North-West Passage by Land*. The book displays by omission Milton's determination that the combined account would not contain any mention of his illness, his frequent outbursts of petulance, or any record that made him look weak or insecure. Such demands are unlikely to have caused Cheadle any righteous consternation. Having arrived safely back in England, and in pursuit of his medical career, any desires to bring attention to possible defects in Milton's personality would have long faded away. In their Introduction, the *Journal*'s transcribers and editors simply, and accurately, described Cheadle's achievements:

> This is the journal of the first transcanadian tourist. Before him others on business, exploration or duty, had crossed overland from Eastern Canada to British Columbia. But Walter Butler Cheadle was the first to traverse the whole country from the St Laurence to the Pacific simply 'for pleasure', for the sheer enjoyment of seeing new lands, hunting the buffalo and visiting the gold regions of Cariboo.

* * *

Nothing further is known of Louis Patenaude and 'Mrs Assiniboine'. However, in 1872, when 'The Boy' would have been about twenty-two, a Benjamin Patenaude was married at Fort Pitt. His parents were described as 'Catherine Moignon and Louis Patenaude, both half-breeds'.

After parting from Milton and Cheadle at Fort Carlton, Charles Alston Messiter headed south and crossed the border into the United States. There, free from having to tolerate Milton's petulant behaviour – which was matched only by his own – and unrestrained by Cheadle's insistence on placing the interests of the group before any individual's, Messiter spent many months roaming around the western part of the country depending upon his wits, his horse, and his rifle. It was a precarious existence, but he survived many clashes with Indians, aggressive cattlemen, and random gunmen. On his return to England, Messiter eventually inherited the family home, Barwick House, in Somerset and was appointed as a magistrate. It was in such peaceful domestic surroundings that he wrote about his adventures in a best-selling account entitled *Sport and Adventures among the North-American Indians,* published in 1890. He died in 1920.

When Milton and Cheadle published the account of their adventures, there was a considerable body of scepticism about the antics – and even, existence – of Mr O'B. All that can be obtained from the few mentions of his activities after Milton and Cheadle had managed to shuffle off their unwelcome burden, was that he obtained work in Victoria as a secretary to a local church. When that employment palled, rumour suggested that he sailed for San Francisco where he stayed for a short time before sailing on to Melbourne, Australia, and, eventually to New Zealand. At that point, Mr O'B disappears from the record; gone but not forgotten. In 1918, a fellow Irishman, Arthur Wheeler, a land surveyor and first President of the Alpine Club of Canada, named a peak in the Rocky Mountains 'Mount O'Beirne', thus demonstrating that distinctions do not always go to the most deserving.

It was not only Mr O'B that was suspected of being a figment of someone's imagination. The headless Indian found in the valley of the North Thompson River was widely believed to have been nothing more than a sensationalist invention meant to 'colour' Milton and Cheadle's account of their journey. In 1873, however, a book was published with the title *Ocean to Ocean, Sandford Fleming's Expedition Through Canada in 1872.* The book's author was the unimpeachable expedition secretary, The Reverend George M. Grant, who gave an account of the search of a possible route for the Canadian Pacific and Intercolonial Railways.

While passing along the same path as Milton and Cheadle, they not only found the headless Indian, but even found his head – and *The North-West Passage by Land* received yet another boost to its sales.

In his book, the Reverend Grant, having direct experience of the route taken by Milton and Cheadle, gave his opinion of their achievements:

> The pluck that made them conceive, and the vastly greater pluck that enabled them to pull through such an expedition was of the truest British kind. They were more indebted than they perhaps knew as far as 'Slaughter Camp', to the trail of the Canadians who had preceded them, on their way to Cariboo; but from that point, down the frightful and unexplored valley of the North Thompson, the journey had to be faced on their own totally inadequate resources. Had they but known it, they were beaten as completely as by the rules of war the British troops were at Waterloo. They should have submitted to 'the inevitable' and starved. But luckily for themselves and for their readers, they did not know it; and thanks to Mrs Assiniboine, and their own intelligent hardihood that kept them from giving in even for an instant, they succeeded where by all the laws of probabilities they ought to have disastrously failed.

And where they 'ought to have disastrously failed', they, and the Patenaude family, succeeded in establishing a trail that made a significant mark upon the map. The Canadian Pacific Railway had decided that it would take its route through the Rocky Mountains at Kicking Horse Pass and then on to Vancouver. Apart from the rugged terrain, the pass had a steep incline which made the train passage extremely dangerous; it was also close to the border with the USA, making it vulnerable to invasion. Eventually, after twenty-five years, a pair of 'spiral tunnels' were constructed that considerably reduced the risks to the trains when using the Big Hill.

One of the leading competitors to the Canadian Pacific Railway was the Canadian Northern Railway, which started at the beginning of the twentieth century to build a line between Fort William and Port Arthur (modern Thunder Bay) and the prairies.

The city of Winnipeg was reached in the last days of 1901, and Edmonton, four years later. Assisted in 1910 by subsidies from the Government of British Columbia, the Canadian Northern Railway line was laid through the Yellowhead Pass before curving to the south just to the east of Tête Jaune Cache. The line (renamed Canadian National or CN since 1960) then passed through several familiar place names, Canoe River, Albreda, Messiter, St Paul, Kamloops, Ashcroft, Lytton, Boston Bar, Hell's Gate, Yale, and Hope, before reaching the city of Vancouver. The trains travelling along the line also pass close by some significant natural features bearing the names Mount Milton, Mount Cheadle, Messiter Summit, and Assiniboine Bluff – mementos to a band of individuals who survived the odds, the elements, and each other.

Index

49th Parallel 15, 174, 183, 190
Abinger, Lord 235
Acapulco 229
Adderley, Charles MP 238
Albreda Lake 145
Albreda River 145, 146
Alcatraz Island 222
Alexandra Bridge 179
Algonquin, Tribe 118
Allard, Ovid 216
Allegheny Mountains 242
Anderson Lake 197
Anderson, Alexander 197
Anderson, Bishop David 89, 105, 106
Anglo-Saxon 14-19
Arrowsmith, John 237
Ashcroft Manor Roadhouse 170, 215
Aspinwall (Colòn) 231, 233
Assiniboine Bluff 160, 251
Assiniboine River 28, 33, 34, 37
Assiniboine, Mrs 96, 113, 119, 120, 124, 125, 130, 139, 144, 145, 149, 155, 156, 162, 166, 186, 248, 250
Assiniboine, The 96, 96, 113, 118, 119
Assiniboine, Tribe 25, 38, 50, 63
Association of the Deaf and Dumb 239

Astor House Hotel 233
Atagakouph 72, 73, 88
Athabasca River 100, 122, 125, 134
Athabascan Pass 101, 102
Atlantic Ocean
Badger 55, 56, 72-74, 82, 88, 89, 91
Bald Mountain 205
Ball, Captain Henry 175
Ballou, Billy 183
Barkerville 205, 206, 209-212
Barnard's Express 214
Barret-Leonard, Charles Edward 207, 208
Barron, Joseph 225
Barwick House, Somerset 16, 249
Bazalgette, Captain George RM 219, 220
Beauclerk, Laura Maria Theresa 240
Beaver Pass House 204
Begbie, Judge Matthew Baillie 201, 217, 218
Bell, Thomas 210, 211
Big Trees Grove 223
Bingham, Mr 164, 167
Bingley, Yorkshire 8, 15, 243, 245
Black, Dr Walter 209-212
Blackfeet, Tribe 36, 43, 47, 50-53, 92-95, 99, 115
Blenkinsop, Mr 210, 211

Bolton Abbey 128, 134, 155
Booker, William 223, 226, 227
Booth, Edwin 234
Booth, John Wilks 234
Boston Bar 176, 179, 180, 216, 251
Bostonaise, Pierre 112
Briggs House Hotel 20
British Columbia 9-15, 21, 62, 91, 104, 164, 166, 173, 175, 178, 179, 182, 189, 193-196, 199, 201, 215, 236, 238, 240, 246-248
British North America 9-12, 15, 17, 28, 98, 112, 166, 168, 174, 179-183, 194
Brother Jonathan 194
Brown, Dr 210, 212
Bruneau, Athanhous 33, 52, 56, 58, 60-66, 70, 74, 83-87, 91
Bucephalus 32, 40, 41, 52, 53, 64, 86, 88, 135-138, 148, 151, 154, 159, 161
Buffalo Dung Lake 135, 136
Buffalo River 23
Bulwer-Lytton, Sir Edward 174, 175
Burgess, Mr 164, 214
Burrard Inlet 182
Bushby, Arthur 187, 188
Butler, Colonel W F 27, 28

Caius College (Gonville and), Cambridge 10
Calumet 39, 50
Cambridge, England 8, 10, 15, 103, 105, 110, 170, 189, 215
Cameron, John 202, 206
Camerontown 205, 210
Camp Lake 7, 59
Canada, Dominion of 10, 240, 246
Canada, Province of 12, 14, 203, 229, 236, 238, 240, 246-249
Canadian Northern Railway 250, 251
Canadian Pacific Railway 257, 250
Canoe River 143-147, 251
Cariboo 13, 55
Cariboo Goldfields 9, 14, 106, 107, 112, 140, 141, 147, 157, 165, 167, 198, 199, 214, 240
Cariboo Lake 193
Cariboo River 193
Cariboo Road 172, 176, 179, 201, 202, 214-217
Central Park 234
Chagres River 231
Champion 197
Chancellor of the Exchequer 237, 238
Chasm 202, 215
Chastellaine, Louis 94, 95
Cheadle Prize and Gold Medal 246
Cheadle, Alberta (community) 247, 248
Cheadle, Sarah Jane 128
Cheadle, Thomas Alec 247
Cheadle's disease 244
Chicago 20, 230, 233
Child of the Hawk 57-61, 65, 68, 78, 81, 85-87
Chippewa, Tribe 23, 25, 34, 38
Clare College, Cambridge 105
Clearwater River 158
Clinton 202
Cochrane, Archbishop 104, 166
Cocker, Mr 210

Colman, George 234
Colonial Hotel (New Westminster) 183, 186
Colonial Hotel, Yale 181
Columbia (California) 223
Columbia River 221
Commodore 191
Company of Welsh Adventurers 204, 212
Cook, Mortimer 171, 172
Cook's Ferry 169-172, 215, 216
Cooper, J 237
Cornish Wheel 207
Cornwall brothers 170, 215
Cottonwood River 204
Count, Mathilda 241, 242
Cowper, Captain 33
Cox, William 207, 209, 212
Cracroft, Sophie 9, 12
Crandell's Hotel, San Jose 224
Crease, Henry Pering Pellew 188, 189, 196
Cree, Tribe 29, 38, 44-46, 50-55, 74, 81, 89, 92-95, 98-101, 119, 128
Crochet River 57, 58
CSS Alabama 74, 228, 232
Cumberland House 43, 98
Cusheon, John 206, 210, 212
Cusheon, Margaret 205
Cuyler, Dr Theodore 242
Dallas, Alexander 104
Darwin, Charles 236
Davis, President Jefferson 168, 197, 233
Delilah 70, 75, 80-86
Delmonico's Restaurant 234
Department of Indian Affairs 109
Detroit 20
Dickens, Charles 199
Dietz, William (Dutch Bill) 193, 205
Dixie, Mr 209, 210
Doane, Captain J W 203, 212
Dodge, Colonel Richard 13
Douglas Lake 195
Douglas, Governor James 190-194, 201
Duck Lake 43

Dunmore, Lord 9, 33, 36, 38
Duntz Head 221
Elliot, Captain George 221
Elliot, Judge 198
Elwyn, Thomas 184
English Camp 219
Enterprise (Gulf of Georgia) 183-186
Enterprise (Soda Creek) 203, 212
Epilepsy 10
Erasmus 107
Eton College 8
Farquharson, James 62, 63, 82, 84, 88, 91
Farren, Mr 210, 211
Ferguson, John 172
Finlayson, Roderick 191
FitzStubbs, Captain Napoleon 207, 208, 214
Fitzwilliam, 6th Earl 14, 181
Fitzwilliam, Lady Laura May 240
Fitzwilliam, Lady Mabel Florence Harriet 240
Fitzwilliam, Lord Henry 241, 242
Fitzwilliam, William Charles de Meuron Wentworth 241
Fleming, Alexander 247
Fort Abercrombie 23
Fort Carlton 36, 40-47, 52, 55, 61-63, 72-74, 78-93, 102, 104, 107, 249
Fort Colville 190
Fort Edmonton 79, 98, 99, 100, 107, 108, 112, 115, 116, 122, 124, 157
Fort Ellice 33, 36, 37, 42
Fort Garry 15, 16, 21, 24, 28, 34, 40, 43, 47, 56, 61, 63, 83-90, 99
Fort George 141, 165, 193
Fort Langley 174, 182
Fort Milton 65, 69, 72, 77, 78, 82, 87
Fort Pitt 91-95, 98, 107, 248
Fort Stevens 221
Franklin, Captain Sir John RN 9, 29, 223
Franklin, Jane, Lady 9, 12, 180, 181, 223
Franklyn, Captain 219

Fraser Canyon 177, 180
Fraser Grand Fork 137
Fraser River 136, 175, 176, 182, 213
Fraser, Colin 115-117
Fraser, Donald 172, 181-183
Fraser, Simon 179
Friedlander, Isaac 225
Georgetown, Minnesota 21-23, 26, 27
Goff, Lyman Bullock 24
Gompertz, George 214
Good, Charles 186-189
Grant, Reverend G M 38, 249, 250
Gray, Mr 16, 17
Great Ormond Street Hospital 243-247
Great Pacific Railroad 21
Grey, J Edward 13
Gugy, Colonel Bartholomew 16, 18
Guillod, Harry 171
Gulf of Georgia 183, 217, 220
Hamburger, Herr 20, 21
Hardisty, Richard Charles 98-104, 109, 113
Harewood Company, The 219
Harewood, 3rd Earl of 218
Harper, Jerome 167-169
Harrison, Captain 215
Hayne, Julia Dean 217, 220
Hector, Dr John 116
Hill's Bar 177, 178
Hind, Dr Henry Youle 9, 107
Hind, William 107
HMS *Forward* 218, 219
HMS *Sutlej* 185
HMS *Tribune* 187
Holy Trinity Church, Wentworth 242
Holyhead 236
Hooker, Sir Joseph Dalton 236
Hope 188, 195
Hope, British Columbia 182, 251
House of Representatives 234
Howe, Julia Ward 234
Hudson's Bay Company 12,

13, 23, 30, 34, 41-43, 47, 54, 55, 58, 63, 71, 84, 93, 98, 100, 104, 113, 114, 163, 164, 181, 182, 185, 187, 190, 195, 197, 210, 212, 216-219, 246
Hutchinson, 'Captain' 19
International 26-29, 35
Irving, Captain William 182, 187
Isbister, Jemmy 79, 84
Jackass Mountain 176
Jackson College, Columbia, Tennessee 104
Jasper House 100-102, 115, 122, 126-132, 141, 150
Jasper Lake 129
Jerking 152
Jessop, John 9
Kamloops 9, 141, 149, 155-169, 197, 214, 215, 251
Kamloops Lake 169
Kane, Dr Elisha Kent 223
Kane, 'Major' 19
Keithley Creek 193
Kicking Horse Pass 112, 116, 250
Kootanie Pass 187
La Belle Prairie 56, 58, 65
La Crosse, Wisconsin 19, 21
La Ronde, Louis 29, 32-36, 39, 40, 45-61, 65-74, 83-87, 91
Labouchére, Henry 190, 191
Lac Ste Anne 114, 115, 122
Lacombe, Father Albert 99, 100
Lady Franklin's Rock 181
Lady Laura, Viscountess Milton 241, 243
Lake Harrison 188
Lake Osoyoos 174
Lake Superior 241
Lascelles, Lieutenant, The Hon Horace, RN 218, 219, 270, 221
Leather Pass 112, 236
Lee, General Robert E 168
Lee, Kwong 218
Leitch, R P 237
Lillie, Alexander 43-45, 63, 64
Lillooet 176, 197-199, 217

Lincoln, President Abraham 168, 225, 233, 234
Linton, W J 236
Little Crow, Chief 34
Little Hell's Gate 155
Little Lake Lillooet 196
London Female Emigration Society 199
London School of Medicine for Women 245
Love, Timolean 101
Lowhee Creek 209
Lundin Brown, Reverend R C 199
Lyons, Lord 234
Lytton 170, 174-6, 216, 251
Macaulay, Aulay 100, 122, 130-134
MacDonald's Hotel, Port Douglas 195
Mackenzie River 41
Maguire's Opera House 224
Mansel, Emily 245
Mansel, Robert 245
Manzanillo, Mexico 228
Mare Island, US Navy Yard 226
Maronde, Isadore 89, 90
Martin, Mr 162-167
Martley, Captain John 218
Marzelle 197
McDougall, John 105-109
McGowan, Ned 177, 179
McKay, Joseph 162, 167-173, 181
McKay, William 38, 39
McLeod River 121
McTavish, William 30, 34
Melbourne, Australia 177, 249
Menken, Adah Isaacs 224
Messiter Summit 155, 251
Messiter, Charles Alston 16-75 *passim*, 75, 82- 91, 155, 237, 249, 251
Mexico 17, 164
Miette River 134
Minton China Company 237
Montreal 19, 33, 98
Moody, Colonel Richard 173, 178-184, 188
Moose Lake 136
Mount Allard 216
Mount Baker 183

Mount Benson 219
Mount Bingley 135
Mount Bucephalus 135
Mount Cheadle 151, 247, 251
Mount Fitzwilliam 135
Mount Martley 218
Mount Milton 145, 251
Mount O'Beirne 249
Murchison Rapids 165
Murchison, Sir Roderick 153, 236
Murgatroyd, Anne 243
Nanaimo, Vancouver Island 219
Nashquapamayoo 66, 67, 74, 76
Neah Bay 222
New Almaden Works 224, 225
New Brunswick 12
New Caledonia 178
New Westminster 166, 169, 174, 179, 182, 186-189, 194, 196, 203, 208, 214, 217
New York 12, 104, 194, 198, 203, 227, 232-234, 240
New York Academy of Music 233
New York Hotel 233
Newfoundland 12, 17, 19, 62
Niagara Falls 19
Nicaragua Slide 179
Nicoll, Captain 219,
Nootka Sound 208
North Thompson River 141, 146, 249
Northampton 104
Norway House 100
Nova Scotia 12
O'Beirne, E F (Mr 'O'B') 103-14, 117, 128-167 *passim*, 197, 249
Ocklynge Cemetery, Eastbourne 247
Ojibway, Tribe 29
Order of the Bath 185
Ormonde, Marquess of 240
Otter 186
Overlanders 9, 107, 113, 141, 146-149, 155, 165

Owl's Club, The 228, 231
Oxford 8, 105
Pacific Fleet 9
Pacific Ocean 140, 222
Palliser Expedition 36, 116, 174
Palmer, Lieutenant Henry RE 173, 174, 182, 205, 215
Pambrun, Andrew 100-102
pan (for gold) 102, 176, 206-208
Panama 11, 12, 203, 206, 223, 225, 231, 232
Panama City 231
Patenaude, Louis (The Assiniboine) 94-99, 110, 113, 114, 117-120, 123-156, 159-162, 165-173, 182, 185, 186, 237, 248, 250
Pavilion Mountain 201, 218
Pearson, Captain 227, 230
Pemberton 197
Pembina 28
Pembina River 117
Perrier, George 177
Perry 102
Phipps Hornby, Captain Geoffrey RN 187, 188
Pickett, Captain George 184, 187 188
Pig War 187
Plains of Abraham 18
Pointe de Meuron 241
Pomme de Terre 23
Popov, Admiral 226
Port Douglas 188, 195, 196, 203
Port Moody 182
Portage La Prairie 35, 104, 107, 167
Poynton, Dr Frederick 245, 247
Prince Edward Island 12
Prince George 141, 165, 193
Prince of Wales 197
Prince of Wales 164
Putnam, Robert 204, 205
Qu'Appelle River 39 40
Quebec 12-18, 229
Quesnel 141, 165, 166, 203, 212-214
Quesnel River 193
Raby Claim 208, 210

Rae, Dr John 29
Red River 32, 35, 43, 74, 79, 88-91, 98-102, 105, 110
Reliance 182, 187, 217
Richardson, Sir John 29
Richaud 40
Richfield 205-207, 210, 212
Ringgold, Dr 224
River Sturgeon 100
Robson Peak 137
Roche á Miette 126-128, 131
Rose, John 205
Rossin House Hotel 19
Rouen (France) 242
Rowand, John 98, 99, 115
Royal Engineers 160-173, 176, 178, 181-184, 188, 215
Royal Geographical Society 153, 236, 237
Royal Hotel, Red River Settlement 106
Royal Marines 178, 183 184, 188, 217, 219
Rubbiboo 80, 140
Rupert's Land 12, 15, 33
Russell Hotel 18
San Francisco 11, 12, 177, 183, 192, 194, 199, 203, 222-228, 249
San Joaquin River 223
San Juan Island, (Gulf of Georgia) 187, 217-221
Santa Clara 224
Sapperton 182
Saskatchewan River 42, 43, 88
Saulteaux, Tribe 95
Schubert, Catherine 165
Scotch Jenny (Janet Morris) 210-212
Scott, General Winfield 187, 188
Secwepemc, Tribe 131 *and see* Shuswap
Seton Lake 197, 199
Shaganappi 32
Sheldon, Professor J P 246
Shell River 56, 61, 64
Shoal Lake 37
Shuswap, Tribe 131, 132, 138-141, 157, 160, 161

Simpson, George 112, 115
Sinclair, Cuthbert 54-56
Sioux, Tribe 23-24, 34, 38,,
    40, 44, 45, 69, 74, 79,
    86, 89-91
Slaughter Camp 149, 151,
    155, 165, 250
Smith, John 61, 63
Snake Hills 96
Snake River 129
Soda Creek 200, 203, 213,
    214
South Thompson River 141,
    163
Spalding, Captain William
    188, 217
Spence, Thomas 172
SS *Ariel* 232, 233
SS *China* 234, 236, 241
SS *Constitution* 225
SS *Golden City* 227
SS *Orizba* 225
SS *Pacific* 220
SS *Scotia* 240
St Albert 99
St Andrew's Society, Victoria
    218
St Anthony 21, 22
St Cloud 22, 90
St George Hotel, Victoria
    184, 186
St John's College, Cambridge
    105
St Lawrence River 194, 206
St Mary's Hospital 243, 246
St Patrick's College 104, 105
St Paul, Captain (John
    Baptiste-Lolo) 162, 163
St Paul, Minnesota 21, 24,
    34, 63, 90
Stage Hotel, Lillooet 197
Stanley Park 182
Stansfeld, James MP 238
Star of the Blanket 55, 62

Steele, James 206, 208
Stockton (California) 223
Supernat, Baptiste 91
Swift Creek 143
T'sek Hot Springs 196
Tait, Philip 84, 85
Tambout 73
Templar 208
Tête Jaune (Pierre Bostonais)
    112
Tête Jaune Cache 112,
    133-148, 151, 153, 157,
    165, 168, 186, 251
The Boy 97, 113, 120,
    123-125, 128-130,
    134-137, 141-145, 156,
    157, 166, 169, 172, 186,
    227, 228, 248
The Fashion (Victoria dining
    club) 127
The Hunter 75-87, 93
The Iroquois, (Louis
    Carapontier) 133-141
The Wolf 80, 81, 93
Thetford, Norfolk 105
Thompson River 9, 141,
    158, 159, 166, 169, 170
Thynne, Captain 33
Toronto 19, 20
Touchwood Hills 41, 42, 84
Trinity College, Dublin 104
Union Club, San Francisco
    223, 226
United States Army 217, 221
United States of America 9,
    103, 166, 186
Van Sickle, Miss 230-233
Victoria (Vancouver Island)
    166, 169, 175, 178,
    181, 184-194, 197-200,
    203-206, 217-220, 223,
    237, 249
Vital, Jean Baptiste 33, 36,
    37

Voudrie, Tousaint 33-36, 41,
    52, 56, 58
Walkem, George 223, 227
Walkenshaw, Miss 225
Walker Dr David 198, 200
Wallace, Dr 221
Ward Beecher, Henry 230
Ward, B Peyton 28
Washington DC 190, 191,
    234
Washington Territory 190,
    191
Wells Fargo 194
Wentworth Woodhouse 14,
    242
Whaddell, Captain Peter
    Brunton 177
Wheeler, Arthur 249
Whisky Punch, The Society
    Addicted to 212, 227-231
White Cloud 44, 45
White Fish Lake 45, 56, 58,
    77, 80, 83, 85
Widow, The (Mrs Wetzner)
    229-233
Wilberforce, Bishop Samuel
    199
Willard's Hotel 234
William's Creek 193, 205,
    208-210
William's Lake 214
Winnebago, Tribe 34
Winnipeg 7, 8, 15, 241, 251
Woolsey, Thomas 101, 104,
    107
Worcester 105
Yale 169-182, 187, 202,
    213-216, 251
Yellowhead Pass 112, 113,
    126, 251
York Boats 43
Young, James Judson
    184-187
Zear 36, 42, 48-52, 56